Desert of Solitude

Refreshed by Grace

LaShawnda Jones

DESERT OF SOLITUDE REFRESHED BY GRACE

BY

LaShawnda Jones

Revised August 2024

Please note: Some names in this book have been changed to protect the privacy of people I have interacted with over the years. Unless otherwise cited and noted, all events are written from my perspective and understanding. This book is only meant to be an accounting of the life experiences that have impacted and matured me spiritually.

May God continue to bless you,
LaShawnda

Desert of Solitude: Refreshed by Grace. Copyright © 2022, 2018 by LaShawnda Jones. All rights reserved. No part of this publication may be reproduced, distributed, used, or transmitted in any form whatsoever or by any means, including photocopying, recording, or other electronic or mechanical methods, without the prior written permission of the publisher, except in the case of brief quotations embodied in critical articles and reviews and certain other noncommercial uses permitted by copyright law. For permission requests, write to the publisher at HarvestLife2020@gmail.com or visit Harvest-Life.org for contact details.

Unless otherwise indicated, all Old and New Testament scripture quotations are taken from the New Revised Standard Version (NRSV) on www.BibleGateway.com©

All word definitions are taken from www.Dictionary.com Unabridged (v 1.1), Based on the Random House Unabridged Dictionary, © Random House, Inc. 2006.

Category: Body, Mind & Spirit/Inspiration & Personal Growth
Paperback ISBN-10: 0-9776179-4-7
ISBN-13: 978-0-9776179-4-4

Front cover image by Deidre Wilson.
Book cover design by Katie Good and LaShawnda Jones.

Printed by Ingram Sparks On-Demand, United States of America.
Second edition August 2024.

Harvest Life
PO Box 2103
Milwaukee, WI 53201
Harvest-Life.org

Dedicated to:

Women
Womanhood
Sisterhood
Femininity
Grace

God is with you, as are my prayers. I believe it, therefore through my faith, I know you are covered by my love.

1 Peter 4:8

Books by LaShawnda Jones

ALONE | All In One: A Solitary Journey
I AM WOMAN: Expressions of Black Womanhood in America
Desert of Solitude: Refreshed by Grace
My God and Me: Listening, Learning and Growing on My Journey
The Process of Asking for, Receiving & Giving Love & Forgiveness
Fantasies: A Metamorphosis of Sexual Attraction
Clichés: A Life in Verse

Contributor
Go, Tell Michelle: African American Women Write to the New First Lady

Calendars
VoLux Full-Figured Calendar, 2005, 2007 (out of print)

Available (e-book & print)
www.amazon.com
www.bn.com
Harvest-Life.org/shop

CONTENTS

Preface: About Desert of Solitude...
Introduction: Wonder-Filled Living ....

FAITH CHALLENGES ※ VERDANT VALLEY

Submitted & Surrendered 10
When I asked, I received 11
NYC is a Life Changer... 12
I asked to be a lover… 14
…and the people said, "HELL NO!" 17
Helping on Empty 24
Love, A Postmortem... 31
Where did my zeal go?... 33
To Be Known by No One 45
First Fruit 47
When Truth Destroys 49
Forgotten 51
Alone vs. Solitude 52
Lessons from Solitude.. 54
Trauma of the Unseen.. 55

WOMANHOOD ※ PRICKLY PEAR BLOSSOM

Be Anything.. 58
To God be the Glory... 59
Progressive Women in a Degenerating Society....................... 62
Womanhood: The Seat of Feminine Power 72
A Collision of Femininity, the Maternal & the Mammy............. 75
He is my sweetness. 80
An Open Letter: Woman to Man 81
When I Think About.. 85

How a Man Treats a Woman 86
Hope of My Life 87
No joy; but good news 95
no words 96
Singleness is not the prize... 98
Without Reservation 105
Nothing beats a try... 108
A Conversation & A Song 111

DEATH & LIFE ☀ DRY RIVERBED

Set fire to the rain… 116
The wanton destruction of life. 119
Good Cop. Bad Cop. Life is not so simple. 124
Tears & Protest 136
Dear Sandra Bland 143
Homemade Radicalism.. 146
Grief Rage Trauma 151
In Memoriam 158
Don't Lead with Your Pain 162
Be Present for the Battle.. 166
Observations of She Who Died Laughing 170
About Granddaddy, Death & Release.. 174
To everything there is a season. 185

WONDER: SELF-CELEBRATION 40 & BEYOND ☀ CELESTIAL SKY

Story of My Beginning...190
Grad School Graduate 196
Montréal, Québec.. 200
Exploring Socialism... 201
A Day in Torino, Piedmont 202
Good morning, Santa Margherita!.. 206
Stormy Nice, France 211
Cannes, France... 216

Grasse, France 222
360° in Geneva, Switzerland 223
Homeward Bound 225

REALITY SUCKS ☀ MOUNTAIN CLIMBING DURING MONSOON

Today 230
Stork Delivery: Uninvited and Misguided 22-year-old 231
If, In Leaving a Place 255
Family Dilemma 258
Complaining is Contagious... 266
Little Tyrants 267
Intrusion, Violation & Destruction 271
Adversarial Fellowship 279
Rethinking Life... 284
Proving Ground... 290
Lessons Learned from Lance Armstrong 294
Prayer & A Song.. 296

GRACE ☀ MOUNTAINTOP

The Journey 300
How do you handle contentment? 301
Once & For All 303
Getting back up again.. 305
Give thanks for what you've been delivered from 320
Thank You, Lord... 322
Love Anyway: My Harvest Lessons 323
Where can I do the most good?.. 327
My Center 329
I'm 41, WTF... 330
Balance of Life 331
Paint & Praise: Your Blessings Require Work!..................333
Bounty in the Desert 338
Mountaintop Perspective 340

Beautify Your Desert 342
Coming Down the Mountain.. 345

I AM ENOUGH :: RETURNING TO THE VALLEY

The End of a Wonder-filled Year. 348
Resistance is Futile, Change is Inevitable 352
Battling Comfort... 354
Woman, Be Restored. 363
Building a Structure.. 368
Starting Off Fresh 371
Road Trip: Riding Shotgun 373
Struggle & Triumph 377
I Give Good Love.. 378
Woman, You Are Enough. 380

EPILOGUE :: SUNSET SILHOUETTES

Journaling through the Journey 386
Media and Verse Lists... 394

PREFACE: ABOUT DESERT OF SOLITUDE

My God and Me: Listening, Learning and Growing on My Journey, the first book about my faith journey, was published in 2009. It is a compilation of stories focused on interpersonal relationships and the impact they had on developing my character and faith. Readers who shared their feedback were effusive about how much they enjoyed reading my story but also thought it was a lot to take in. They felt the pages were too dense with words and required frequent pauses to reflect on what was being shared.

In *Desert of Solitude: Refreshed by Grace* I continue sharing my faith journey through my intrapersonal relationship and the challenges of sustaining a faith-filled life practice. This book explores my internal process for seeking peace, understanding and acceptance of who and where I am in life.

Keeping in mind what my readers have shared with me, this volume has fonts and pages that are well-spaced and easy to read. Breaks and transitions in the form of poems, notes, and journal entries have been added. Additionally, suggestions for related songs and sermons are the last line of many passages.

This volume was created to be read as a multi-media message. It began as video messages to myself to keep moving forward no matter the obstacles. Links to songs and sermons from other creators that also encouraged me are shared as well. All referenced media are indexed in the back and available on Harvest-Life.org under the "Books" tab. I encourage you to pause and experience the full-bodied message in the various formats provided. My greatest hope is for you to receive enough nuggets to nurture in your life and plant into someone else's.

Meditation Verse: *Deuteronomy 30:15-20*

See, I have set before you today life and prosperity, death and adversity. If you obey the commandments of the Lord your God that I am commanding you today, by loving the Lord your God, walking in His ways, and observing His commandments, decrees, and ordinances, then you shall live and become numerous, and the Lord your God will bless you in the land that you are entering to possess. But if your heart turns away and you do not hear, but are led astray to bow down to other gods and serve them, I declare to you today that you shall perish; you shall not live long in the land that you are crossing the Jordan to enter and possess. I call heaven and earth to witness against you today that I have set before you life and death, blessings and curses. Choose life so that you and your descendants may live, loving the Lord your God, obeying Him, and holding fast to Him; for that means life to you and length of days, so that you may live in the land that the Lord swore to give to your ancestors, to Abraham, to Isaac, and to Jacob.

INTRODUCTION: WONDER-FILLED LIVING

People travel to wonder at the height of the mountains, at the huge waves of the seas, at the long course of the rivers, at the vast compass of the ocean, at the circular motion of the stars, and yet they pass by themselves without wondering. ~ Augustine of Hippo

THE African philosopher, Augustine of Hippo, remembered as Saint Augustine, pondered that people travel the world to experience wonder yet pass by themselves without wondering at all. We become used to ourselves, used to our lives, our surroundings and our situations. We live life thinking we are common – that there's nothing special about us, indeed that our very ordinary days are as good as life gets.

In my late thirties, I fell into the darkest of pits. It was deep enough to obscure any spot of light within myself. The harder I tried to climb out, the deeper I sank. Eventually, I settled uncomfortably into a despair that made a future impossible to envision. After a while, it no longer mattered, I was ready to be done with this life. I laid down at the bottom of my internal pit and waited for the day I no longer have to worry about getting up. Thankfully, that day has yet to come. No matter how low I fall, there's a push in my spirit to get up and continue walking. An insistent whisper urging me forward.

Friday, June 11, 2010

Here we go again. I'm just floating around passing time and taking up space. Another day, weekend, summer, year with no one to share any of it with. Not talking about the people who pass through with sincere deposits into my life. There's no one with me day in or out, during any hour with plans or hopes to be around for the long haul.

I'm tired, Father. So very tired. Exhausted. Hurt. Bereft. Rejected. Abandoned. Lonely. Sad. Heavy-hearted. Angry over it all. I don't know what to do with it, except come to You and ask You to please take all my burdens away. In the name of Jesus, Father, please.

You put so much in my heart and I yearn for it all more every day and each day Your blessings seem further away.

What am I missing? What am I supposed to be learning? What should I be seeing or hearing? Where should my focus be? I believe my focus is on You. My hope is for all You want for me. I'm doing my best to live, think and love according to Your Word. The more I do, the more isolated I become here.

My most discouraging lesson has been learning to hide. Repressing my feelings and thoughts. Keeping them to myself. Which naturally leads to keeping to myself. I want to share and remain open, but the pain of rejection is debilitating. The scorn and superiority of the People (Your creation) halts me in my tracks. Now I just want to keep my Self buried within me. Protected. Soothed. Safe. Calm. At peace. No harm can come to me if I'm shielded, right? Of course not, not when You're shielding and protecting me. I want... need Your protection, Father. I need Your covering. I need Your peace and reassurance. In the most gracious name of Jesus, I pray! Thank You, Father. Thank You, Abba.

A few years marked by feeble attempts to reanimate myself passed by. Around my thirty-eighth birthday, depression had exhausted me, and I became determined *to be* different by the time I turned forty. There was no way I wanted to be stuck in the same pit drowning in emptiness at the beginning of a new decade of life. The thought of anchoring to a goal with a timeline became my lifeline.

Nearly ten years prior, I had invested a year towards a master's degree program and the credits were approaching expiration for transfer. Finishing something I had begun so long ago became a very worthy goal and focus. Fixating on something other than my emptiness allowed hope to trickle in again. Thoughts of a better future began to lift the darkness.

Turning forty was a milestone that deserved excitement and celebration, even if I was alone. It was important for me to know that even if there was no one to celebrate with me, I needed to honor my own life. It would be more than one day of self-appreciation; it would be *a year of wonder-filled living!*

Not long after making the decision of focusing on the wonder of life as I approached my fortieth year, I was accepted into a graduate program at The New School. A very apt name for my life stage. Within weeks of starting my graduate studies, an opportunity to purchase a brand-new co-op apartment in East Harlem presented itself. Truly, the combined stress of buying a co-op and pursuing a graduate degree in New York City while working full-time in a top global firm kept my mind off of depression.

Sometimes stress and busyness can be a blessing. That year, the wonder was *abundant*.

The emptiness I had lamented for years became an unexpected fullness that overflowed in unimagined ways. It led to a commitment to focus on the abundance in my life instead of what I perceived as lack.

Perhaps I spoke the revelation into fruition. Perhaps God used my empty darkness as an opportunity to display His creative power and faithful care in a way I couldn't misunderstand or misattribute: GOD *IS* the wonder which fills me.

> *wonder: a feeling of surprise mingled with admiration, caused by something beautiful, unexpected, unfamiliar, or inexplicable.*

How many of us spend our lives wandering and wondering? Searching outside of ourselves for direction, instruction and satisfaction? Trying to figure out how we can dominate, control or eliminate our issues and our foes? Dedicating our lives to someone else's vision, purpose and grand scheme? Adhering to lies, misdirection and trickery because that's all we know? How many of us are stuck in a rut because life simply stopped flowing in our immediate favor; we reached a bottleneck or a fork and decided it would be easier to just stay put? Easier to decide to not move forward.

In all the ways life comes at us, and in the countless ways we analyze our lives, we rarely give ourselves the benefit of wonder.

Desert of Solitude: Refreshed by Grace explores my journey to recognizing myself as a wonder. This truth, which is exceptionally hard for many to accept about themselves, revealed itself slowly and concretely over the span of three years.

When was the last time you felt surprise and wonder at the beautiful creation you are? When was the last time you embraced the unfamiliar and inexplicable in your life?

The Bible speaks of God's wonderful works, His miraculous creation, as expressions of His everlasting love. Psalm 139 is an ode to humanity as well as God. "*I praise You, for I am fearfully and wonderfully made. Wonderful are Your works; that I know very well* (v 14)." Humans are the Creator's wonderful work.

You are a wonder! Your wonderfulness is not dependent on money, employment, family, friends, network, possessions, status or anything else. You are a wonder because you were created that way.

Though the experiences shared in *Desert of Solitude: Refreshed by Grace* were written in a symbolic desert – New York City – processing them led me to a geographic one – the Sonoran Desert in Sothern Arizona.

There's something incomprehensible, yet encompassing, about deserts. The vastness. The dryness. The endless natural beauty and matchless sunsets. The silence. There is such majesty and awe in the thundering silence. My soul and spirit were crying out for all of it. Dry bleached bones. Dehydration and death. All the imagery an arid desert conjures up is truth. As is the ferocious refreshing of the monsoon rains and the invigorating desert breeze. The evening sky is no less miraculous. A map of eternity laid out overhead. Stars without number stretching as far and deep as the eye can see, revealing more and more the longer our eyes gaze upward.

> *My heart overflows with a pleasing theme; I address my verses to the king; my tongue is like the pen of a ready scribe.* ~ Psalm 45:1

The desert appears to be nothing. From a distance it looks to be a vast empty space incapable of sustaining life. To the contrary, the desert embodies everything important for life. Space for clarity. Gentle breezes to revive the soul. God's Breath of Life breathing into empty vessels. The unrelenting separation of darkness and light graces us as a beautiful illustration of the need for both and the purpose of each. Every stage of life is a wonder.

It is impossible to experience such an understanding living in cities. Nature is washed away by artificial light and vainglorious darkness. Manmade enticements deaden souls to the need for nature in all its vast starkness and bounty. The contrasts and seemingly opposing truths in nature lead to a better understanding of our true selves. Cities on the other hand, make it easy to spend a lifetime pursuing false ideals and empty goals while cultivating identities that don't resemble who we truly are.

Desert of Solitude: Refreshed by Grace is an exploration of the lows and highs of living my faith and the understanding revealed along the journey. Joy is present throughout, though at times it may be difficult to identify. Sorrow is more apparent, but please remember sorrow allows for joy to be experienced in a deeply encompassing way. By and large, the stories in this volume carry us into understanding that a wonder-filled life is a by-product of embracing the wonder that is humanity and, more specifically, embracing the wonder of our own spirit-filled personhood.

LaShawnda Jones
New York, 2017

Listen to: *Desert Song* by Hillsong

FAITH CHALLENGES

※

VERDANT VALLEY

SUBMITTED & SURRENDERED

January 29, 2014

My Dear Heavenly Father, I come to You, submitted to Your Authority, surrendered to Your Grace, yet scared of all that I don't know about my future – scared that it will continue being only me. No loving, supportive husband or endearing loveable children of my own.

I'm hurting, Father. I'm angry. I'm confused.

I thought I was living according to your Word and instructions.

I've been honest with You, myself and with people, but my honestly has only driven people away. I've spoken truth and I've expressed my needs, my hurts and my hopes. In return, people have laughed at me, cursed me and cast me aside.

I no longer want to share myself (my thoughts, my revelations or discoveries) with anyone. I just want to huddle in a corner and wait for the world to end. I don't want to reach out to anyone else. I don't want to live for countless more years knowing that NO ONE in this world finds me worthy of their love and friendship. Worse yet, knowing I am no man's choice for wife. Add to that, the mask on my last friendship from Milwaukee has fallen off. Finally, seeing that relationship as it is cast me into a deep melancholy this week. I've been sinking into a depression for a while and had no will to fight it this time.

WHEN I ASKED, I RECEIVED...

When I asked[i] for courage, Abba exposed my enemies.
When I asked for strength, Jehovah gave me challenges.
When I asked for wisdom, El Shaddai graced me with adversity.
When I asked for understanding, God intensified my struggles.
For patience, Yahweh-Rapha gave me a heart for people.
For a home, El Shammah made me a constant visitor.
For financial security, Jehovah Jireh blessed me with talents.
When I pleaded for love, El Elyon revealed Himself to me.
In place of a man, Elohim made me a self-sufficient woman.
In place of a family, Abba Emmanuel guided me into solitude.
Instead of a fabulous life, Yahweh-Rohi sat me in a wilderness.
I learned that life is not about getting what we want.
El Roi guides us into becoming who we need.

NYC IS A LIFE CHANGER

Bless the Lord, O my soul, and do not forget all his benefits — who forgives all your iniquity, who heals all your diseases, who redeems your life from the Pit, who crowns you with steadfast love and mercy, who satisfies you with good as long as you live so that your youth is renewed like the eagle's.
~ Psalm 103:2-5

NEW York is known as the city that never sleeps. It has a reputation of being lively and entertaining, but being deprived of sleep feels like a waking death. Sensory overload happens almost immediately. From there many bad habits form.

I used to be a morning person. After a dozen years in the City, I took a scouting trip to Tucson, Arizona in consideration of a possible move. During that first visit to Tucson, I learned I still naturally rise with the sun. However, in a city densely populated with buildings early sunlight rarely reaches bedroom windows. Add to that unending stimuli coming from every possible direction throughout any given day. Getting to sleep is hard when you can't calm down or relax. By the time I decompressed after work, I could get about five hours of sleep before repeating the cycle.

Living in a high-octane metropolis turned me into a night owl. Before I moved to the City, I wasn't too fond of coffee or alcohol. By the time I was ready to leave the City, I wasn't fully awake unless I had a coffee by 11:00am. After that time, not even expresso could liven me up. Wine is also a staple in my fridge, and I've considered taking a mixology class to learn how to make my favorite cocktails. The City changes people drastically because we all need to figure out how to get by.

Additive personalities populate both sides of my family. Addiction and vice have ravaged my people for generations. Drugs, alcohol, sex, greed, you name it, I have several relatives for each vice. People want what they want and have no concern for those they hurt to satisfy their urges. I grew up seeing what a lack of self-control does to individuals and their and their relationships, therefore self-discipline has always been a deep need for me.

Prior to living in New York City, i.e. before I turned thirty, I intentionally stayed away from anything I could lose control to. No smoking, no drinking, no excessive partying and no casual sex. Therefore, acquiring an appetite for alcohol of any kind was a big deal.

Truthfully, when I first moved to the City, I wanted to explore some of the things I wanted to be free of. I felt tainted, used, abused, discarded, and unwanted. Why not sample the wild side? At the time I thought the freedom and access to explore fleshly pursuits, things I would never want to see in the light of day, was a worthwhile venture during my early adulthood. I made motions to immerse myself in the underbelly of the City, but the underbelly spat me out. Each time I walked away from potentially dangerous situations unscathed, I was more assured of God's grace and guidance enveloping my life.

On the surface, I was attempting to act my age and do what all the thirty-somethings were doing. However, I had never been able to act my age and freely engage in sexual expression. So, the social scene and I had nothing in common. Within six months of relocating to the Bronx from Milwaukee, it was painfully clear that my time in the Big Apple was not going to be anything like Sex in the City, my secret wish. Disappointing realization at thirty, however, not so much in hindsight on the other side of forty.

I ASKED TO BE A LOVER...

You shall not hate in your heart anyone of your kin; you shall reprove your neighbor, or you will incur guilt yourself. You shall not take vengeance or bear a grudge against any of your people, but you shall love your neighbor as yourself: I am the LORD.
~ Leviticus 19:17-18

AT the beginning of my faith journey, I asked to be a lover. It was a sincere request, yet also unimaginably naïve. The response has been a constant assault against my personhood, beliefs, ambitions, goals and life. All my interpersonal relationships have since been plagued with rejection, hatred, jealousy and sabotage.

Long ago, I prayed for patience in front of a friend. She *tsked*, shook her head and said, "Be careful what you ask for. Get ready for situations that will make you practice patience." To date, life has trained me well in patience. Asking to be a lover also put me in situations to practice love. When I realized what I had opened myself up to, I could only continue on course with an affirmative, "Here I am, Lord! Use me!"

The young Believer in me was eager and hopeful. I wanted to be the first to reach out to embrace the lost and fallen. I wanted to love God's people. More than that - I wanted to be a messenger and conduit of His love for His people.

The passion and commitment were certainly there, but my understanding was not. I didn't comprehend the magnitude of what I was asking for. I thought I was ready to love people in their natural state. Without their masks, when they were no longer attempting to hide themselves or their motives. I thought I was ready for love to work through me. I assumed all I needed was to be a willing vessel, remain open, offer my humanity and resources. In my mind, being willing to give what was needed when it was needed was love and the resistance to love would be temporary - so short term as to be unremarkable. The most off the mark assumption was that the ugliest rejection could only be "*no, thank you.*"

Unfortunately, the overarching lesson learned was that *"no, thank you"* would have been a kind response. People who resist love aren't polite. Some don't say anything or respond in any way. Some resisters go out of their way to show how little love means to them. They find a wound to grind salt in. They dig out new wounds. They weaponize affection and wage aggressive assaults. Resisters build barriers to hide behind while making accusations and belittling love and all its glory. Persistent love resisters can effectively distract the lover from their purpose, effectively causing them to stop practicing love. Resisters are testers who are intent on proving or disproving a person's commitment to love. Will the wannabe lover hit back? Will they hate back? Will the hopeful lover give up?

Looking back on early growing pains, I see beauty for ashes in the scorched landscape of my interpersonal relationships. When I asked to be a lover, God removed the scales from my eyes and released people to be who they are. Seeing so much undiluted hatred and resentfulness made it impossible to excuse behavior. People may need love, but many don't act like they want it; they don't know how to receive gentle care and concern.

I asked to be a lover and God gave me so many opportunities to learn how to respond to pain, rejection and hatred. He allowed so many chances to bounce back from attacks on my personhood, my vibrancy, and my faith. I would like to say that I got through the experiences with flying colors, but you already know I went into hiding. My passion faded. My light dimmed. My determination wavered. My understanding became dust, and I was ready to give up on everything.

Loving people is not easy. Love is not soft and fluffy. It's not rosy and light. Love is an anchor, a rock, a foundation and a door. It's stalwart, fearless, a transformer of life. It knows no time and it inhabits countless forms. Love is an expression of spirit, life and truth.

I asked to be a lover and I was remade. Beginning with new eyes, a purified heart and fresh understanding. I asked to be a lover and God began transforming me with every interaction.

There is a time for love. When we aren't ready for it or when we are indiscriminate about whom we give our love to, it can destroy us.

Love is not something to be forced onto people. It cannot be demanded. It cannot be bought. It cannot be ignored or neglected. Love is not to be taken lightly. Love is a responsibility. It's strong, harsh, consuming and eternal. It's unquenchable and indestructible. Love is a commitment. It's a way of life or a way to death. There's no escaping it. Love is to be lived fully or you will come to believe life is not worth living. Love is everything. Without it, we have nothing.

When the time is right, loving others will not be a traumatic ordeal. Until then, practice with care.

Listen to: *True Love* by Phil Wickham

...AND THE PEOPLE SAID, "HELL NO!"

> *And this is the judgement, that the light has come into the world, and people loved darkness rather than light because their deeds were evil. For all who do evil hate the light and do not come to the light, so that their deeds may not be exposed.*
> *~ John 3:19-20*

HUMAN beings are the teaching interface in the world. Our interactions with people provide lessons that are experienced in the physical and manifest in the spirit. What we learn is our harvest. What we pass on or give to others is our tithe. Unfortunately, in the thick of life, it's hard to keep this process in mind.

My first blog post *"Can I love you?"* explored the concept of lovers being beggars. It expressed the deep desire to reach out to everyone within my proximity with openness, joy and acceptance of who they are. Five years later, I felt completely defeated and infected. Tainted. Depleted. Jaded and hated. Nearly ten years after writing that post, none of the people I had earnestly sought to love were an active part of my life. Worst still, they were no longer welcome in my life. Today, their removal is viewed as a blessing. This process taught me that love will be rejected repeatedly. People will hate for no apparent reason, but I can still choose to respond in love.

The whole process of reaching out and getting rejected, being available only to be ignored, offering help but getting passed over, issuing invitations only to be stood up, opening up only to be continually shut out was cyclical pruning. God's ruthless cleansing and uprooting made room for His Spirit to fuse more deeply with me.

After cycling through this process many times, I developed a hardness that coated my heart and thoughts. Compassion was no longer hanging on my sleeve. A shrewdness and discernment developed. That's not to say I became hard-hearted. To the contrary, my heart became extremely tender. The breaks and the cracks expanded it in ways I couldn't possibly imagine beforehand. It feels and sees more now than ever before. It is also more guarded than before. It's no longer open to anything or everyone who simply crosses my path. My heart is operating on an invitation-only basis which keeps me free to shake the dust of inhospitable environments from my feet and keep moving forward.

Love and hope go hand in hand. Once upon a time, love was pure hope for me, and hope was loving innocence. When my heart became tainted, my hope began to dim. We cannot know how deep or resilient hope is until we experience its revival after a period of devastation. Yet, once a period of hopelessness has been overcome, it's impossible to fully lose hope again. The trick is to continually bounce back.

During the most painful periods of rejection, hope became a dark murky morass. There was no vision or passion. This is not a report claiming that love failed - for that would be an impossible lie. This progress report is about people I've encountered who have not been interested in a love that looks like me, sounds like me, feels like me. It hasn't been difficult to observe how people are not interested in sharing time or conversation with me. There are certainly those who are content to dump their trash into my ears, mind and life, but those same people choose not to share any measure of their joy or happiness with me. By and large, people have only chosen to sow their darkness into me, even as I attempted to sow my light into them. I now have an awareness, an understanding and strength to reject all such offerings. As far as the question of eternity is concerned, Light has already won, but within the expanse of my physical life, the daily battle with darkness is overwhelming. I am no longer willing to risk my grip for those who are unaware of the damage their cavalier attitudes inflict.

What is shared between people molds the relationship they have. Think of the things you're willing to share with your friends. What you choose to share defines that friendship from your perspective. By the same token, you can get a good idea of how you're viewed by your friends by what they choose to share with you. The same analysis can be used with any type of relationship.

In my 9 to 5, I support two executives who have no interest in me as a human being. How do I know this? Because they do not ask questions about my life – my day, my week, my weekend. There's no interest in developing me as an employee. The verbal exchanges are only about what they want me to do for them and when they want it done by. The senior executive doesn't share anything about her life either. When I ask about her trips, vacation, holidays, she barely gives a stilted reply of "It was fine." The junior executive is perhaps more frustrating because he attempts to feign interest in speaking to me occasionally by talking about his kids and showing photos on his phone. However, as soon as I interject a comment, he shuts down the "conversation," tells me what he wants and makes an escape. At this point, I've supported these two for over three years. When I started with them, my energy was high, and I was eager to perform. Now, there's no interest in getting out of bed for work. These daily interactions have literally been a slow death.

It's important to be the best person I can be in every situation and encounter. Being my best self doesn't mean I'm always anyone's idea of a *good* person. It means I constantly work on being present and engaged, available and honest as I move through this world.

Authentic has become an overused word that is rarely embraced as a state of being. Some folks think my straight talk is too harsh. I don't' gossip; I provide my insight on situations. Speaking in platitudes has never been my thing. Being nice is a false sensibility. I do my best to be kind, but folks misunderstand kindness, truth and honesty.

For as long as I can remember, I've spoken my every truth and shown up earnestly as my authentic self, no matter the pain connected to doing so. My truth and authenticity may not always be pretty, fluffy, bouncy, joyful or anything the world prefers, but it has always been me at my most basic level – raw human.

This journey has shown that even though I have striven to be open, honest, sincere and accepting of people as they are, those same people were not interested in accepting me as I am. Over and over again that's what the disregard, neglect, rejection and general hatred amounts to. Whoever I am, whatever I am seen to represent is not wanted or respected. There is no appreciation or applied value.

> *People walked by and insulted Jesus and shook their heads, saying, "You said you could destroy the Temple and build it again in three days. So, save yourself! Come down from that cross if you are really the Son of God!"*
> *~ Matthew 27:39-40*

In my deep disgust, I remembered Jesus on the cross. He too was rejected by the masses. Bodily, brutally, horribly. When I remembered all Jesus suffered, I asked, *"Dear Jesus, how did you keep yourself from stepping down from the cross and killing everyone cheering for your death? Certainly, you could have done that and then climbed back up onto the cross to give Your Life for the rest of the world?"* Ruminating on how Jesus, in all His power and glory, could continue to fully execute God's plan for His life IN THE FACE of hatred and WITHIN HEARING of shouted blasphemies humbled me in such a profound way. The revelation of that bit of darkness, rebellion and willfulness in my heart was painfully humbling. How did a lover come to aspire to hatefulness?

Nevertheless, not my will, but yours, Father.

Since the beginning of our human story, people have been saying, "hell no; no thanks; that's ok; uhhh… I'll pass; maybe next time" to God, the Creator of everything known and unknown. God grew a paradise. Adam and Eve wanted something else. God gave individuals the right to rule themselves and their territories. People asked for a king to rule them instead. God provided a sacrifice to absolve mankind of all its sins in the person of Jesus Christ. People choose continually not to believe or accept the sacrifice. Jesus lives as an example for all to follow, yet so many give up seeking along the way. Even Lucifer rejected his purpose. God gave Lucifer the gift of music and the responsibility to bring the light. Lucifer wanted the human experience and waged war in Heaven to obtain it.

I don't want to say *hell no, no thanks* to my Lord and Savior. I don't want to be at war with Light and Joy. I don't want to be so beaten down by the world that I give up my anointing because of weariness and disappointment.

It was in asking Jesus how He kept from destroying the people who not only eagerly sought to destroy Him, but actually taunted Him to destroy them, that I better understood the choice to love as an amazingly burdensome responsibility. Now I'm learning to love through faith.

When I embarked on my listening, learning, and growing journey with God, I thought the process would only produce more love, joy, peace and wisdom. The world teaches that love is a soft thing – warm, cuddly, tender, and weak. Perhaps those who bask in the labor of someone else's love experience warmth and softness, but those who labor to love… well, we weather tempestuous storms, debilitating uncertainty and endure heart-breaking on-the-job training. We don't immediately see the benefits of the humiliation, shame, loneliness, sadness, abuse or temptations that hammer at us throughout the workday. But when we get to a certain point on our walk, we are able to look back and see where one humiliation prepared us for the next… until humiliation was no longer a concern. We see how shame shrouded us in darkness… until we decided to cast off the weight of shame and expose ourselves to more light. We can look back and see how loneliness felt excruciating for a time… but it was only in our aloneness that we were able to draw closer to God. There is a reason for everything connected to our life. There is a purpose for each season we enter on our journey. Keep walking. Keep trusting our Lord and Savior. Choose to love by continually choosing to receive the Love presented to you.

Meditation Verse: Matthew 26:15-26

While Pilate was sitting there on the judge's seat, his wife sent this message to him: "Don't do anything to that man, because he is innocent. Today I had a dream about him, and it troubled me very much." But the leading priests and elders convinced the crowd to ask for Barabbas to be freed and for Jesus to be killed. Pilate said, "I have Barabbas and Jesus. Which do you want me to set free for you?" The people answered, "Barabbas." Pilate asked, "So what should I do with Jesus, the one called the Christ?" They all answered, "Crucify him!"

Pilate asked, "Why? What wrong has he done?" But they shouted louder, "Crucify him!" When Pilate saw that he could do nothing about this and that a riot was starting, he took some water and washed his hands in front of the crowd. Then he said, "I am not guilty of this man's death. You are the ones who are causing it!" All the people answered, "We and our children will be responsible for his death." Then he set Barabbas free. But Jesus was beaten with whips and handed over to the soldiers to be crucified.

Listen to: He Knows by Jeremy Camp

HELPING ON EMPTY

*My God, my God, why have You forsaken me? Why are
You so far from helping me, from the words of my
groaning? O my God, I cry by day, but You do not
answer; and by night, but find no rest*
~ Psalm 22:1-2

ON a winter's morning the year I turned forty, I walked to Central Park from home to record the first video message for the project that would become *Desert of Solitude*. The working title was *A Year of Wonder-filled Living*.

It was a sunny forty-three-degree day with sparkling heavy fresh snow on the ground. Living near the northeast corner of Central Park afforded daily convenient access to enjoy nature in the wilderness in the center of Manhattan. This corner of the Park was never crowded with tourists. Locals dotted the benches surrounding Harlem Meer, a large man-made duck pond stretching from Fifth Avenue to just beyond Lenox Avenue and 110th Street to 106th Street. New Yorkers jogged or walked the winding paths. There was a fishing spot where it was common to see old-timers teaching young people how to prepare bait and cast a line. Personal trainers occupied grassy sections for their clients. It was one of my favorite spots in the City – beautiful and full of life no matter the season.

On this particular morning, I walked through the Park along Fifth Avenue to 105th Street where there's two parallel paths in the center of the Conservatory Garden that are double-lined with trees and benches. During spring, summer and fall, the trees create a full canopy which feels almost cocoon-like by blocking out much of the traffic sounds along Fifth Avenue. In the winter the sense of canopy remains despite the sky peeking through the spindly, reaching branches.

My walk ended at the center of the first tree-lined path. Sitting on a bench, breathing in the quiet tranquility of the space, listening to the wind whistle through the empty branches occasionally adorned with twittering birds, I prepared myself to share on camera.

The first message surprised me. Being a pretty blunt person, straight talk is rarely a surprise. Due to a lifelong practice of journaling, there's a deep awareness and acknowledgement of the hidden scary thoughts that seemingly spring up from nowhere. Despite my frequent self-communication, the overwhelming sadness that flowed from me when I began speaking into the camera was completely unexpected. I thought I had overcome some of the things bubbling up from my deep well of sorrow.

The idea of helping on empty began to form in my mind as a way to describe my state and desire to keep moving forward.

For several years prior, I had been wallowing in pain, aloneness, rejection, sadness, depression and exhaustion because I wasn't willing to accept my solitary life. Despite living in a city of nearly 8.5 million people, working at a global firm with 220,000 employees, and attending a church with over 8,000 other congregants, I had no meaningful relationships with anyone. No shared meals, no shared histories, no shared days. I functioned within a routine that didn't require thought, intelligence or passion. Frankly, none of it required my presence. Being so painfully aware of how dispensable, replaceable, unremarkable I was to people was emotionally debilitating.

Confronting my thoughts and emotions regarding the state of my life was difficult because I hadn't always been that person.

More importantly, I knew it was not the person I would be in the end. However, the road between where I was and where I believed I was going was not clear.

Despite being single all my adult life and without family for half of it, being alone continues to be a difficult topic to talk and write about. The difficulty is primarily due to the fact that living a single life had never been my desire or intention. Though I had never enjoyed dating, because most men became sexually aggressive almost immediately, I held on to an abiding belief that eventually I would click with a man who would become my life partner. Each passing year of my solitary thirties saw this hope diminish more and more. The abundant thinking I embraced for my fortieth year included embracing every hurt, pain and hidden thing within me. When I began to look inwardly with compassion, I no longer felt compelled to run from my loneliness or to demonize it. I began to embrace it and acknowledge the many ways it could be enjoyed. And expanded.

Yes, I am alone. No, singleness is not a death sentence. I owe it to myself to stop living as if I am already gone from the world.

Deciding to embrace my solitude didn't mean I no longer wanted a partner in life or that I suddenly enjoyed my own company above all others. Embracing solitude was about honoring my life in every moment, no matter the condition or status. In the face of disappointment, I wanted to focus on joy.

This state of growth needed to be embodied. The process taught me to sit still and accept being carved, shaped and changed – a requirement for the *Holy Spirit Training Course for the Ministry to Come*, i.e. life.

The question I contemplated earnestly was, *If I can't accept my life as it is today, how can I possibly be prepared to receive everything to come tomorrow?*

Remaining in faith requires consistent conscious decision-making. The ability to hold on to God's promises derives from a steady belief. This belief makes way for an understanding of being fully blessed in every past, present and future moment. There is nothing lacking in me or my life. God is not waiting for my life to exhibit certain elements to make me whole or to make me worthy of His Grace. Everything I need to be, I am already – a vessel and conduit of grace.

Helping on empty is about embracing every experience and feeling, processing them into edible fruit and presenting a banquet for those who want to partake.

For a long time, I have understood that every moment of pain and everything I've perceived in the world as a negative attack on my life, against my belief, a violation of my personhood, who I am, who I want to be, targeting my future, my dreams, my vision – everything that I've experienced as a negative has always benefited me. Always. No negative situation has ever done more harm than good. Even the most unbearable things have blessed me on the other side of healing. In every single instance. Even knowing that, emptiness has a way of camouflaging an entire life. In the dark moments, my thoughts centered on not being where I wanted to be, not having what I had asked for, not being able to identify God's promised blessings or any true friends. The descent would deepen into a lamentation – *Where is my husband? Where are my children? Where's my family? Where is my joy? Where is my joy?*

Since childhood, I have prayed consistently for a home and loving family. In my late teens financial security was added to my prayers with a request for Gods provision. That day in the Park, I had been well aware and greatly appreciative of God's exceeding provision and care of me. He had provided a space in a city I had always wanted to live in but had been beyond my scope in every way when I first arrived. A home big enough to begin a family in and comfortable enough to host friends in. Jehovah had provided a foundation to offer to others everything I've ever asked for. It was imperative to focus on what had already been provided, what I had already been guided through and the lessons so diligently taught. In essence, that's the root of helping on empty.

There was no husband, but there was still belief that one would come. No children, but I trusted that the opportunity to nurture and love someone was near. My life was a staging area for the family I could see so clearly, but they remained so very elusive.

∞ ∞ ∞

Focusing on the absence of a man and children in my life kept me in an emotional prison wallowing in sadness, disappointment, and a whole lot of self-doubt. *What could I have done differently? Who should I have said yes to? Did I try hard enough? What kind of woman am I? How can I possibly be enough for anybody? What if I can't handle what I'm asking for? What if being alone is the blessing?* Such circular thoughts breed dissatisfaction and depression if they aren't stopped. They will envelope and suffocate with their intensity. Dissatisfaction became the backdrop of my insignificance. A narrative of being nothing and meaning nothing because there is no one around to make me matter. My inability to see my value because what I wanted hadn't manifested meant that I was devaluing everything else that had. God was manifesting *me*.

When I made myself insignificant, I devalued the God I claimed to have a personal relationship with, the God I could not see but whose Spirit transformed my life, whose Presence I felt throughout my being and who continually provided for me in ways I couldn't explain. I devalued the sacrifice of His Son, my Savior Jesus. When cognizant of destructive thoughts, I aggressively root them out because I refuse to repay Grace with ungratefulness. I do not want to miss everything God has for me in any given moment.

∞ ∞ ∞

It has been extremely difficult to continue moving forward, to maintain an open heart, to repeatedly offer a gracious spirit, to greet each new day with hope, to let go of hurts even as they continue to hurtle towards me. My strength has not saved me from hiding. Sometimes burying my head in the snow, sand, dirt or under my sheets was the best I could do to maintain. Many times, avoiding the world was the only way forward. Unfortunately, every time I hid, I also kept my blessings, talents and gifts hidden. Though hiding was the preferred way to practice self-preservation, it became harder to re-emerge after each episode.

Self-preservation has been my way since childhood. The earliest, most painful lesson I remember is speaking up in defense of myself when no one else would. My experiences forged me into a fighter and survivor. These core characteristics are embedded and formed a woman who thinks like a doer and provider. Perhaps that's why I've been put in situations beyond my ability and understanding to do for myself. Maybe that's why God's provision is the cornerstone of my journey.

As in all things, coming full circle with self-preservation brings a different understanding than it began with. At first, it was a way to protect myself from external forces. Eventually, closing down neutralized the ability to receive anything and stunted internal growth.

∞ ∞ ∞

The full circle of emptiness brings the realization that whether achieved by being drained or choosing to pour yourself out, emptiness is a blessing. Emptying out is a process that repeats in a loop throughout our existence. Every time I get rid of all the things I prop myself up with, I am left with an unformed silence which amplifies God's voice.

Emptiness is the only state that can be filled.

Despair, quietness, aloneness, solitude initially appear as unbearable burdens. However, if they are fully experienced, they will contribute to a harvest bountiful enough to nourish many. It's in these dark lonely spaces where God is received as Sovereign, Creator, Savior, and All-in-All that we can easily submit to being held, guided, and comforted. Being within His grasp is the best place to accept how dear and precious we are. Indeed, how His Spirit makes us resilient enough to endure all things.

Helping on empty means whatever we are called to do, *we are able to do* – no matter our perception of positive or negative. In fact, we are more than able, we're fully capable because God has already provided everything we need to perform on His behalf when He calls.

Listen to: *Lord I'm Ready Now* by Plumb

LOVE, A POSTMORTEM

I once loved
With a purity of
Hope
Before
My love was tested
For conditions
By one who
Sought to break me
Now I love with an
Expectation
To be hurt
He meant me no good
So, he presented
No good to me

Interesting
I didn't see that when
I saw us

This is why the world has
A shortage of Lovers
Those who love openly
Are hated viciously
By those they bare their
Hearts to
And each time the Lovers
Choose to love again
They are aware
Their love is poured from a
Tainted and ruptured vessel
From which it takes
Longer to give
And is harder to receive

This less pure
More defined
Conditional love
Hopes for little and
Expects the worse
Lovers become less willing
To love those who don't
Love them
And that's how Lovers
Disappear from the earth

WHERE DID MY ZEAL GO?

> *I can testify that they have a zeal for God, but it is not enlightened. For being ignorant of the righteousness that comes from God, and seeking to establish their own, they have not submitted to God's righteousness. For Christ is the end of the law so that there may be righteousness for everyone who believes.*
> ~ Romans 10:2-4

IN recent years, I've been forced to face harsh realizations about my faith and the faith practices I witness around me. These realizations came in the form of mental asides, afterthoughts, mild irritations, and frequent frustrations.

When I was on Facebook, my feed occasionally displayed the rapturous updates of young Christians – early to mid-thirties, who had committed or re-committed themselves to Jesus Christ after having loads of fun in the world. The cynic in me often thought how great it must be to do everything one wanted to do in one's adult life and still have the opportunity to return and declare one's love for Jesus.

The weary Christian in me often remembers when I was also extremely passionate about my pursuit. Yet prior to my thirst for Jesus Christ, I, too, was excited to explore the ways of the world. There was something in me that resented not being wild in my youth as I began to age into the background of life.

Basically, my image of Christianity was dragging me down.

In the world the "church" is all about fellowship meetings – eating, singing, and telling your neighbor (the person or people standing near you in service) that you love them or you're glad to see them. "Church" is advertised as a ministry outreach to the poor, the broken, the injured, the rejected, the spiritually lost. It becomes a routine, or a series of goals centered around missionary trips, church plantings, fund-raising, and sister or satellite churches in far-flung locations. Colloquial "church" is outward experience focused. It's about being seen, having the "right" friends, current fashions, socializing and inciting rapturous applause accompanied by a chorus of *amen* for paraphrased scripture. Colloquial church has become a ritual of obeying men who imagine they have cornered the market on God's Word.

In the world, "church" is about a network or a special clique. A group of people who stick together as long as they have the same confession of faith (not to be confused with the *practice* of faith) and nothing is expected of them outside of the church walls that isn't well-publicized far and wide for the effort.

"Church" mimics the world. *Lights...camera...action!* You're on...now perform! Perhaps that's why I've become so dissatisfied with the people I encounter in "church" and self-proclaimed Christians outside of church. What I've noticed is that people repackage worldly goods and try to sell it to Believers as godly fruit. Personally, I don't want to use anything the World had first as an expression of my faith life. And before you think the world had Jesus first, I'll remind you that in the beginning was the Word and the Word was with God.

To sum up my frustrations, I've been looking for the Christ in Christians. As diligently as I've searched, I've rarely encountered Christ in "church" settings or church-goers, however, I've certainly encountered Jesus in many other places and people outside of church.

My "church" experiences have not been about showing love or being love. They haven't been about openness, honesty, availability or acceptance. I've experienced more rejection in the "church" and by "church folk" – through relationships and service in ministries – than any other area in my life (and I've certainly known great rejection in other areas). In my experience, church organizations choose to operate like businesses but aren't nearly as conscientious with their "human capital" as businesses generally are. I've had more difficulty trying to volunteer for various ministries in various churches than I've had becoming a volunteer for senate campaigns.

Hillary Clinton's 2006 New York Senate Campaign required a background check, a phone interview and an in-person interview. A bit much in my opinion at the time, but her husband was a former president of the United States of America. I got it and got over it. However, that's nothing compared to the steps required for volunteering at my third church in New York City.

∞ ∞ ∞

Modern "churches" appear to be geared towards conversion and beginners in the Word. There seems to be very little focus or substance for the seasoned Believer.

Where is the fellowship or prayer circle for those who have loved themselves empty? Or for those who have become so disillusioned, the world begins to look like salvation? Where is the church for the Believer with no intention of returning to the world? The person who's just trying to get through a humdrum day, week, month, or year? The person passing time with no desire to waste their time. Where's the church for the person who isn't lacking in faith, but may simply be in an in-between time, waiting for the next assignment? Where's the church for the Believer who simply needs a hug because it's Wednesday? Where's the community that actually reaches out within itself? To the Believers who are still hurt or newly hurt by its members? To the Believers who need more than words, who need to be shown how loved they are? Those who need someone to show up in their daily life? Need to know how much they matter in the chain of events that surround their existence. Where's that community that heals itself, covers itself, embraces itself and then radiates itself to surrounding communities? If church folk actually took the time to get to know each other, and made the effort to appreciate their neighbor, instead of just telling them that they're glad to see them during service, they would be a much more gracious people when they encounter the world outside of their community. They would be much more radiant in their workplaces, on their travels and in their politics.

Frustration grew from several years of actively desiring and seeking a Christian community in New York City and realizing no tangible relationships had developed from the effort.

From high school through my twenties, I considered myself a professional church visitor. The first church I felt a connection to was my high school friend's church. I attended as her guest for eight years. Afterwards, I visited churches here and there and sought out historic churches on my travels.

The first congregation I joined in New York City was one I had watched on TV while living in Milwaukee. They broadcast from Los Angeles and had a satellite church across from Central Park at the corner of 96th Street in New York. They provided a Word-based teaching while always insisting the congregation read the Bible for our own understanding. We weren't expected to accept the teacher's interpretation as law. We were taught not to.

The teachings and experiences in this congregation catalyzed me. Shortly after setting foot in the building, I began studying the Bible like I had never been able to do before. Teachings included scripture quotes from multiple versions of the Bible. This opened me to looking for a version I could read easily. When that happened, my comprehension expanded exponentially. I committed my life to Jesus Christ and received my adult baptism at that first church.

I was consistently active in at least four ministries at a time and attended nearly every monthly special event. I was there for most Sunday morning services and Thursday evening Bible Studies. My life was the "church" for the time I was there, and boy, did I grow! But I didn't conform to every part of that congregation's culture.

The best thing I learned during my time with that congregation was "to study and show myself approved." I am a literal learner and doer. If the Teacher is telling me that everything I need for my life is in the Word of God, and all I have to do is study the Word, then that's what I will do. So indeed, growth was miraculous when I went from not reading my Bible to studying it faithfully. Every word was the most succulent nourishment for me. My world became new, leading to renewed vision and understanding. That's where the rapturous passion comes from – breathing in the life of God's Word is the source of zeal. Experiencing God's Word as refreshment is sustenance. The Word continually revives and propels.

All things, stages and cycles eventually come to an end. Shortly after a dubious and disturbing change in leadership, I sought a new church home.

The second church I attended in New York City was much smaller. Eventually, it would feel like a cult. They focused on theology. Primarily, what western thinkers think of God's Word… and how to best summarize the Bible. For six months I attended one or two small group sessions a week in addition to Sunday service. My quest has always been to seek a closer and stronger connection to people. Ideally, small groups would be a way to achieve that.

My primary lesson from this second congregation was an awareness of how important it is to maintain independent thought and my own understanding of God's Word.

The small group sessions became a forum for the leadership to exercise more control over the thinking (therefore, the beliefs) of the attending congregants. Most of us were young adults who were new or alone in the City. Easy prey.

The small group leaders had their agenda and instructed group members not to interrupt their teachings and to hold our questions. Mind you, this was billed as a discussion group. I did what made sense to me. I asked questions, shared my opinions and made requests. When they shut me down in the meeting, I followed-up via the Facebook group page by sharing scripture with everyone. The small groups weren't Bible-based. They were sharing from a workbook that essentially re-imagined the Bible. I was blocked, reported and shunned from the group meetings. The "church" leaders thought my pointing out scripture was disruptive to their teachings. With agreement, I said, "If you're teaching the Bible wrong, and I'm sitting in front of you, yeah, I'm gonna say something." After speaking with the head pastor one-on-one (he led one of the small groups I attended), I decided that I needed to preserve myself and find another congregation.

After a six-month break, I decided to attend a service at what would become my third congregation in New York. When I began writing this book, I had been there for four years. Throughout the first year, I sat quietly in services and soaked in the teachings. There was no desire to get involved beyond greeting people near me in service. At the beginning of the second year, I went to Israel for a Bible Study Tour that followed Jesus' ministry route.

Three others from the congregation also went. Together, we joined other groups from around the world. Again, I thought it would be the beginning of great relationships. It wasn't.

∞ ∞ ∞

After returning from Israel, I applied join the children's ministry as a teacher. To participate in the church's ministries, an online application was required. If you were unable to apply online, dates were provided to the congregation for in-person opportunities to apply. General interviews or information sessions were held monthly. During these sessions a four-page paper application needed to be filled out requiring two references who also attended the church and knew the applicant "well." After handing in the application, applicants were required to attend the New Believers class about the "church's" beliefs. All this took place on weeknights.

If the references panned out, you would have to return for an in-person one-on-one interview within the next month or two. During the workday. This process was extended over two or three months for me. That's effectively more of a process than most jobs I've had. During the time I was applying to join a ministry at Church #3, I was a bonded employee working on the executive floor of a top global bank on Park Avenue where the bosses of Wall Street sat. To get that job, all they required was fingerprints, background check and an interview. Within a week I had a desk assignment.

Becoming a volunteer at church shouldn't be more difficult than becoming a volunteer for an ex-First Lady of the United States during her senatorial campaign or working on an executive floor on Park Avenue in the financial capital of the world. Nor should it be based on who you know or how well they think they know you.

The problem was, I had learned how to hide. I had run up against some powerful controlling spirits and abusers of authority in my prior two congregations. My faith and trust in people who claimed to be followers of Christ had taken some brutal beatings. I needed to heal and wanted nothing more than to sit quietly in the back of the top balcony, far away from the pulpit, unseen and unheard. I was hurt but I wasn't willing to forfeit hearing the Word spoken to a congregation. Nor was I willing to sit without serving.

As a result of hiding so well, I didn't have any personal relationships with anyone in the church. The three other people from the congregation who had gone to Israel with me a year prior were the only people I could reasonably reach out to for references. One was an elderly woman whose son had asked me to keep watch over during the tour. The other two were a couple; the husband played an instrument in the church band; the wife was a repressed and frustrated new mother. We had distantly friendly interactions while touring Israel. When we returned, they politely avoided me.

Generally speaking, I'm outspoken. There were a few occasions during the Israel trip when I went head-to-head with life-long ministers and missionaries who spoke in hate-filled tones about populations they were "ministering" to around the world. The couple from my church didn't approve of my calling folks out for their racism and prejudice. The husband, who is German, had actually shared a "testimony" during a prayer session in Haifa, a city nestled in the shadow of Mount Carmel, about the fear he experienced daily as a white man in Brooklyn living near a mosque. That trip was a lot. It was eye-opening and heart-breaking. It presented a painfully clear view of what passes for Christian leadership and education in the world.

The German's wife agreed to be a reference for my application for the Children's Ministry.

Eager to teach, I accepted what I could get.

It seems like a lifetime ago.

This is where my zeal has gotten me in the "church" – not wanting to share space or speak to professed believers in person. Truly tragic... and a waste. I have a heart of light I want to share, and it has been rejected at every turn by people who profess Christ. This has been a struggle to comprehend and overcome. How much do I push back? How long do I sit out? How long do I keep to myself and shield my light?

Even as a seasoned Believer, I felt like giving up on my ministry application. Eventually, I survived the process only to deal with an egomaniac in the Children's Ministry who insisted that my availability be what she wanted rather than what I could do. During that time, my corporate job ate up about fifty hours a week and I was desperately trying to manage that down to give more time to my full-time graduate studies. Still, I was offering the Children's Ministry two Sundays and a Tuesday night a month, however, I anticipated that later in the year my availability would change to one Sunday a month for a while. Unfortunately, the head of the children's ministry needed to control and dominate the situation. My offering and fore-sharing wasn't enough. She claimed my lack of "general availability" made me unfit for the ministry's needs.

I made a complaint to the church administration. They allowed me to speak but I didn't get my post back. That was quite a devastating blow. No matter what I did in life, I couldn't get close to anyone or engage fully with meaningful activity.

It took another year or more before I even considered applying for another ministry. When I did, it was for the online prayer ministry specifically because I could do it remotely and wouldn't have to deal with people directly. They required a new application with references. I didn't feel comfortable asking for another reference from a woman who clearly didn't like me. My inability to provide references from the congregation I had attended for a number of years ended my application process.

I've never been interested in burying my talents, but I never thought my biggest spiritual struggles would be within the congregations I considered myself a part of.

Fortunately, these experiences were not the end of my faith. Instead, they have combined to create a solid experiential foundation to grow from.

Though Church #1 gave me a solid foundation, or perhaps because they did, I was in danger of idolizing my pastor. When he was dismissed, I wrote to him and his wife declaring my support of them and outrage at the senior pastor, who lived across the country and visited monthly, terminating him with no notice to the congregation for a disagreement that sounded very political. I vowed to follow the man I considered to be my primary pastor wherever he went. Luckily for me, they never responded to my letter. They ended up moving to Georgia.

The conflict at Church #2 showed me the power and value of faith. When the head pastor and I sat down for a one-on-one, he exposed himself by speaking about his manipulations and need to control the congregation. He understood he wasn't feeding his flock with a pure Word. He was redirecting and misguiding people with philosophy and theology. He would perhaps quote one scripture during a sermon and read whole passages from theological essays. Because I was taught to read the Bible for myself, I knew the Bible was self-referencing. Anything you need to understand has an explanation and background somewhere in the book. Sitting in church listening to someone read someone else's ideas on what was written seemed ridiculous to me. I shared as much. My challenge was met with such aggression, I saw him and his cohorts clearly.

The best lesson for understanding my faith came towards the end of that conversation. Perhaps he was attempting to flatter my ego, but I saw the truth of his words. His church was renting a room over a storefront on the Upper West Side off of 72nd and Broadway. They wanted a bigger space. He told me I had a faith unlike anyone he had met before. He believed Jesus but he didn't consider himself to have faith. For that reason, he was asking me, a woman of faith, to petition on his behalf for a meeting space. I made one call on his behalf, then put distance between us to get away from the fire I saw engulfing him.

The layers of bureaucracy in Church #3 taught me that appealing to a higher authority in the world will never bring the justice I need. My "church home" is not a building or congregation. Everything I need for true connection and relationship is within me and the One I seek is never far from me. Accepting this keeps me balanced, whole and focused.

∞ ∞ ∞

The conflicts with church leaders vividly exposed the controlling spirit attached to my life. All the leaders attempted to control some aspect of me – my mind, my faith, my time, my voice, my beliefs, my actions. Throughout the years, there have been many very deep moments of helplessness and hopelessness. Times of disbelief and unbelief, long periods of self-doubt.

Ultimately, I want to belong someplace, I desire a community, I want to connect with people, I'm looking for leadership and I would rather not stand alone. The overall lesson is *community is nice, but it doesn't trump a personal relationship with God*. No man, group or organization takes precedence over the Word of God. Their reputation, education or experience doesn't weigh in their favor against God. If their words or behavior do not ring true or line up with the Word as I read it and understand it, I have to remove myself from their influence.

Self-preservation can also be resistance.

It's paramount that we not only cultivate our personal relationship with God, we must also protect and nurture it. Cultivation, protection and nurturing means limited, reduced or no exposure to harmful elements with a focus of positioning, directing and feeding the relationship only good, healthy food for growth and strength. This relational source infuses all other interpersonal relationships as well.

TO BE KNOWN BY NO ONE

It must be me.
Weird. Defective.
Incomplete.
Off-putting. Irrelevant.
Unable to truly connect.
Wasted years. Deferred dreams.
Colossal amounts of time and energy
building a life around relationships,
weaving in love and flexibility,
Willing to be what was needed.
Straining to see God in the unlovable,
ungrateful and unrepentant.
Attempting to stand when
I could barely crawl.
Receiving the burdens of community
without the benefits.
Where is my shelter?
Whom can I lean on?
What does a close
companion look like?
Being fully available in every area
drains a life of spirit.
Devoted worker --
long hours, weekends, holidays
as needed.
No questions, only willingness
to adjust my life with
a desire to give
all of me, some of me,

whatever of me was needed.
Now there's none of me that
hasn't been discarded.

It must be me.
I see love.
People know how to show love,
yet refuse to show me love.
I see friendships.
People know how to be friends,
unfortunately, not to me.
I see supportive work environments,
but I'm always outside the circle.
How did I get outside the matrix of life?
How did I come to exist
outside of the norm –
on the outskirts of relationships –
when all I wanted was
to offer the best of me
to everyone I encounter?

FIRST FRUIT

DURING my thirty-ninth spring, which happened to be my second spring in my East Harlem co-op apartment, I planted my first garden. My apartment had a 10x15 foot enclosed patio attached to it which was plenty of space to create a potted garden semi-retreat.

The garden was started with the intent to cultivate something that would nurture me. Something I could give attention and love to and receive the fruit of that effort from the garden's harvest.

The memory of my first harvest is special. I was in awe at every step of the process. The biggest plants with the biggest fruit were planted as seeds. To witness a seed sprout, grow, flower, and produce fruit is to witness the miracle of life. Gardening illustrates God's abundant grace and provision in such a colorful and experiential way. Each step of the process reminded me of how we are to give the first fruits of our crops to God. That reminder led to exploring the question: *What's so special about that first crop?*

As a beginner gardener, the significance of first fruit represents:

- Firming of a vision
- Seeing a plan come together
- Importance of process
- Manifestation of a promise
- Need for love, attention, and care
- Fullness of time
- Commitment and development of the Gardener

Consider this: there was a seed that was nothing by itself. In fact, the seed was debris from a dying or shedding plant. It fell to the ground with no awareness that anything was possible beyond the fall. The fallen seed was embraced by the earth and watered by the weeping sky. From such love, attention and care, the forgotten seed germinated. Life sprang up and it became a plant reaching for the sun. The plant grew and multiplied with branches, leaves and flowers. It provided beauty and nourishment. All because it was refreshed with care when it was dead and buried.

If we are to partake of such miracles daily, the least we can do is give thanks and honor the Master Gardener with a taste of what He's provided us.

WHEN TRUTH DESTROYS

> *"I baptize you with water, but there is one coming who is greater than I am. I am not good enough to untie His sandals. He will baptize you with the Holy Spirit and fire. He will come ready to clean the grain, separating the good grain from the chaff. He will put the good part of the grain into His barn, but He will burn the chaff with a fire that cannot be put out."*
> ~ Luke 3:16-18

SOME time ago, a woman told me she thought my directness in sharing my truth was courageous. Somewhat bitterly, I responded, "People can't handle their own truth, so my truth has been destructive. None of the relationships I've spoken directly in have survived my words."

"That's why I think you're so courageous," she continued. "You're living free as you are, not as other people will have you be. You're not restricted to their view of you because you are so direct about where you are and what you need."

Since that conversation I have thought of the many relationships that changed drastically or ended because I exposed myself in truth. Then I thought of how each of those relationships would probably still be as superficially unsatisfying and emotionally frustrating had I held my tongue. There is no virtue in wearing masks of false communion. No one is served by friendly façades, believing in the vanity of shallow relationships. I mourned each relationship that didn't survive the fire and gave thanks for the people and the lessons they taught me.

It was never my desire to come to the end of people, but I've come to learn of that when we are able to see the true limitations and weaknesses of human relationships, only then are we truly open to the incomprehensible vastness of possibilities available through our personal relationship with God. The whole of the Bible is an instruction manual on how to be in right relationship with our Creator. He even presented Himself in the flesh to model His Book of Instruction for those in need of visual aid. Jesus exhibited the nature and purpose of relationship. When we get that understanding – the understanding of the truth of Jesus Christ – everything that burned up in our life when we first learned to be true to ourselves, ceases to matter. It was all chaff in the wind. The fire of truth refines that which is true and created to endure, it destroys the falseness of everything rooted in the flesh.

FORGOTTEN

I am forgotten.
Therefore, I have
Stopped remembering.

ALONE VS. SOLITUDE

BEING alone in the world is different than living in solitude. Perhaps the difference is in the concreteness of aloneness and the option of solitude.

"Alone" is a contraction of "all in one," yet we're socialized to shun aloneness, or singleness. Being alone is a paradox.

Aloneness is raw truth, a lie, a blessing and a curse. No matter our family and community environment, we all arrive into the world by ourselves. We experience limitations differently. We may have familial and communal connections, but what we take away from those will be unique to our point of view and understanding. How we encounter and respond to life will be based on how we processed everything that came before.

Long ago, I realized my inability to see greatness in myself was a result of the way relatives treated me in my youth. In time, I learned my specialness isn't predicated on anyone acknowledging it. Neither is yours. It's essential to recognize what makes us unique. Acknowledging our gifts builds appreciation. We each have a responsibility to ourselves and our lives to grow beyond limitations.

Being alone highlights the absence of others. There is no one to turn to, to learn with, to show up for, and no one to show up for you. Emergencies and milestones are the hardest. Solo celebrations eventually feel hollow. After a while, nothing seems worth observing.

Solitude is calmness, clarity, confidence and quiet.

Solitude highlights the completeness of self. It gives time and space to reflect on environments, situations, and relationships as well as their impact on your entire person. It's a process of inward seeking, self-evaluation and self-understanding. Solitude leads to acceptance of yourself as embodying everything needed for a fulfilling life. Nothing outside of you will benefit you more than what's inside of you. Solitude provides daily examples of how you are enough for your life. You learn to trust your ability to be or obtain everything you need.

Reaching for solitude in aloneness leads to freedom. The struggle is getting comfortable with being alone. This involves releasing worldly views about the quality of life a single person can have.

Though I have learned to embrace my single life and protect it fiercely, there is still a deep yearning for companionship. Unfortunately, over the years when I've reached out and invited people in, I've been disappointed by their inability to be companionable in my space. There's usually a big clash due to unspoken expectations. After the inevitable discord, the guest is viewed as a disturber of my peace. Without fail, they're ousted and not invited back.

The tug of war was necessary to get to a point where I am no longer willing to sacrifice the peace I know for the company of unknowns.

When life is full of relationships, it's nearly impossible to focus inwardly. Since single people are not accounted for in the framework of society, most cling to attachment in an effort to be seen. Often societal norms set us on a life course with an outward focus, keeping people devoted to a timeline and schedule that rarely represents what they actually want for themselves. People pursue cultural and traditional symbols of good living without understanding what it is to actually live well.

LESSONS FROM SOLITUDE

solitude does not always equal loneliness
company rarely equals companionship
inviting others into my peace often taints it
someone who can sit quietly with me is a rare find
relaxing and balancing can be daily activities
solitude needs to be protected
home becomes sanctuary
open doors require filters
when the invited become unwelcome
invitations must be withdrawn
to reclaim a peaceful home
the strongest filter is a closed door

TRAUMA OF THE UNSEEN

Many traumas ripple through a life
Remembered forgotten long ago feeling like now
How to tell what's real or simply
Perception from trauma tinted lenses
Impossible to know if the
Traumatized have no awareness of their state
One revels in solitude because loneliness
has become a way of life
Quietness broken by occasional conversations
with strangers labeled as friends.
True friends don't allow friends to rot
Unseen. Unheard. Unfelt. Unknown.

WOMANHOOD
☀
PRICKLY PEAR BLOSSOM

BE ANYTHING

I had such bright
hopes and dreams
when I believed
I could
be anything
I tried
strived
over-achieved
if thoughts manifest reality
the American Dream
wouldn't be
unreachable
and life would be
different
all I truly wanted
was freedom to be me
without threat, violence
shame or compromise
how tragic
being me
proved to be
the hardest thing

TO GOD BE THE GLORY

I give all the glory and credit to God for the woman He has created me to be and for the woman He is continually forming me into.

I'm in awe of how He has designed and chiseled me according to His vision and plan. I am amazing! I am wonderful! I have the capability of being fully authentic and absolutely fearless!

Emotionally, I was chased into hiding a number of years ago. Slowly, over the last couple of years I have struggled to return fully into the light. All of me, all at once – continually and persistently. I didn't think I had any appreciation for the darkness until I began to explore the illusion of my own invisibility. I could sit back and watch life happen to others. I could give myself time to sulk over my wounds. I could plan and fantasize about a more perfect tomorrow... thereby minimizing the triumphs and worries of today.

When did I begin to believe the lies about me? When did I first believe, like a memory, the false image of what my life would be? When did I stop appreciating my own power? When did I stop recognizing my own beauty? Wonder of wonders, I am here! Of all the impossibilities in the world, I have developed a voice that has cowed and destroyed demons attached to my life and banned them from my present and my future. Of all the unthinkable happenings in the world, a neglected and forgotten girl-child grew into a fiercely independent and productive woman who seeks to love and nurture those in her care.

We look to others for safety and security, but humans are not equipped to give each other the safety and security we truly need. We yearn for partnership and community, but each can demolish our awareness of our true self. A good portion of my youth was wasted waiting for someone to rescue me from a living nightmare. Then one day, God provided an opportunity for me to be my own hero. He rescued me, but He GAVE ME the will to stand up and walk, the opportunity to reach out and seek helpers, and the voice to speak against the violent oppression in my life. When I look back on what I thought my heroes would look like throughout my life – mom, dad, uncles, aunts, grandmothers, a husband, education, faith, fitness, a good salary – I am relieved that none ever lived up to my needs. For if they had, they may have become idols in my heart and mind. Instead, when I look back on how I escaped and survived disasters throughout my life, I see the weak little girl, the awkward teenager, and the lonely solitary woman (internal images of myself) who decided to get up and walk through the doors God opened for her. I see me guided and protected by my Heavenly Father. The only one able to make a way through cement boxes thrown into the deep sea of hopelessness. I have learned through the long years of my desert crossing that God provides beyond the needs of our human relationships and beyond our understanding of His master plan. In my relationship with my Father God, through His Son Jesus, and by His Holy Spirit, there is nothing I lack.

There are battles He fights for us and there are battles He sends us into for victory in His name for His Kingdom. Our job is to learn to hear the difference... discern our obligation to His instruction. Nothing we encounter or overcome is for our lives alone. Our Heavenly Father has made it His business to build victorious warriors. Know your battle. Learn your strengths. Keep praises to God on your lips and songs to Him in your heart.

There is so much that seems to be missing from my life when I choose to focus on my emptiness. On the other hand, there's so much that's amazingly awesome when I choose to focus on my fullness.

Each step of our process and growth is a choice. Don't believe the lie that where you are is where you are meant to remain.

Everything in God's Kingdom is about forward motion, progress and growth. Don't eat the lie that what you have is all you are meant to keep.

God intends to bless us so we can bless others. Don't internalize the falseness that who you are today is all you will ever be. You were created to *become* so much more. Your life is your testimony.

Today is a building block for tomorrow. Embrace the fullness of today – opportunities to love, deepen your faith, embrace heartache and joy, share your story, be hospitable, offer refreshment – whatever today has for you to give or receive, do that... so tomorrow, you will answer similar opportunities with the wisdom of experience and the patience of a teacher.

Listen to: *You Say* by Lauren Daigle

PROGRESSIVE WOMEN IN A DEGENERATING SOCIETY

> The history of mankind is a history of repeated injuries and usurpations on the part of man toward woman, having in direct object the establishment of an absolute tyranny over her. To prove this, let facts be submitted to a candid world. [2]
> ~ Elizabeth Cady Stanton, Declaration of Sentiments

THE Women's Movement, also known as the Feminist Movement, began within the Abolitionist movement by African-American women demanding basic human and civil rights in the 1830's. Maria W. Stewart and Mary Mapps Douglas were prominent early speakers directing their commentary towards African American women.[3] From the beginning, the movement has been a series of events and ideas proclaiming the intelligence and value of women to their husbands, families, communities and nations. The history of the feminist movement is a study of the continuity of thought and process from two streams of consciousness. Black Women were fighting on multiple fronts – to eliminate slavery, to gain citizenship for African-Americans and to get equal rights for all women. Some white women joined the Abolitionist Movement, but their main goal was the equal rights of white women to white men and the right to vote could help them achieve that. Nearly 200 years later, Black Women are still fighting for basic civil and human rights for themselves and others. And white are still fighting to be equal to white men.

The overwhelming public knowledge about the Feminist Movement is skewed towards the goals and actions of white women in the movement. Very little is known, taught or shared about the Black Women who quite literally put their lives on the line to demand justice and equality. Therefore, the dominant culture of the Feminist Movement focuses on the dominant culture in America – whiteness.

> You white women speak here of rights. I speak of wrongs. I, as a colored woman, have had in this country an education which has made me feel as if I were in the situation of Ishmael, my hand against every man, and every man's hand against me.
> ~ Frances Ellen Watkins Harper

Neither group of women had in mind the goal of taking over the male role in the household or society. Their primary goals were to become equal partners and citizens. That shouldn't be an outrageous idea requiring two centuries of agitation, protests, and legislation here we are. Seeking the right to vote was basically a request to speak, be heard and seen. However, the quest for equal rights has led to the skewed belief that a woman who wishes to be equal to a man is a woman who places little value on her femininity, ergo her sexuality. As a result, we have evolved from a society that idealized the mystique of femininity, thereby respecting it on some level, to a culture that over-sexualizes and objectifies the female body in every medium possible, thereby degrading it.

> "Now, in view of this entire disfranchisement of one-half the people of this country, their social and religious degradation—in view of the unjust laws above mentioned, and because women do feel themselves aggrieved, oppressed, and fraudulently deprived of their most sacred rights, we insist that

they have immediate admission to all the rights and privileges which belong to them as citizens of these United States." In entering upon the great work before us, we anticipate no small amount of misconception, misrepresentation, and ridicule; but we shall use every instrumentality within our power to effect our object.[4]"

~ Elizabeth Stanton & Susan B. Anthony

∞ ∞ ∞

The first stage of the Women's Movement, took place throughout the 19th and early 20th centuries[5] and was primarily focused on getting women the right to vote and the right of female representation in public office.[6]

The second wave took place from mid-to-late 20th century.[7] It is known primarily as a sexual revolution and characterized by the image of women burning their bras in the streets. Sex without commitment was billed as a personal freedom by the feminists of that generation. From there the battle for reproductive rights was engaged.

In *Four Waves of Feminism*, Martha Rampton writes, "Whereas the first wave of feminism was generally propelled by middle class white women, the second phase drew in women of color and developing nations, seeking sisterhood and solidarity and claiming 'Women's struggle is class struggle.' Feminists began speaking of women as a social class and coined phrases such as 'the personal is political' and 'identity politics' in an effort to demonstrate that race, class, and gender oppression are all related. They initiated a concentrated effort to rid society top-to-bottom of sexism, from children's cartoons to the highest levels of government.[8]"

In the 1990's, the third wave of feminism embraced diversity and change and the notion that there is no all-encompassing single feminist idea. The third wave sought "to challenge or avoid... the 'essentialist' definitions of femininity, which often assumed a universal female identity and over-emphasized the experiences of upper-middle-class white women.[9]" According to Rosemarie Tong in *Feminist Thought*, the third wave was a response "to the perceived failures of, and backlash against, initiatives and movements created by second wave..., and the realization that women are of 'many colors, ethnicities, nationalities, religions and cultural backgrounds.'" In other words, there is no universal womanhood. Therefore, Black Women do indeed stand alone. It's not a comfortable truth, but it is the way of the world.

The third wave informed my thoughts on femininity and women's rights, on body autonomy and identity. Insomuch as the historic agendas of the various stages of the feminist movement in the United States have not defined me, nor have they adequately addressed the woman I choose to be, I have come to consider myself to be post-feminist. Or more directly, I refer to myself as a Womanist who is concerned primarily with honoring womanhood. That's not to say that I have not started off in life in a better position than my predecessors. I am of course eternally grateful for the commitment, contribution, dedication and sacrifices of countless women through the centuries whose efforts to better the world for themselves, and the women who followed, have brought us to where we are today.

As with any movement or revolution, the end goal has to be narrowly defined so that successes and failures are easily identifiable. However, narrowly defining feminism – the rights of womanhood – is almost as restricting as leaving women without a voice altogether.

By and large, women around the world still function and are treated as if they have no representation or will to speak up for themselves. Women in Western societies are certainly forerunners in the Women's movement, but there are still women within Western cultures who are abused, victimized, and violated in countless ways. This is truly unfortunate for a population of women who have access to education and laws to protect them. The greater tragedy rests with women who live in countries where laws don't even speak to their existence. These women have no recourse for safety and dignity within their communities other than the good will of their male relatives. This is where the narrow objectives of the various stages of the feminist movement have fallen short of their lofty goals. As Dr. King said in his Letter from a Birmingham Jail, "Injustice anywhere is a threat to justice everywhere. We are caught in an inescapable network of mutuality tied in a single garment of destiny. Whatever affects one directly affects all indirectly.[10]"

When Western women believe they are free, they are laxer with the responsibility of freedom they have for those without it. An American woman cannot live with true freedom of feminine expression if her sisters around the world are being sold and used as sex slaves. Or if her sister in the office next door thinks the best way to break through the glass ceiling is to never marry or have children. When women's bodies are continually violated all over the world, no woman is really free to express her femininity without constraints. Therefore, the freedom touted in the Western cultures is an illusion.

It is not only expedient that women who are favored by advances in cultural norms and attitudes reach back, out and over to women who are still oppressed by unchanging norms and attitudes, but the same women who are seeking to progress society must also include the men and boys in their households and communities. Society is changed and culture is transformed, household by household, community by community. No one has more influence over the formation of a young mind than the mother feeding, nurturing, guiding starving or ignoring that mind. In this regard, many women have set aside their power and silenced their own voices within their own sphere of influence.

Representation is great. Protective laws are an awesome boon. Equal pay for equal work product is satisfying. Being respected for saying no and maintaining boundaries is empowering. However, none of those situations can stand against the tidal wave of societal transformation waiting to happen when each boy a woman raises grows into a man who honors and respects the intrinsic value of every female he encounters. Equally transformative would be each girl growing into a woman who is aware of both her value and the value of all her sisters. Such women would be as the women of Bethlehem said Ruth was to Naomi – better than seven sons.

∞ ∞ ∞

> We are not a charity – we are a global change movement. We have no interest in patching up this system as it is. We support women leaders and visionaries in grassroots communities who are changing the traditions, structures, norms, givens, politics, laws, and religious imperatives of those communities. We believe in all-out change and revolution, and we know nothing less will suffice if we want to end violence and save the planet.[11]
> ~ Eve Ensler

RAINN (Rape, Abuse & Incest National Network) is the largest anti-sexual violence organization in the United States. Their legislative agenda includes fighting sexual violence with DNA, improving services for victims of sexual violence, protecting children against sexual predators and campus safety.[12] RAINN has been a leader in tracking, analyzing and sharing statistics they compile and information they gather on federal and state sexual assault policies and laws. With this experience RAINN pushes forward to continually improve sexual assault policies and laws around the United States. A few of the most staggering statistics RAINN reports[13] are:

- ❖ Every 73 seconds an American is sexually assaulted
- ❖ The U.S. has an average of 433,648 victims (age 12 or older) of rape and sexual assault annually
- ❖ 1 in 6 American women has been a victim of rape or attempted rape in her lifetime[14]
- ❖ 15% of sexual assault and rape victims are under age 12
- ❖ 82% of all juvenile victims are female
- ❖ 90% of adult rape victims are female
- ❖ Approximately 70% of rape or sexual assault victims experience moderate to severe distress, a larger percentage than for any other violent crime
- ❖ 37% experience family/friend problems, including getting into arguments more frequently than before, not feeling able to trust their family/friends, or not feeling as close to them as before the crime

According to the World Health Organization, sexual assault victims are:

- ❖ 3 times more likely to suffer from depression
- ❖ 4 times more likely to contemplate suicide

- 6 times more likely to suffer from post-traumatic stress disorder
- 13 times more likely to abuse alcohol
- 26 times more likely to abuse drugs

The International Rescue Committee (IRC) is an organization that focuses on a wide array of global humanitarian issues. Primarily, the IRC is committed to empowering and protecting women and girls around the world. They provide:

- Health care, counseling and safe spaces to survivors of sexual violence in more than 17 countries
- Annual training and education of 2.5 million men and women in ways to prevent sexual violence
- Economic empowerment programs which increase women's income and ability to provide for themselves and their family
- They work to strengthen national and international laws against sexual violence and the exploitation of women

According to the Women's Empowerment and Protection page on the IRC website, "Violence against women is one of the most widespread of human rights abuses. One out of every three women worldwide will be physically, sexually or otherwise abused during her lifetime. During times of war and conflict, sexual violence is used to terrorize and humiliate women and girls. Survivors often suffer further victimization by family and society. The IRC works to break this cycle of violence by helping survivors to heal, delivering care to victims of sexual assault, and by bringing women together for mutual support.[15]"

One in six American women and one in three women worldwide being violated during their lifetime sounds like a legacy that's too closely joined for freedom to take a full breath.

The consequences of violence against women are debilitating emotionally, mentally, physically, sexually and spiritually. The psychological and social consequences are equally devastating, as the prevailing stigma associated with sexual violence often leaves women isolated and increasingly vulnerable. The trauma a survivor experiences goes beyond her own suffering, also rendering great costs to her family and community.[16] In an effort to combat this devastation, the IRC operates grassroots campaigns geared towards encouraging women to speak out and share their experiences within their communities. The IRC also reaches out to boys and men in an effort to change the cultural attitudes that support abusive environments towards women.

Crimes against femininity – girls and women – are not isolated or rare. Atrocities against girls and women are committed each hour everywhere in the world. No woman of today's generation can truly claim to be progressive unless she is working to improve the lives of women who are being destroyed by the rage of some men and the nonchalance of others. The primary focus for progress may not be the same for every group of women in the world, but we are all in the same boat attempting to navigate and eliminate the violence against us.

Throughout history, men and women have had various roles across cultures, religions and regions of the world. When looking closely, nuances of progressive thought regarding women, family, community and society based on faith, geography and cultural norms can be identified.

In America, the struggle for women to obtain the basic rights of citizenship and to execute the privileges thereof has led to the idea that being like men is prize. Unfortunately, the more women have sought to be like men, the more degenerate society has become. Women are the maternal and moral compass of every level of society. We provide wisdom, guidance, compassion and insight. The feminine balance and complements the masculine. Families, communities and nations need all the gifts women have to contribute. Don't abdicate what you have because of the false promise of masculine femininity.

WOMANHOOD:
THE SEAT OF FEMININE POWER

> *So, God created humankind in his image, in the image of God he created them; male and female he created them. God blessed them, and God said to them, "Be fruitful and multiply, and fill the earth and subdue it; and have dominion over the fish of the sea and over the birds of the air and over every living thing that moves upon the earth." ~ Genesis 1:27-28*

WOMEN are powerful. Our strength is deeply rooted in our ability and desire to nurture relationships. We have been formed with a creative energy that births life in many forms. We can do things that men cannot do. Just as men can do things women cannot do. That's okay because men and women were made to complement each other. To partner together and co-manage the life of their joint choosing.

Over the past few years, I have come to the realization that the feminist agenda has diminished femininity. The essence of womanhood is buried deeper and deeper into rhetoric and nonsense with each new political agenda women and men dream up regarding equality between the sexes.

When I was younger, I screamed for equal rights and recognition as loudly as the next liberated woman. However, as I have grown and matured in my womanhood, I realize that there is nothing about manhood that I want or aspire to be. I have come to view the feminist political agenda as a battle cry for aspiring to maleness.

I am not equal to man in terms of having equal form and function. Nor do I want to be viewed as such. I am not interested in being slapped on the back, punched in the face or wrestled to the floor. I am not interested in nose-to-nose combat or shoulder to shoulder competition for rewards that appeal to men either. I AM A WOMAN. I was created purposefully and significantly different from a man. I function differently. I think differently. I desire differently. I pursue differently. I plan differently. I live differently. Women and men are different beings. That is okay.

No man is my equal. No man can nurture and birth life within their body. Manhood is a completely different process and experience than womanhood. No man is going to understand firsthand the monthly flow of my blood or the ache of my breasts. No man can fully empathize with my swelling or my birthing. Nor can any man fully appreciate all my concerns about pregnancy – the ability to become pregnant, the desire or lack of desire to have children, the capability of carrying a healthy child to term, the timing of pregnancy, location of birth and considerations of how to bring a child into the world - in a hospital medicated into oblivion, or cut open to accommodate a doctor's schedule or someplace focused on my peace of mind and spirit. Women have a creative power that is fed from a spiritual well. And we are losing touch with our true selves with each successive generation that buys into the "think-like-a-man/be-like-a-man" foolery.

Women have a different seat of power than men do, which leads to a different expression of power than men have. We've been throwing away our power because we think what men have is so much better. It's not. Men depend on us much more than we depend on them. Ask one. Then ask follow-up questions. His love or his hate of womanhood is going to be rooted to a woman who was prominent in his life and therefore had great influence in the man he has become.

American women have allowed themselves, and men in general, to minimize the importance of family. The man may be the natural authority in the home, but the woman is the true power. She holds everything together. Why has this become so abhorrent? Power and authority when joined together is magnificent. Women are the incubators and birthers of generations. Yet we have allowed the deterioration of society to make us feel as if we are only sexual organs, objects of desire, paychecks and a vote. That's what a strict adherence to the feminist political theory has gotten us. We've degenerated ourselves, yet we are looking to men to build us back up. We have the power to recreate our public image and we are more than capable of doing so.

Women have the power to change how we are represented in the media and the substance of our representation via entertainment. More and more we have delegated the raising of our children to society-at-large, entertainment, schools, neighborhoods, friends and extended family. We lament over a disconnected society without acknowledging that we disconnected from our homes first. The family is the first unit of society. When we disregard our power and influence within our family (with our spouse, children and other family relationships) we also disregard our power and influence in larger societal circles.

COLLISION OF THE FEMININE, THE MAMMY & THE MATERNAL

DURING the second summer of my graduate studies, I participated in the *Democracy & Diversity Seminar* hosted by the Transregional Center for Democratic Studies at the New School. The seminar is a semi-annual event based in Wroclaw, Poland.

As a champion of women, it's very rare for any woman to make me uneasy, but there was a young American woman whose attention rubbed me the wrong way and made me very uncomfortable. She was in her early twenties and came across as someone who was not comfortable, or familiar, with taking responsibility for her actions and well-being.

After putting up with her clingy and somewhat demanding, off-putting behavior for nearly two weeks, a series of interactions over the course of a couple of hours blew my top. My responses to her became rude, abrupt and dismissive.

We were in a two-week program studying global social movements in a country and culture neither of us could communicate in. There were stressors all around. More so for me as the only Black Woman discussing racial and ethnic injustices in a group of white people from various countries. Throughout the totality of our time in Poland, this young woman would randomly ask questions like, "Will you carry me? Can you hold me? Will you be my pillow? Come here so I can lean on you! If I get drunk, can you make sure I get to my room?" At one point, in total frustration, I asked, "All these men here and you're asking *me* to carry you? Seriously?"

I'm not dainty, but I am still a woman. Nor am I a laborer or muscle for hire. Her comments were an offense to my womanhood. Her inappropriate requests were an affront to my femininity. I assumed she took my solid, generous build (i.e. large, hardy Black Woman) as something of a workhorse or mammy-servant-woman at her service.

It wasn't until a few days before our departure from Poland, that a broader interpretation came to mind: perhaps she was flirting! I can only say that like a good portion of America, I was pre-occupied with race during this time. It's possible that what I took as ridiculous, sometimes disrespectful, treatment due to my skin color and voluptuous proportions could have been pure sexual attraction. I admit to being rather slow here, but, in my defense, I can't always tell when men are interested either.

Assuming this interpretation of her behavior is true, one of the last things I said to her in frustration, may not have had the intended effect. A group of seminar participants had gathered on the hotel patio for a birthday celebration. She walked through the group to stand in front of me. In a sulky tone, she said, "I'm tired. Can you pick me up?"

In a flash of anger, I curtly said, "Should I whip out my breast so you can suckle at the teat too?"

In retrospect, what I mistook as shock could have been a flash of ecstasy. Who knew? I really thought she was looking at me as a "mammy figure" and it pissed me off. Additionally, she had a habit of randomly poking, tapping and hitting me. I don't do "playful hits" with anyone; neither do I accept anyone touching my body as if they have a right to. No one is going to get comfortable touching me when and however they want without my permission. She was in serious danger of getting beat down for violating my bodily autonomy.

As she left the gathering, she touched my shoulder and said, "See you later."

Beyond flabbergasted, it was in that moment I realized she was very much aware of my femininity while trying to engage with my maternal physicality. She had shared stories of how her parents had been distant during her formative years, which contributed to the thought that maybe she was looking for a mother-figure. No wonder I mistook her clinging, touchy-feely behavior as attempts to turn me into her mammy.

The suspicion she was attracted to me rather than being intentionally racist, calmed my need to confront her in anger. If she was struggling with her sexuality, I didn't want to be the person to push her into hiding or shame. Nor did I want to crush a young woman who was beginning to explore or understand her sexuality. However, I had no intention of continuing to receive her abrasive attentions. Male or female, unwanted physical advances are still a violation.

A couple of days later, a group of about ten of us went exploring the city. We split up for lunch and agreed to meet in the town square at a certain time to return to the hotel together. Shortly after the meeting time, this girl and the person she was with hadn't shown up, so the rest of us spread out around the square to look for the two of them. When they were spotted, someone signaled, and we all reconvened in the center of the square. As the group was gathering, she approached me with a balloon twisted in the shape of a sword and started hitting me with it. I told her to stop hitting me and asked her what her problem was. She said she was "punishing me for being late".

Who the f----... woosah.... Who are you to punish me for anything? That didn't make it out.... I pulled myself back.

All I could manage to say was, "We weren't late. You were on the opposite end of a large square and we're all foreigners." Someone else said, "No one specified a landmark or building to meet at."

For the rest of the afternoon, when I thought about that exchange, my blood boiled. When I could think somewhat clearly, I concluded she was treating me like I belonged to her – a pack horse, of sorts, a worker at her disposal. It took all my home training to not go all "angry black woman" on her.

All my theories about her behavior linked back to race.

It has been my experience that people of all walks of life will attempt to put people in boxes that fit their ideal, stereotype or perception of who a person is. Their behavior accompanies their misconceptions. Their words outline their thoughts.

Black Women are seen differently than any other woman in the world, if we are seen at all. We are described as angry, loud, hyper-sexed, always available, diligent workers, nurturers, surrogate mothers, loyal friends, aggressive fighters, and emasculating partners. We're seen as less than or what others want us to be. Our needs are not assessed. Our voices aren't heard. Our pain doesn't register on society's consciousness. A sliding scale is put on our beauty and usefulness. We are desired as workers, yet our contributions are not valued as long as our name and image are attached. We are courted as voters yet disrespected as citizens. We are lauded as the genesis of the world yet can rarely find partners to share our lives with. We're good for a tumble but deemed unworthy of longevity. Our services are demanded, but who's serving us?

Folks will do their darnedest to make you conform to their image of you. Part of the mission of my Year of Wonder-filled

Living was shedding the parts of me that conformed to the demands of others, while amplifying my vision of myself.

I am a nurturing woman... with boundaries. I am a lover... with conditions. I am available... on my schedule. I am a sexual being... for someone I consider worthy of sharing my body with. I stand. I fight. I shout. I am woman. I am human. I am a being of amazing complexities, nuances and fluidity that cannot be confined to one dimensional containers.

Some may only see my potential as a mammy. Their shortsightedness is not my problem. I know I am the fruit and the seed of the Mother of All Life. Therefore, Life flows from me in every possible creative way. No matter what others see, the Feminine and Maternal are always present.

HE IS MY SWEETNESS.

He is my sweetness.
When we aren't right
He is the source of all my
Bitterness.

AN OPEN LETTER: WOMAN TO MAN

> *When Jesus came to the area of Caesarea Philippi, He asked His followers, "Who do people say the Son of Man is?" They answered, "Some say you are John the Baptist. Others say you are Elijah, and still others say you are Jeremiah or one of the prophets." Then Jesus asked them, "And who do you say I am?" Simon Peter answered, "You are the Christ, the Son of the Living God." Jesus answered, "You are blessed, Simon son of Jonah, because no person taught you that. My Father in heaven showed you who I am. ~ Matthew 16:13-17*

DEAR Man:
What others say about you will never trump what I see in you and believe about you.

Though my day-to-day feelings about you derive in part from your treatment of me, my vision and knowledge of you is God-given. You may think the accolades of others will win me over. You may also think that what you do for others will make you shine brighter in my eyes. You would be wrong on both counts. You can bend over backwards for everyone in the world, but if you aren't willing to even stand up and face me, why should the opinions of others matter to me? Your relationship with others is about you and them. They have nothing to do with me. They do not create space for the possibility of us. For that reason, I am not impressed by what other people think of you because their experience of you is not representative of my experience of you.

Right now, in this moment, my struggle is seeing everything you are willing to do for others while remembering everything you have been unwilling to do for me. This knowledge continually leads to resentment, bitterness and separation.

Your struggle is admitting you are in error; that you have squandered time and taken love for granted. Pride is the downfall of every man; however, all is not loss. You, my dear Man, are a conqueror. Should you choose to accept your assignment, you can make everything right with just a word.

You love the Word of God, but you won't speak a word to me.

You enjoy life, but you won't share yours with me.

You yearn for the light, but you keep me in a shadowy pit.

You admire modesty but the way you waste time is the most painful extravagance to witness.

You think you're humble, but your spirit strives against me in a rage of hurt masculine pride.

You think love and war are synonymous. They aren't. Love may be confrontational, but it is not destructive. War is targeted violence and willful destruction. Creating and maintaining conflict is not an expression of caring.

You go on and on about love and grace, but what love and grace have you shown to me? Where is your mercy? Where is the love of Christ for the woman you would have as wife?

I do not hold a grudge against you, but I will not fight endlessly with you either. I know what you want; I know what you need, but I can't force you to receive anything from me.

I have been equipped to nurture, love and honor your life with my being. I have been created to share your breath and expand your life.

I have prepared for you, but I am not willing to be everything I can be to a man who is content to be nothing more than a disconnected observer of my life.

You will not drain me dry, leaving me nothing for myself. I won't allow it. God has shown me too much of Himself in me for me to throw myself away according to your whim.

I will not support a man who doesn't support me. That would be energy you take from me without replenishing. Your confidence should not cost me mine.

I will not attempt to stand beside a man who has no interest in standing beside me. To do so invites heartbreak every hour of every day.

I will not chase anyone who is not pursuing me. I am the good thing you are responsible for shepherding, but I am also responsible for where I choose to go. You lead, I follow. When you stop leading, I stop following. Remember that.

Relationships are built on mutuality and thrive on reciprocity. I cannot build with someone who is constantly attacking me. Passive aggressive behavior is violent in nature. You may "only" be emotionally dismissive, neglectful, and stoic, but each instance is an attack on everything I see in and believe about you. Such behavior attacks everything I understood about us from the vision I was first given.

If you want a woman who will sit at your feet and praise you continuously while you spend your time and energy praising everyone else, then you have my blessing and encouragement to keep looking for her. I am not the woman for you.

If you want a woman who will encourage you, despite your refusal to acknowledge her words, then again, I say, I am not the woman for you. Go in peace and live a joyful and bountiful life elsewhere.

But... If you want a woman who will strive to communicate with understanding and who will use her tongue only to bless and lift you up, then I say I am your woman.

If you want a woman who will walk, run, dance and ride through life with you in all its triumphant glory and devastating tragedy as a partner – hand in hand, shoulder to shoulder with arms linked – I am your woman.

If you want a woman to build with – from scratch or from leveraged land and materials – I am your blessed goodness. I am your wow-factor.

If you want me, you must recognize you are joining with a woman who knows her place in God's Kingdom. My place is not subordinate to you. My place is one of honor, not disgrace or shame. My place is by your side as co-ruler of all we are blessed to supervise and manage as stewards. My joy in you derives from your recognition of your place in my life.

Be the man you were created to be, bone of my bone, flesh of my flesh, breath of my breath, joy of my joy. Be true to God. Be true to yourself. Be true to me.

Meditation Verse: Song of Solomon 3:1-4

At night on my bed, I looked for the one I love; I looked for him, but I could not find him. I got up and went around the city, in the streets and squares, looking for the one I love. I looked for him, but I could not find him. The watchmen found me as they patrolled the city, so I asked, "Have you seen the one I love?" As soon as I had left them, I found the one I love. I held him and would not let him go until I brought him to my mother's house, to the room where I was born.

Listen to: Say You Love Me by Jesse Ware

WHEN I THINK ABOUT

When I think about
How I loved
I mean
How I wanted to love
Each time I tried to love
Or rather how the love I offered
Was always rejected
When I think about love
In this world
My heart breaks
All over again

HOW A MAN TREATS A WOMAN

THE way a man treats a woman says a lot about the man. Though there's something to be said about what the woman allows, much more is illustrated about the man's character.

The way a Man of God treats a Woman of God says even more about his deeply held beliefs and the one he truly serves. When a man who claims to be a Brother in Christ is dismissive of and disrespectful towards a Sister in Christ, he should be viewed as being dismissive of and disrespectful towards the Spirit of God living within her. God's indwelling Spirit transforms character and changes behaviors.

If you are contemplating a relationship with someone who treats you as "lesser than" – second to them and somewhere behind others – step back and walk away. From Genesis to Ephesians, partnered man and woman are called as one, joined together as one life, one faith, one belief. Man is instructed to care for his wife as he cares for his own body. This language speaks to unity and equality. If you enter a relationship where your selected partner does not view you as their equal partner in life, then you are signing up for a long, arduous uphill battle.

Meditation Verse: Luke 6:45

A good man brings good things out of the good stored up in his heart, and an evil man brings evil things out of the evil stored up in his heart. For the mouth speaks what the heart is full of.

HOPE OF MY LIFE

THROUGHOUT my thirty-ninth year, I mentally catalogued my life. The results were stark and depressing: single, never married, no children, no immediate family or close friends. In truth, mine felt like such a worthless existence, void of substance.

Though the promises I held dear were ever present, there was no evidence of pending manifestation. Promises of a husband, children and a full, gracious home. Outwardly, all the trappings of an amazing, abundant and wonderful life adorned me, but every day I became more achingly aware of how empty abundance is with no one to share the overflow with.

The beginning of my life was enriched with a large family. Both my mom and dad came from large families, the majority of whom were within close proximity. The utopia of my youth was bouncing between my grandmothers' homes, at first across the street from one another and later a block down from each other.

For the majority of my adult life, I've lived alone and away from all family. Most of that time was in New York City where personal interaction is the minimum for survival in the city. +My parents and two of three siblings are deceased. The remaining living sibling has withdrawn completely from all who love her. Other relatives have never really cultivated a personal relationship, so no one has visited me in my space. And I have long since grown weary of visiting people who make no effort to participate in my life. As a result, I became extremely lonely. Painfully so. Yet even the extended grief-stricken loneliness didn't stop me from gleaning.

Though I have never been in a relationship or experienced any intimacy with a man, I have had deep and abiding feelings for one. As I have matured in age and temperament, my social circles and interactions have narrowed significantly. As a consequence, opportunities to meet a compatible partner are disappearing faster and faster.

This is not the life I envisioned for myself. When I was young and full of hope, I dreamed of love and fantasized about passionate romps. I thought I would always be surrounded by love and light. Now the only love and light I receive is what I give to myself or what I allow myself to receive in passing from strangers. I believe God communicates His presence through the strangers who cross my path because they cannot possibly know what I need in the moment they are giving me everything I need to get by.

New York City is viewed as a thriving cosmopolitan metropolis full of life, adventure, opportunity, and options. A city capable of answering any dream, hope, lust, thought or fantasy. If you can think it, you can find it and get it in New York City. It's a city with something for everyone. With a little creativity and a smidge of perseverance, everyone who steps foot into one of the five boroughs can find a niche they could enjoy for as long as they want. It takes much more effort, perseverance, and even planning to remain focused on your overall goals, and to achieve that one thing you first came to the City to accomplish.

Living in the Borough of Manhattan keeps you a stranger to neighbors, colleagues and passersby alike. Everyone operates in their own personal bubbles. There's no time for anything other than getting to where you're going as quickly as possible. Every day is a rush, and the daily goal is to get through everything on your schedule.

For the first eight months after I arrived in the City, I lived in the Bronx. The Bronx is the only borough on mainland United

States. Every other borough is an island or part of one. Staying in the Bronx upon my arrival in the City was good for me. I rented a renovated garage in a neighborhood of single-family homes. For a while I was able to keep my car. The ability to explore lessened the culture shock as the Bronx felt very much like the Midwest to me. At least it did where I lived close to the border of Westchester County. The county line was directly behind my apartment. The neighborhood I shopped in was similar to the neighborhood I shopped in in Milwaukee, my home prior to New York.

After the Bronx, I moved to Harlem, a neighborhood on the island of Manhattan. Harlem is where I built my life. Within a few years, I was able to purchase my first home in East Harlem, also known as El Barrio and Spanish Harlem. The neighborhood had long been culturally Hispanic and had the highest population project housing in the city. My co-op building was a brand-new build and part of the wave of gentrification sweeping the last affordable neighborhood in Manhattan.

As a homeowner, I was eager to get involved in my building management as well as the larger community politics. For the first two years, I participated in building subcommittees, attended building events and began hosting a book club. I was vocal about the rights of the homeowners and pushed back against unfair board pronouncements. Unfortunately, the sense of belonging and merging with a community never happened. All my neighbors were either distantly cordial, completely stand-offish or straight-up hostile.

The environment was a far cry from what I had envisioned my first home and community to be. My vision had been of a space where neighbors interacted socially and shared a comfortable comradery. Before I knew what community was, I was dreaming

of being part of one. Yet, I ended up in a city with a largely impersonal culture. Where people put equal value on minding their business and staying out of people's way. There was no pocket of the community that I could fully identify with, therefore, there was no place I felt I fully belonged. The stark summary of my time in New York is *stranger at home, a stranger abroad*. That disconnect and inability to complete a safe landing is quintessential New York City.

Around this time, shortly before my fortieth birthday, I took a hard look at my life. The only thing I was getting up for was work. There was nothing else going on in my life. Nothing to look forward to on any given day. Just a job as an executive assistant, a role which received very little respect and offered even less opportunity to advance. I was pigeon-holed, despite having an advance degree and more business sense than most of the people I worked with. Unfortunately, my primary manager saw no value in supporting my efforts to advance my career at the company. Without her support, no one else saw a reason to honor my requests for a transition to another department. Add to that long hours and lack of connection and there's no wonder that I began sinking into a pit of depression, fatigue and frustration. The counterbalance was a healthy paycheck that paid my mortgage, debt payments and vacation expenses which lead to complacency. Choosing to remain stagnant made my life unproductive.

∞ ∞ ∞

Prior to my psychological downward spiral, travel renewed my vision and ambition. My family moved around a lot when I was a child. At first new beginnings were an adventure. By my teens, I wanted to stay in one place for more than three years. Staying put and building a home base would be doable if frequent travel was possible. Exploring new places provided different perspectives. Traveling to experience new textures, colors, languages, flavors and art became a passion until the world stopped fascinating me. After several years of traveling alone, the sense of adventure gave way to extreme loneliness. No travel companion meant no shared plans or experiences. When I returned home, there was no one to share stories or photos with. Travel started to feel like an empty pursuit. The real tragedy of a solitary life is having no one to share memories with.

∞ ∞ ∞

There was a man who represented hope for my future. I saw him as the promise and the prayer. During the years I wallowed in the darkness of my despair, thoughts of him were my only joy. If ever there were a man of my vision, a man I felt an indefinable spiritual connection with, he was it. He consumed my focus for a dozen years. All because he seemed to see me. He listened and spoke with a gentle awareness that put a lifetime of fantasies to flight. His infrequent casual greetings on Facebook made my whole body smile, but his smile spun my heart into a whirlwind. He became my dream and all I wanted in the world.

Shortly after Christmas, during the time I was evaluating my life, he reached out and oh so casually shared his plans to vacation in Jamaica in early January. I was very aware of how he kept tabs on me from a distance and I had been sharing on Facebook for months that I needed a beach vacation but couldn't think of where to go. Just as casually, I told him Jamaica was on my short list.

He said, "Cool. If we're both there at the same time, maybe we can meet up."

I giddily replied, "That would be nice. I'll keep you posted."

He lived in Milwaukee, where I met him during my youthful, nubile late twenties. I moved to New York City a couple of years after we met. Often, I've imagined how my life would be different had he asked me to stay, or simply asked me out with the intention of exploring the possibility of us. He didn't. I left. But I remained hopeful and ever ready to return if he would just say something.

Through the years we remained in contact via social media, email and texts. Occasionally, we met for coffee or lunch when I returned to Milwaukee for visits and events. At the time of the email exchange about Jamaica, I hadn't seen him in person for over four years. The thought of meeting up on a sunny, hot beach, away from our daily lives was a temptation I'm sure I don't have to describe. In my mind, our time had finally come. A decade of me holding on and waiting for him to recognize and claim me as his woman, his wife, and the eager mother of his children would finally pay off. I traveled to Jamaica with a heart full of hope and a conscience pre-silenced of guilt. I envisioned our first meeting on a resort beach. Different visions developed in my mind, of course, but each vision culminated in a long over-due embrace and a shared vacation from that moment on. Perhaps the ultimate fantasy was me laying my claim on him in every way possible, leaving no room for doubt by jumpstarting our togetherness in the tropical paradise of Jamaica.

Short story shorter, none of my hopes manifested. He never showed up for me. He never made actual plans to meet me on the island. That would've been fine if that was all. He poured salt in the open bare wound my heart became. He launched a social media campaign posting videos and photos of him and his buddy having a blast exploring Jamaica off the beaten track. It was an epic bromance showcased so exuberantly with the boyish charm

I had been so drawn to. Feeling like the butt of a cruel practical joke, I felt compelled to save some face and show how great my solo culture-focused vacation was with my posts as well.

"It looks like you're having a blast," he commented on one of my photos.

"I am," I replied.

Whatever game he was playing or point he was trying to prove, either hit me dead center or missed me completely. I could never tell what his intent was. I'm sure I asked. I'm equally sure he didn't give a real response. Whatever it was, he shattered me in a way I hadn't thought was possible.

That episode hurt me so deeply, I refused to think about it for over a year. I thought I would break from the callous randomness of it all. The pain didn't just come from the rejection. I was overwhelmed by the calculated way he set me up to look forward to spending time with him and then dismissed me without a word or consideration for my time or plans. I had been fine living my life. Thinking of him occasionally in the background of my day. No one told him to reach out and plant seeds of possibility and hopeful beginnings I hadn't even thought of.

He not only pulverized my heart, he destroyed my spirit. The pure, fragile, open and gentle spirit of love I had worked so hard to protect from the harshness of the world. The spirit of love I had attempted to guard against his cavalier attitude. The spirit of love that is always so willing to forget past hurts and grievances and embrace each new moment with a full embrace. That spirit of love was on full display when he expressed an interest in seeing me.

When I returned from Jamaica, I was unable to face myself. Which meant I was also unable to write. The hope I had been clinging to allowed me to make a fool of myself. I had thrown my heart at the feet of a man who nonchalantly trampled it underfoot. Repeatedly. I wanted to blame him, but truthfully, it was my desire to be a lover in body and spirit to him that left me exposed. For that, I could only blame myself. This incident was an anchor that sank me deeper into the pit. Unable to recover gracefully, I floundered. Unable to overcome the hurt and rejection I began to spiral. Everything in life that had given me joy turned to sorrow and ash.

Finally, my heart became desensitized and I was able to rip him from the place of honor he held in it. For a while, nothing seemed able to penetrate me. There was no light, no hope, no joy. For years, he was the hope that kept me afloat. Then suddenly there was absolutely nothing on my horizon.

I won't pretend to know why it was necessary for God to bring me to the end of my hope in such a way, but I do know this ending was the beginning of a new me.

Listen to: *Thy Will* by Hillary Scott & Family

NO JOY, BUT GOOD NEWS

May 17, 2015

It's been a while.

I've had no joy to report and my heart and soul were exceedingly tired of recording sorrows, disappointments and loneliness.

That being said, I didn't mean to be silent for so long. I've missed journaling. I've missed this form of communing with myself and my God.

Part of me thought that recording a year of my experiences for publication would be enough. Its' not. Writing words for the world to see takes different spiritual energy than writing from my wounds in order to acknowledge my healing. When I write to myself, it's impossible to hide, so enlightenment is always imminent.

I have no joy to report, but I do have good news.

I've completed graduate school! In five days, I will graduate with my Master of Arts degree in International Affairs with a concentration in Media & Culture. The past two and a half years have not provided the education I hoped for, but it has provided a deeply enriching one. I know the path and focus were orchestrated by you Father God. Your Spirit is forever my guide. I'm continually amazed by Your work in my life!

NO WORDS

what can i say
how can i speak
i gave you all the words
i wished to live
only to watch them die
from your carelessness
i have nothing to say
other than
what's been spoken
nothing to give
other than
what's been offered
you seem to want
more than i have
other than i am
someone not me
to that what can i say
other than
you once took my breath away
and i didn't mind
each gasp for air meant
you were near
for your closeness i
willingly traded my breath
until you took it as your tribute
and turned away
walked away
stayed away
how can i speak when

you never returned
never acknowledged
my sacrifice
you held on to my life
kept me choked
in an inattentive grip
weakening my gift
day by day
slowly killing me
painfully destroying
all i had to offer
yet you expect to revive me
simply by loosening your grip
from a distance
how can you breathe life
into me
from a distance

SINGLENESS IS NOT THE PRIZE.

SOME years ago, I heard a pastor teach about the importance of correctly identifying God's words in the Bible which are distinctly different from other speaker's words in the Bible. He was teaching out of Job and after pointing out people's fondness for saying *"the Lord gives and the Lord takes away,"* he railed at the congregation, "Stop attributing bad things to God!"

Job spoke those words in prayer as an expression of his understanding of the happenings in his life at that moment. However, the reader knows that Satan had asked for and received permission to take everything Job had in an attempt to prove to God that Job's praises would turn to curses when his blessings were removed from him (Job 1). That's quite the extreme to test a theory.

As I approached forty, I looked back on my first twenty years as a single adult. Over the second decade, my thoughts on sexual purity had evolved. When I began studying the Bible in my early thirties, presenting my body as a holy sacrifice was not a difficult concept for me because I didn't think I would be single for long. However, as the years marched me into my forties, there has been little joy in my singleness.

For two decades, I attended engagement parties, bachelorette showers, baby showers, weddings, births, housewarmings. I accepted five requests to be a godmother before starting to decline requests. I've seen friends marry, fight, cheat, divorce, then start over with new spouses and personalities. I've been present through some of their struggle with disease, elder care and the agony of sexual identity with the young ones. After a while celebrating round two other people's milestones became a chore. Most especially for the friends who aggressively pursued their individualism at the expense of their union and families.

As an honorary presence, I have witnessed people's lives from within their doors but outside their family. A precarious position that is welcome as long as they benefit. At the hint of disagreement, friendships weren't just put on ice but my access to the sense of family they provided, and the joy of their children was also removed from my life. That has led to a lot of grieving and more hardening than I had ever thought possible. Observing families as a guest is no substitute for having one of your own. After a while, you decline invitations and avoid inclusion because being "like" family isn't the same as being family.

In my extended family, older female relatives struggle with aging and ill-health on their own. They may have married in their youth and collected a roster of men over time and raised children they thought would be a blessing in their old age, but in the end, bitterness was their only companion.

Singleness is a blessing for a time, but not for a lifetime nor for every season. Often, I've shared that I'm happy I didn't marry before I turned thirty. Thirty is when my life turned completely in the direction of God. My spirit of gratitude for the fact that He brought me to Himself as an individual, not as part of a couple or a family unit. He isolated me to expose Himself and through this process, my identity is being revealed. It's a true blessing to be able to walk out my belief and understanding in my own time and space. It has helped me develop a very strong faith and a powerful voice. I thank God for His meticulous care of me. Since I committed my life to Him, my priorities have changed, my vision has sharpened, my purpose has become more defined, and I hold tighter to His Truth. The most prominent truth I've held onto is, "It is not good for man to be alone (Genesis 2:18)." These words are attributed to God as He prepped to create Chavah, the first woman and mother of all life. We know her as Eve. Before Eve, God's creation was good. After Eve, all of creation was *very* good. Partnering man and woman tipped the scale.

My internal struggle has been to reconcile God's proclamation in *Genesis 2:18* with Paul's words in *1 Corinthians 7:8-9*:

> *Now for those who are not married and for the widows I say this: It is good for them to stay unmarried as I am. But if they cannot control themselves, they should marry. It is better to marry than to burn with sexual desire.*

Paul said explicitly, *'it is good for them to stay unmarried as I am."* I believed that to a certain degree, but I didn't truly get it until I saw an online conversation thread where a woman cited Paul's words in *1 Corinthians 7:28-29*:

> *But those who marry will have trouble in this life, and I want you to be free from trouble. Brothers and sisters, this is what I mean: We do not have much time left. So, starting now, those who have wives should live as if they had no wives.*

To the woman's credit in the conversation I read, she was pointing out that she and her husband had individual callings from the Lord. I appreciate that, but an individual calling does not mean it cannot or should not be a shared pursuit by both husband and wife. It certainly doesn't mean that one partner should follow their calling to the exclusion of their spouse.

Further down in this passage Paul laments that spouses are distractions from God's work. I will argue here that a spouse is intended to be a blessing of completion and unity. Don't misunderstand me. Yes, we are complete as individuals. Yes, we are complete in our relationship with God, Jesus and the Holy Spirit. But there is also another dimension in which God has allowed for completion – a marital relationship in which He has joined two people. This joining and unity is echoed throughout His Book of Instruction.

It's important to note Paul again explicitly states in *verse 25, "I have no command from the Lord about this; I give my opinion."* Paul's preferences are not the foundation of our faith. We are not called to be like Paul. We were not given Paul's breath, spirit or life. Yet *1 Corinthians 7* is laced with Paul saying *"I wish you could be like me… I command… and in my opinion (verses 7, 8, 10, 12, 17, 25, 26, 28, 29, 32, 35, 40)."* Paul's opinion, even though it's in the Bible, does not equal or trump God's Word. The only thing God said was *not* good about His creation was that man or woman (i.e. humans) being alone. That is significant.

For Paul to call singleness good, in his opinion, is in direct opposition to what God called it. For Paul to extort married people to act as if they were single is not the call of service God requires of us. A great part of our service to God is serving the people He has put in our care. We are to be helpers and ministers to our spouse. We are to be teachers and guides to our children. We are to be truthful and honest leaders in our communities. More importantly, we are to decrease as individuals so that Jesus can increase in us.

Our call is to become more Christ-like, to grow more fully and purely into the original image we were created in. The spouse God has blessed you with is not a distraction; and your work together – in one another, in your family and in your community, through the Holy Spirit – is kingdom preparation and building.

I have seen many debates over the years revolving around people trying to make Paul's words fit their present-day circumstances. Paul provided great teachings, but he is very clear about when the Holy Spirit is urging him to speak and when he is speaking on his own. I think we need to be careful to distinguish between the two voices. When we do that, it's not so difficult to apply Spirit-led words to our life.

That takes me to the seemingly waning blessing of singleness. Truthfully, singleness has taught me to look after myself, to think of myself and focus on myself. I am my only priority and primary obligation. No matter how I may try to focus on other people, every day is filled with my life issues, and I admit, I'm actually sick of myself. It would be wonderful to have someone else to focus on and look after. Not in the way of around the clock caretaker, but as a partner and stakeholder in the life details of another person. Singleness doesn't provide that opportunity.

As a single person, every relationship in your life feels transient (if you're paying attention to how people come and go, that is). Singleness leads to an independent individuality that takes us away from the deep benefits of unity and community. Single people are not included in social groups the same way married couples or families are. We are limited to a certain type of social interaction. Usually a very shallow social interaction – comic relief, entertainment, etc. Single people aren't necessarily trusted for their dependability and commitment. Meaning, on many levels, we are included with the expectation that we'll exercise our freedom to get up and go whenever the mood strikes. A right I've exercised many times.

I stopped committing myself to friendships that changed drastically shortly after vows were spoken. I stopped inserting myself into family settings that treated me as a refreshing change to the redundancy of their stability. I left jobs that drained me spiritually and mentally. Over time, I've learned to step out on faith with boldness and expectation.

During my singleness, I have been able to tune my life, my heart and my ears to God's voice – His whisper, His urging, His guidance – with a sensitivity that I may not have been able to develop had I not been alone for a time. My faith has grown and deepened because I had no one else to depend on or look to other than God. My internal seeking and questioning have become layered because my communication with God is mostly silent – my thoughts, my musings, my writing. My Lord Father has been my one and only constant and our relationship is not part of what I term a "waning blessing." My relationship with God is an eternal blessing that I would never wish to live without. What has waned is my need for solitude and any belief that singleness is a step above or equal to being joined to another.

There is richness in merging your life with another person. This indefinable wealth is evident in any couple that has acknowledged the goodness of their union. There's a wisdom, understanding, acceptance, appreciation, patience, in-it-togetherness, that most singles don't really get. At any sign of marital trouble, we singles ask questions like: *Why are you putting up with that? What's in it for you? Why won't you leave? Why not just do what makes you happy? Why aren't you taking care of yourself? Do you really have to put up with this?*

Every single person who has asked any variation of these questions to a married friend or relative has undoubtedly heard in response: *He's my husband. She's my wife. We have a family. It's not that simple.*

Singles don't get it because, singles don't have it. For us, it usually is that simple, because we have only ourselves to think about. That's why single people change so much when they get married – if they're doing it right. Human beings are meant to change. We are meant to grow. We are meant to evolve from singleness to unity with another. Singleness is not the prize. Oneness and unity in marriage is the gift to cherish.

Listen to: *Still Rolling Stones* by Lauren Daigle

WITHOUT RESERVATION

I've been thinking –
perhaps I had an epiphany –
I thought of how I was willing,
begged God actually,
for the boon of being
with you. To my mind,
you were the greatest
possible gift.
Then it came to me
this desire to give, give, give,
to love you with all
my heart and mind
to worship and praise
your body with mine –
it was all wrong.
I was backwards.
I've been requesting things
which would not satisfy me
in the long run.
Yes, I want you.
Yes, truly I want all
I've petitioned God for.
I do. I love you.
But there is something I want
much more than the pleasure of
pouring my life into yours.
There is something I need more
than my prayer answered.
Something I deserve more than

being a giver who receives
nothing in return.
My epiphany showed me
that more than anything
I want and need to be loved and
desired unreservedly.
It showed me you should be
the initiator and I should follow.
When you give of yourself, cover me,
pour your life into me –
those will be my true gifts.
When you choose to love me
with your heart, mind and spirit…
choose to join your body with mine in a
symphony of worship and praise…
Those are acts worthy of my devotion.
I was sitting and thinking –
what I wanted was so limiting.
What I was shown would open the heavens.
My efforts have proven useless against your inaction.
So, my love, I must back away from temptation.
I must resist the urge
to supplicate myself at your feet.
Resist my obsessive longing and
suppress the desire to shower my gifts on
a man who does not value
or reciprocate such devotion.
I must resist that part of me until
you present that part of yourself to me.
Your gifts will replenish and revive
even as your presence restores.

Your love will cover
even as your strength shelters.
When you join your gifts to mine
we will experience our greatest blessing.

NOTHING BEATS A TRY

I don't think I ever really thought about the meaning of "nothing beats a try" until after I tossed those words over my shoulder towards a man as I sashayed away from him.

It was a shortly after my fortieth birthday and male attention was a rare thing.

There was a stretch of time in my youth when I thought the onus was on me to help encourage a man to get up and start wooing me. In my teens and twenties, I was all for putting myself "out there" with the men I was interested in. My *modus operandi* was to directly state my interest. If memory serves, I declared myself to three males in my lifetime. The first time was to a classmate my sophomore year of high school. The second time I was twenty-five, gleefully single and trying to live *the life*. The third and final time I outed myself to a mating prospect, I was thirty-four and ready to merge my life with his in matrimony. All three of my crushes had similar responses: silence, followed by avoidance, and then awkward "hey buddy" chats.

Eventually, it clicked that directly expressing my attraction and intentions to a guy is a surefire way to chase them away. Until, of course, they want something, that is. Two of the three remain in occasional contact. Honestly, I think I'm a self-esteem boost for them... or perhaps more like a trampoline to touch on when they're having difficulty with their life choices.

On the flip side, the men who made an effort to woo me – took time to get to know me, showed up for me, *declared themselves* – those men were too much for me. Too available. Too intense. Sometimes, too controlling. They wanted too much too soon. I tried being present with a couple of them, but they were in *woman-barefoot-and-pregnant* mode when I was still trying to figure out who I am and how I fit in my own skin, not to mention where I fit in the world. Now that I'm world weary and ready for barefoot-and-pregnant myself, those men who were too much fifteen years ago would be perfect for me now. Unfortunately for me, they have what they were looking for: wives and homes filled with children.

Finding a mate as a forty-something black woman is completely different than looking for a good match at twenty-five. It's like I've become invisible. In addition to that, the mating culture has completely changed in the last twenty years. Today, technology rules all areas of society. The men who lacked initiative before non-verbal indirect communication became a norm, now lack imagination and drive. They can't see beyond their phones, their profiles, friend lists or connections. Basically, men are no longer trying.

What I perceive as the lack of male effort and initiation could very well be a local phenomenon and the by-product of spending my thirties in New York City. Making truly personal connections in New York is a painfully impossible endeavor. It's a city where relationships are mostly transactional (do this to get that) and social activity (meet up for food and events). Very little time is spent actually getting to know people in a personal way.

On a larger scale, the lack of male effort is endemic of a national culture where men think they're doing women a favor by stepping back, doing nothing and shutting up. Men are not true allies or partners to women when they supplicate their masculinity to a feminist agenda. Nor are men empowered by aggressively wielding any authority or position they may have over a woman to subjugate her. When interacting with a woman, a man is best received when his sense of self is not threatened by interaction or confrontation with her femininity. By the same token, women are not truly empowered when men are emasculated. A woman is empowered when her sense of self is not threatened by interaction or confrontation with a man's masculinity.

As much as women need to voice who they are, men also need to contribute their true voices to the conversation. It's the blending of our individuality that creates great partnerships. Not domination and subjugation. Dominance has no partner; neither is it rooted in love or respect.

Listen to: *No One Ever Cared For Me Like Jesus by Steffany Gretzinger*

A CONVERSATION & A SONG

ON a *blah* night during a low energy week, I was walking across 14th Street near Union Square after class. A young homeless man called out to me as I walked past with a classmate, "Can you buy me something to eat?" This is a common question in New York City. I do what I can when I can, and basically keep it moving. I asked him if he knew what he wanted. He said yes. We went into the restaurant he was sitting in front of. My classmate followed. There was a line; he and I got in it. My classmate had a large bag, so she stood off to the side.

While we waited, I started asking him questions. *Are you a student? How long have you been homeless? Where do you normally stay? How long have you lived in New York? How are you doing overall?* He answered some of the questions and deflected others, but he was very adamant in telling me what bothered him about the world. "How am I doing," he repeated. "How should I be doing when so many people hate me? People hate me because I'm gay. They hate me because I sing, and they don't want me to. They don't want me to be anything, and they tell me that. But I'm not going to hate them back. And I'm going to keep singing."

I looked him in the eye and said, "Can I share something with you that I've learned over the last twenty years?"

He looked taken aback. "I shared that with you because I thought you wanted me to be real," he said cautiously.

"I do. Thank you for sharing. I just want to save you some time and energy. From the last twenty years of my life, I can tell you: people don't hate you because you're gay. People hate you because people are hateful, and they usually hate themselves. People are being people. Don't over-complicate it. I can't tell you how often I asked myself, 'Why me? Why are people treating me like this or that? What if I was different? What if I did what they wanted me to do? What if I was a better person?' But you know what? None of that mattered. People hated me because they wanted to. Hate is what people do. I had to learn to appreciate who I am. You need accept who you are. When you accept all the various aspects of yourself, other peoples' thoughts about you will no longer matter. Learn to appreciate yourself. Learn to love yourself."

He looked a bit dreamy-eyed and touched his head to my shoulder for a second – I wasn't expecting that. Then he looked me in the eye and asked if he could sing me a song.

"I'm not one to silence anyone's voice. Please do." We were still in the middle of a slow-moving line. He began singing *I Still Believe* by Brenda K. Starr. Mariah Carey was her back-up singer and later covered the song. He had a beautiful voice. Halfway through I began lip-syncing along with him. My heart was lifted, and I believe he lifted the hearts of several people in the restaurant also.

When he finished, I had more questions for him, as did my classmate and soon we were at the register. He ordered his meal, and I asked him his name before we parted ways. "Brandon. My name is Brandon."

After leaving the restaurant and parting from my classmate, I searched online for the lyrics and was rewarded. *"If there's one spark of hope left in my grasp, I'll hold it with both hands. It's worth the risk of burning to have a second chance...If we believe that true love never has to end, then we must know that we will love again."* I needed a song and desperately needed a word too. Brandon had started his serenade off with *"You looked into my* eyes...." as he gazed into mine. His delivery and demeanor touched me deeply.

A few minutes prior to meeting Brandon, my classmate had seen someone from another of her classes. She walked up to the woman and said, "Do you see me? When you see me, say 'Hi' and I will do the same." The woman was taken aback; however she didn't seem to take it literally at first. She asked, "How do you mean, 'Do I see you?'" However, by the end of their conversation she revisited the blunt statement and answered succinctly, "This is the first time I am seeing you and I did speak."

Brandon gave me this kind of clarity.

One of my gifts is seeing people as they are. I hear the things they don't say. I feel their pain, confusion and their sense of loss. They willingly reveal themselves, until they realize they can't shake me off at the next turn. In understanding their pain, I'm able to follow them when they withdraw and hide within themselves. I invade their emotional hiding places and lovingly confront their fears. All this happens through conversation.

People reject openness, honesty, truth and love. Every friend I've gained through conversation has been loss the same way. People are happy to tell you what they think you want to hear, but they can't stand to share the truth of themselves. I have no problem with sharing my truth, but my openness has been the beginning of the end of my friend and family relationships. After so many endings, I had started to despair that I could ever love people beyond their rejection of me.

Blessings to Brandon for sharing his truth in a random encounter in Union Square. I was able to follow his light out of hiding when he reminded me that I will indeed love again.

Listen to: *I Still Believe* **by Brenda K. Starr**

DEATH & LIFE

DRY RIVERBED

SET FIRE TO THE RAIN...

MY dad, whom I call by his nickname, Peewee, died three years before I wrote this letter. It was originally written for a publication about father-daughter relationships. The letter so poignantly represents the nuances of love and forgiveness that it ministers to me every time I read it. It has been a truly cathartic contribution to my healing from the damage Peewee inflicted on my life.

Dear Peewee,

I know if it is at all possible, you are somewhere stalking my life. Indeed, you cajoled your way into my dreams until I torched the images you planted in my mind. I was so torn when you died. The little girl who will always love her daddy wanted so much to go to your side during your last days on earth, but the little girl you abused and violated needed to know that she was a welcome presence at your bedside. You didn't call for me, so I didn't go. I would have come had you simply asked.

You and I have both come a long way from the torment you inflicted on me and the rest of our family, but we didn't come far enough. We left the pain behind, but not the residue. We walked into the light of forgiveness but clung to the shadows of shame. You said you loved me, but you never showed me. I have misjudged and misunderstood love for this reason for most of my life. I started off expecting far too little of people who claimed to love me and now I'm in a place where I hope to see the love of Jesus Christ exhibited through those who claim to love me. What an impossible scale to live on! On one end, the extreme of a depraved reality; on the opposite end, an everlasting ethereal promise glows.

I don't want to blame you, but I can see that I have sadly become a hard person to know and love. I don't want to blame you, but I learned about the natural ugliness of mankind far too early and deeply to be completely full of grace towards all my neighbors. I don't want to blame you... but I still hurt.

I still ache.

I still cry.

I didn't think any of my tears would ever have your name on them again, but they do. I don't want to blame you for not loving me, yet I blame so many other people for not only not loving me, but not accepting me, not embracing me, and not wanting me. What a burden this has been! What a deep well of sadness I can never seem to climb out of. What a horrible cycle I keep perpetuating in my life.

So, I am writing to tell you: I set fire to the rain. I burn up all the pain you gave me. I throw into the consuming fire everything you would have your legacy be. I am not the little girl you destroyed. I am the woman God's Love has built. I will cling to my Heavenly Father's eternal promise of hope, love and peace with every fiber of strength He graces me with. I will live in His presence and protective covering now, today, forever, as He wills it.

Only through God's grace can I dig deeper still and say that I truly wish, with all the heart of an orphaned child, that you had not only loved me, but that you would have allowed me to love you back. I wish that you had given fatherhood a real chance at any of the many points you were forgiven and embraced.

I didn't mourn the man you were, for there was no love there. I didn't mourn because of regret, for I did everything I knew to do. I mourned because the hope of reconciling our relationship died with you. I cried because I will never know what it is to have a right – good, decent, open, honest, and productive – relationship with you, my earthly dad. I mourned because your choices led you to death long before you stopped breathing.

Your sister told me you accepted Jesus Christ on your death bed. I pray that is the case; as I prayed at the time that God would have mercy on your soul. Yet, even as I prayed that in the end you accepted peace and love into your heart, I received freedom to let you go. I release you. I declare that you no longer have any authority, any influence, any suggestive power in my life, on my life, over my life or through my life. Nor will you have any effect on my husband, our marriage or our descendants. Nothing that you were, nothing that you tainted will spill over into my present or my future. For that I thank God continuously, for He has made me new apart from the ashes of my past... apart from you.

Listen to: Set Fire to the Rain by Adele

THE WANTON DESTRUCTION OF LIFE

Witnessing the wanton destruction of life in every corner of American society has had a painfully life-altering impact. The overwhelming repetitious nature of murder, being forced to bear witness to murder and then listen to reasons why murder is justified has darkened the lens through which I view the world.

How does a people – a community, a society, a nation – watch men, women and children get beaten and murdered, usually with bystanders recording or doing nothing, then read the sanitized summaries in mainstream media, and think we are an advanced civilization?

America is primitive.

Witnessing such egregious hatred on a regular basis in a national context has profoundly changed me. Knowing this level of violence has been consistently increasing for centuries is mind-blowing. Each instance has punctured and cauterized my heart in such a way it's impossible to see any innocence in the world. It has broken parts of me. In many ways, being a witness has radicalized me.

Human beings are being hunted and killed because other created beings assume they have the right to destroy life.

Giving the benefit of the doubt when state representatives murder unarmed, unsuspecting or cooperating citizens is not an option anymore. There aren't two sides to hear, see or understand. What happened before doesn't need to be known. One person usually has the support of the state and a gun. The other person is already subject to the state by jurisdiction and has an absolute right to breathe, live, move, speak and question any threat to their personhood. Imagine all the all the people throughout the history of this country who didn't resist their own murder because they believe obeying and complying would get them home safe. The horror!

Popular culture is rabid about animal rights. Some folks would have everyone believe animals are people. Others claim some people are animals. Dogs and lions have the right to life. Yet, Black people, poor people, Muslims, Mexicans and women, forfeit their right to life the moment they're born according to popular culture.

Popular culture is wrong.

People are people. Human beings have an inalienable right to life. No matter how a person is described, they have a humanity that cannot be denied or explained away. No *however, but,* or *if only* can change that. There's no sliding scale on what constitutes a human being.

Human beings deserve to be treated like human beings. How do we do that? One way is to recognize everyone you encounter is created in love even as you recognize you are created in the same love. Respect is rooted in treating others as you want to be treated. Most of the world's population has been mistreated for as long as empires have ruled in the land.

It is unfortunate that we have to announce, chant, insist, scream and demonstrate that *Black Lives Matter, Women's* rights are human rights, no child should be left behind, beg for same sex marriage and family rights, or constantly remind ourselves Lady Liberty is an open invitation begging for *the tired, poor huddled masses yearning to breathe free.*

The hatred of people has changed me. I haven't succumbed to internalizing it in a way projects from my being, but I have come to scoff at the concept of non-violent protests. Nothing has been non-violent about any protest in this country.

Collectively we come together to assert our right to life, liberty and justice because of unjustified homicides. The premise of marches is violence. The words marchers scream roar from their tortured spirits:

We can't breathe!
Get your knee off our necks!
Stop bombing us!
My body my choice!
Pay fair wages!
We're hungry!
We're homeless!
We're poor!
We are not yours to kill and destroy!
What happens to a dream deferred?
We too are America.

Our turmoil, fear and trauma are rooted in the violence that fuels the world.

It's hard to focus on life when death remains so aggressively front and center. Ultimately, I always come back to the fact that the abusers, murderers and oppressors of the world were created by the same God who created me. We share a connection to humanity and creation rather they choose to exhibit that knowledge or not. My one comfort is the sure knowledge that murderers are killing and eliminating themselves even as they think they are ravaging God's creation with their hatred. The world will not remain in darkness forever. It's impossible to do so. God is light and love and He chose to create human beings in His image. We reflect light and love. The hatred and death many choose to cloak themselves in is not eternal and will come to a very definite end.

Change is slow, but it's also visible. Technology allows the general public to bypass mainstream media and its sugar-coating of state-sanctioned violence. Members of the public can share information in real time across the globe and participate in joint action immediately. The internet and social media have drastically changed how injustices are perceived, received and responded to. Technology has increased awareness and participation in protests against injustice and inhumane treatment around the world. The laws and systems haven't yet changed, but by creating mass awareness and community activism there is hope they will eventually be overhauled.

Life will win. Life has to win. Eventually, everyone will recognize themselves in the abused, downtrodden, uncounted and eliminated. Eventually, the dominant culture will recognize that they weren't just killing "others," they were also killing themselves. Perhaps then they will see we are all created equally in love. Hopefully, some of the rest of us will still be around.

∞ ∞ ∞

Days after the Grand Jury in Ferguson, Missouri decided not indict Darren Wilson for the murder of Michael Brown, an unarmed teen who was found guilty and executed for walking in the street on his way home, I wrote, *"Let Ferguson – and the United States – burn!"* The sentiment came from a place of raw fury and blinding frustration at my – our collective – inability to create change instantaneously or as needed. Raw fury burning through me was a very unusual and unsettling feeling. Unfortunately, this emotion has been fanned continually in recent years.

Shortly after the Grand Jury decided not to indict Darren Wilson's for anything, several more murders of unarmed Black men (Rumain Brisbon,[17] Phoenix, Arizona) and boys (Tamir

Rice,[18] Cleveland, Ohio) by police officers across the United States were reported with supporting videos. Additionally, a Grand Jury in New York City decided not to indict at least one police officer, Daniel Pantaleo, for the murder of Eric Garner[19] in Staten Island, New York. Mr. Garner, who was found guilty of standing on a street and allegedly selling single cigarettes, was jumped by five to six police officers, several sitting or kneeling on his restrained body and choked to death on the sidewalk. As he was being murdered, he repeatedly exclaimed, "I can't breathe!" The recording we have of Mr. Garner being murdered have eleven utterances of "I can't breathe!" His murders continued to choke him, kneel on him and otherwise restrain him. Until death.

When the man the world saw literally choke Eric Garner to death was not even INDICTED for any level of assault or bodily harm, my rage boiled over. As it cooled, it crystalized.

The news kept reporting how "rioters were destroying property." Much of the public then condemned protesters as unruly, destructive nuisances with nothing better to do than destroy their own communities. So, the summary refrain became: *it's unfortunate this person loss their life but the police were just doing their job, what are Black people so upset about?*

Seriously? Police officers around this country are killing unarmed PEOPLE – CITIZENS they take an oath to protect and serve – without any fear of condemnation, consequences or prosecution and the main concern of those watching is "be careful of other people's PROPERTY?"

Throughout every report on the demonstrations and rallies, pro-property advocates lamented *"How can 'they' destroy their own community?* Who are the "they"? The people who were supposed to stay in ghettos? In neighborhoods cut off from "civilized" society?

While the tone-deaf oblivious Americans are mad because buildings are burning and cars are being overturned (usually by paid government operatives), the traumatized Americans are yet again undone by the killings of people who have been burned, shot and suffocated. "They" – fellow Americans - are mad because humans are being categorized, and treated, as meaningless in this country.

Why don't the lamenters think of "they" as "us"? Why is no one talking about how America continually destroys its own? How America hates its own. People with a conscience are infuriated with Americans who ignore, diminish and murder human beings.

It boggles the mind how anyone can hear a story about a brutal, unjust killing, see other people respond in pain by demanding the killer be arrested, charged and prosecuted then exclaim that the destruction of property is too much to bear. Even in the midst of a city burning, those not impacted by the terror of over-policing are more concerned with preserving property than human life. Their focus keeps them enslaved to a system that destroys countless lives daily.

What is wrong with this country? What is wrong with people who justify the killing of ANYONE over a presumed suspicion of selling or stealing a cigarette? Would they be okay with their children being killed over such minor things? Certainly not. It boggled the mind that so many are okay doing to others what they would not want done to them.

When did we become such a deadened society? Perhaps our end was written in the beginning of colonial rule, when the first European murderers claimed this land as their new home. This country began with deceit, theft and genocide. It was built on the backs of kidnapped, tortured and enslaved African Peoples on land usurped from Indigenous Peoples. Property has always been driver of American greed and bloodlust. The American Dream is to acquire and profit. American foreign policy is about subduing and puppeteering other nations for the benefit of American imperialism. Our democratic capitalist ideology is not for the benefit of all the People. Capitalism works towards monopolies. Soon America will lose the appearance of being ruled by government, as various captains of industry take over the right of rulership based on their profit share and lobbying portfolios. Capitalism is the true foundation of this nation, and it will also be its downfall.

> *"You cannot serve God and wealth." The Pharisees, who were lovers of money, heard all this, and they ridiculed Him. So, He said to them, "You are those who justify yourselves in the sight of others; but God knows your hearts; for what is prized by human beings is an abomination in the sight of God. ~ Luke 16:12-15*

Everyone has the right to live free of harassment and the threat of death. However, much of the population in this country and throughout the world, has not been able to practice that right in their daily lives.

The burning of Ferguson is a REACTION to continued blatant injustice in one case that is rooted in a history of blatantly sustained inhumane injustices toward a specific group of people in this country. If the out-of-touch Americans want a *reasonable reaction*, then 'they' should insist on *reasonable justice* being applied in every facet of these United States of America. Had the bare minimum of an indictment been issued for Darren Wilson when he murdered Michael Brown by shooting him four times in the back then leaving him in the middle of the street uncovered for hours in the hot summer sun, then neither the first protest nor the second would have happened in Ferguson. The people have a right to expect law enforcement officers to be answerable to the same laws they are responsible for enforcing. Upon hearing the grand jury in New York City saw no reason to hold Daniel Pantaleo accountable for killing Eric Garner, all I could think or write was: *I'm out of words.* Rage had burned me up and I couldn't maintain the anger that swallowed my words.

Yet my heart and spirit demanded action. My soul cried out to express its anguish. That night I marched.

Words failed me, but my voice did not. With thousands of other marches, I shouted through the streets of New York from Union Square to Times Square. I stood in solidarity with millions of Americans who were also outraged by the assumption of power the police have taken upon themselves.

Two comments within my hearing enraged me enough to shout directly at the police officers while demonstrating my outrage with my feet and presence. The first was when a police officer threatened to arrest people if they sat down in the street. Sitting in a street is not a crime. Sitting in a street that is occupied by people standing and chanting while being closed to traffic presents no danger to anyone. The second comment was shouted by a cop as we walked through the streets. "Get on the sidewalk!" "No, we're taking the streets," we chanted. "Do as you're told," the officer shouted back. For that he got an infuriated, "I don't have to do as you say," from me. Apparently, the fact that Michael Brown was killed shortly after he flippantly refused to walk over to Darren Wilson when he was waved over seems to be lost on police officers. Police officers themselves are *not* the law. Their job is to uphold the law. Satisfying their egos is not an obligation of citizenship.

The police essentially justify their killings of civilians by two sets of reasoning: 1) The person did not obey them; and 2) they feared the person, i.e. they thought the person was a personal threat them.

No other citizen can get away with murder by saying their orders were not obeyed or they feared the victim would harm them, yet we allow police officers to kill indiscriminately simply by claiming their own lives were in danger. Their sickness is the sickness of the nation.

The people need to continue to speak up, show up and stand up for those whose voices and lives have been taken from them.

Meditation Verse: Luke 18:4-5

For a while he refused; but later he said to himself, 'Though I have no fear of God and no respect for anyone, yet because this widow keeps bothering me, I will grant her justice, so that she may not wear me out by continually coming.'" And the Lord said, "Listen to what the unjust judge says. And will not God grant justice to his chosen ones who cry to him day and night? Will he delay long in helping them? I tell you, he will quickly grant justice to them. And yet, when the Son of Man comes, will he find faith on earth?"

GOOD COP. BAD COP.
LIFE IS NOT SO SIMPLE.

OVER the last decade, there's been a lot a commentary on the majority of cops being "good." Every time *cops* and *good* are mentioned in the same sentence, I cringe. Popular opinion assumes cops are good because they wear a badge representing their public service. The only *bad cops* are those who kill on purpose with no good excuse, because *good cops* don't kill unarmed people randomly.

Essentially, the translation of *good cops don't kill unarmed people*, is *bad cops are good up to the point they kill* someone the public deems worthy of living. That's not the measurement of judgement we are provided in the Word.

> *And as you wish that others would do to you,*
> *do so to them.*
> ~ Luke 6:31

Police officers are human and created of the same dirt as the rest of humanity. They are not inherently good. They do not supply safety or generate trust simply because they wear a uniform and a badge. Neither do you.

People who encounter you – the people you serve in your own life – know you mean no harm when you do no harm. They feel safe because you do not threaten them or hurt them or others they know of. They trust you because of the continual trustworthy behavior you exhibit. This is not a perfect equation, but it's generally applicable to most lived experience.

Where else in society does *not killing* another human being determine ones' goodness? How did the bar get so low for those who took an oath to protect and serve the public? Being a good person begins with doing no harm to others and generally entails a combination of many small daily actions imparting one's nature, intent, and personality to others.

It would do us well as a society to hear stories about police officers who act with integrity, treat the people they encounter (even known criminals) with respect, and make wise decisions with the full knowledge that every decision they make has an impact on someone's life, especially their own. Those stories are few and far between. Unfortunately, the common stories involve police brutality, abuse of authority and the murder of civilians.

Since I began following the stories of police and civilian assaults on Black bodies, my mood and world view began to darken. An impotent rage engulfed me for a time. The knowledge of my helplessness and inability to effect change was debilitating. It seemed the more I focused on the anger and outrage, the angrier and exhausted I became. The more helpless I felt. The amount of injustice in America is overwhelming. Each subsequent killing added new layers to the inherited trauma of living as a Black Woman in America. Eventually, I learned to refocus the dark energy warping my mind and spirit by documenting the protests and marches igniting across the country.

Thinking about the many ways humans find to justify hating and killing each other is a demoralizing exercise. Quite honestly, I can only do what I can do. And doing all I can do does not solve the worlds' problems. I know that. But it's in the doing that we get caught up in what's been done.

I don't want to be caught up and focused on the wrong actions that have been done to me or to others. I have to continually remember that the people who are okay with injustice, state-supported murder and torture, the rape of women, the abuse of children, the separation of families, basically the subordination of any human being, are still people who Jesus died for. He did not die just for me. He did not only die for believers. He surrendered His life so that people the world over, throughout time, may have access to true life – eternal life. Jesus died so every human being would have the choice of a spiritual life. This is the action I choose to remember each time the happenings in the world conspire to make me forget.

> *Jesus called them to him and said to them, "You know that those who are considered rulers of the Gentiles lord it over them, and their great ones exercise authority over them. But it shall not be so among you. But whoever would be great among you must be your servant, and whoever would be first among you must be slave of all. For even the Son of Man came not to be served but to serve, and to give His life as a ransom for many."*
> *~ Matthew 20:25-28*

Fear will not rule me, neither will those who peddle it. Fear is not of God. So, in fear, there is no good thing.

Hatred is an awesomely powerful emotion. Though the hater rots from the inside out, their venom negatively impacts those who observed their acts of hatred, read their hateful words and listen to their hate-filled speech.

Hatred and fear are interconnected and reflective of each other. They both spread like an infection. Anyone who knowingly operates in fear or hate is not trustworthy nor can they provide safety. Yet nearly every officer who makes headlines for killing unarmed people claim they feared for their lives and, almost universally, their fear has been upheld as a valid reason to kill.

Even more disturbing, the murderer's fear usually receives an outpouring of public compassion and support while their victims are dehumanized and vilified.

Once upon a time, bravery and courage were honored characteristics of public servants, especially for police officers, but the rhetoric surrounding state-sanctioned murders coddles these trained killers. Bravery and courage are the result of overcoming fear; cowardice is the result of giving in to fear. Police officers who are too afraid to perform their job with integrity, respect and honor should have, at the minimum, enough self-awareness to step aside and leave the job even if only to protect the public from their trigger fingers. If they are unable to make the call themselves, their fellow officers and supervisors should step in and guide them towards the exit.

For the general public, fear is not justification for taking a life. However, across America, being white and saying you feared for your life is sufficient justification for police officers to commit murder. Claiming to be afraid in order to be exonerated of murder is a privilege for a select few within state-approved and orchestrated situations. Black police officers and those of other ethnicities, are more like to be indicted and do time, whereas white police officers are rarely even indicted. Nowhere is it socially acceptable for women to kill men they fear, even in violent situations where a man has abused or violated a woman. White women who kill their husbands out of fear are treated like any other oppressed group – prosecuted to the fullest extent of the law. But a white woman who kills a black person, well that's an allowable homicide.

Several times over the last few years, I had to step away from my social media feeds because unfiltered public opinion about the value of Black Life stirs up deep anger and frustration. Since

I've been paying attention to all the trending killings by police officers and civilians (since Trayvon Martin's killer walked free), I've become more and more outraged by the failure of police chiefs, mayors, district attorneys, prosecutors and grand juries to see and prosecute murder for what it is. On top of that, I've become even more outraged by the willingness of members of the public, fellow citizens and residents, to justify murder as a necessary rebuttal for sleeping on a park bench, walking in the street, playing on a playground, walking up a dark staircase, bringing dinner home to the family, driving to the grocery store, standing outside a convenience store or shopping in the toy aisle. It's incomprehensible to think that anyone can break these actions down to their simplest form and still conclude that these human beings deserved to be shot and killed in the midst of their respective actions because of another person's fear or hate. Wrong is wrong – no matter the job, uniform or badge worn by the perpetrator. Murder is murder.

What comes after outrage? Who can sustain anger and frustration due to ceaseless hate and violence against humanity? Centuries of human trafficking, genocide, rape, torture, family separation and overall oppression. Centuries of being denied basic human rights. Of having no civil recourse for injustices. Whose rage can burn indefinitely?

No one's. Truly, it's impossible to sustain an extreme level of rage for any extended period of time. Eventually, you need to pull back and tend to your trauma and acknowledge your grief. Fortunately, organization can be sustained. Organized protests, marches, legislative measures can be managed by a community of individuals who can tap in according to their capacity.

The saturation of mobile camera phones throughout the public has exposed horrors in modern context that we swore had been rectified in the 1960's. The Civil Rights Movement had supposedly resolved the issue of our rights and social standing. We were no longer being lynched. We were equal citizens under the law and free to come and go as we pleased. This is what we all thought. Until camera phones allowed us to compare notes from the far corners of the country. Sanford rose up. Ferguson caught fire. New Yorkers flooded the streets and shut down highways. From Baltimore to Oakland, Chicago to Houston, Milwaukee to Phoenix and all points surrounding and in between, we were no longer able to pretend that the atrocities of the old South weren't woven into the very fabric of Americana. This nation was funded by trafficked human beings, and built on their broken bodies. The ineptitude of the enslavers fostered hatred for the endurance of those thy enslaved and oppressed.

If a thing is rotten to its core, how long do you attempt to cutaway the rot before tossing the whole thing into the trash?

The year after Ferguson exploded, Milwaukee County prosecutors refused to indict Christopher Manney, the police officer who killed Dontre Hamilton, an unarmed Black man with documented mental illness, who was sleeping on a park bench. At that point, I threw up my hands, laid down and rolled over in prayer. *What is the purpose of all this, Father? How will you be glorified through all this violence and hatred? What do you want me to do?* I awoke the next morning with a will to write.

I believe that purposeful prayer is part of the solution, and I know that prayer has always been a response of those who fight oppression across the world. However, it needs to be used in collaboration with action. Community action. City action. State action. Federal action. Global intermediaries. All levels of society and government have a role in making America hospitable for all its residents.

I am an instrument secure in the hand of my Creator. God is my safety and in Him is all my trust. He is just and He will not be mocked. His ways are above our ways. Those who think they are free to live without consequences for taking human life without cause will learn in time that God's vengeance will be much more than they can bear. With this knowledge, I urge all police officers who have killed, to repent. Turn yourselves in, ask for prosecution and make reparations to the families you have shattered and to the communities you have betrayed.

> *Whoever sheds the blood of a human, by a human shall that person's blood be shed; for in his own image God made humankind.*
> *~ Genesis 9:6*

America's biggest stumbling block is its refusal to acknowledge and make meaningful amends for everything done to groups of people in this land in the name of discovery, expansion, revolution, commerce and capitalism. Making amends look like giving Indigenous Nations back their lands (if that pushes cities away, so be it); giving the promised land and livestock to descendants of enslaved Africans; removing personhood from corporations and making sure their destruction of human life, sacred lands and natural resources is halted. This would be the beginning of progress. From there, everyone needs to learn to view every natural person as human, individual and part of a global community. To achieve this, it may be helpful to eliminate categories such as black, white, gay, lesbian, old, young, criminal, thug, immigrant, citizen, employed, unemployed. We label everything and everybody. The more labels we have the easier it is to think we are all completely different when we aren't. Societal structures create the illusion of barriers and divisions. We as a people need to overcome the corrosiveness of the societies we've built.

Meditation Verse: Ephesians 4:1-6
I therefore, the prisoner in the Lord, beg you to lead a life worthy of the calling to which you have been called, with all humility and gentleness, with patience, bearing with one another in love, making every effort to maintain the unity of the Spirit in the bond of peace. There is one body and one Spirit, just as you were called to the one hope of your calling, one Lord, one faith, one baptism, one God and Father of all, who is above all and through all and in all.

TEARS & PROTEST

May 13, 2015

I'm sitting on a partially shadowed bench in Union Square Park listening to sounds. Sirens screeching through the streets. Blaring horns rushing through traffic. Music blaring from indistinguishable distances. Entangled lovers kissing on nearby benches. Conversations between friends. One-sided phone chats.

Tears have been streaming down my face for more than a half hour. Like a running faucet dripping in a silent steady stream. Sitting here blowing my nose like a trumpet heralding the end of rainy season. Or not.

Deep sigh.

I hope no one notices my distress. I just returned a call of my own in an effort to distract me from this onslaught of sadness and loneliness that's been creeping up in a well-known and well-battled way. Triggered by the reality of being unwanted and unchosen by every significant person in my life. And knowing that even in the less significant relationships, I am not chosen for who I am, but for how I can benefit a situation. It's a truth I try not to dwell on too often because it reminds me that there is indeed something about me that repels people. There's something about me unable to truly connect in any significant way with other human beings. How have I nearly reached forty without a real friend or family member to celebrate anything with? Each graduate is given two tickets for the ceremony, and I don't even have two people for my tickets.   There's no one. I mentioned my upcoming graduation to my sister and invited her to attend – mostly so I could see her. She said she would come, but I know she won't. She has successfully avoided me for many years. I've managed to resist the sting of rejection in years gone by, but there's no more salve for that wound. There's a friend from work who I've been social with over the last few years, last year we discussed her coming to my graduation, but since those conversations our relationship has cooled into more of a casual acquaintanceship. I find myself thinking that graduating alone is representative of my daily life. This connecting thought made my deep well of sadness bubble over.

Despite all that has gone well in life, the absence of anyone to share anything with makes me feel like an abject failure.

God put the thought of this memoir in me at the beginning of the year with an exclamation: "Watch what I'm going to do for you!" I'm watching, Lord – I've been watching for years. I don't want to look anymore. That's the sad truth.

Tears are dripping in a steady flow again.

I don't want to wait with expectation anymore, Father.

The same hope that keeps me alive is also killing me. The desire for love produces only anguish.

I keep visualizing the women I know in their fifties and sixties who've given up.... Or rather given up in public; how can anyone put away such a yearning in private? In the emptiness of their home, the vacancy of their hearts and the coldness of their beds? What woman ever stops yearning for arms to hold her and a voice to counsel her? What woman is satisfied with the barrenness of her own space when she's been given the heart of a nurturer and counselor?

Remembering these women, the sisters who have born the burden of loneliness before me, I think, "Ah, they didn't give up on the hope. They gave up on God." Knowing full well they found other ways to satiate their longing for companionship and community. Unavailable men. Foster or adoptive children. Latch onto family units. Volunteer their life away.

I don't want to give up on you, Father. And I don't want to drown in a well of my own tears. All praises to You. Good night.

∞ ∞ ∞

After getting up from the park bench, I went searching for food. I hadn't eaten in over ten hours. This morning, I was working feverishly on my final project for my final class which met tonight. I stumbled through my final presentation tonight. The first low. From there I went into a free fall and I'm still falling.

Got home a short while ago. After finding a quick bite to eat, I went to Barnes & Noble to look for books by Eve Ensler. I met her last Wednesday night a block away from Union Square during a protest against police brutality. The demonstration was a show of support for the uprising in Baltimore, Maryland following the in-custody killing of Freddy Gray[20].

Within a couple of minutes of the march starting from Union Square at the corner of 16th Street and Broadway, the police attacked the front line of the marching protesters. They were blocking the sidewalks and had a show of force in the middle of the street. The intent was to scatter the crowd before we got started. As the crowd tried to get past them, they began pushing and shoving en masse. It was sort of terrifying. It was like a melee. I had never seen anything like it. I almost went down from the shoving the police were giving to the front of the crowd. This was the second march I took part of and the first time I experienced fear for my safety and life. Not from the demonstrators – the outraged public – but from the police officers charged with keeping law and order. They were the ones acting disorderly in their attempt to keep the crowd trapped between avenues. We hadn't even marched the length of a city block yet. The vast majority of the demonstrators were still in the square yelling towards the front trying to figure out what was going on.

The police do not seem to be aware of the rights of the people. They think they are the rule of law and that their militarized presence should automatically subdue the public into inaction and inertia.

It was in the midst of the chaos they created that I had the presence of mind in my newfound fear for my safety to step out from the press of the two opposing groups. When I got up on the sidewalk, I noticed a steady stream of marchers slipping through a gap in the police line. A gap between scaffolding and a building. I squeezed through and walked to next corner, Sixth Avenue. It was at this corner that I watched with bemusement at a crowd of police intimidating a peaceful group of demonstrators in New York City. "I've never seen anything like this," I said aloud.

A voice next to me chimed in, "Amazing, isn't it? This is our City," she yelled at the police.

I echoed her and we began a sideways conversation, both keeping our eyes on the police surrounding us and the movement of the demonstrators. Before we decided to walk around the block to get back to the back of the crowd, I turned to her and said, "I'm LaShawnda, by the way." She introduced herself as Eve. Lovely name, I told her. We meandered around the block, constantly checking our phones along the way. I was looking for text updates on how the demonstration was being rerouted and Eve was expecting to meet up with a friend in the crowd. After reconnecting with the larger crowd, we turned towards 14th Street and walked across to Seventh Avenue. On the stretch between Broadway and Seventh Avenue, one of us asked the other what we did for a living or what our motivation was for being part of the demonstration. I responded that I was writing my thesis on eliminating discrimination and thought a short documentary about the protests would complement it nicely. She responded that she worked for One Billion Rising Revolution and V-Day. I paused. I blinked. My head tilted to the side. "Eisler? Ensler? Eve Ensler?" She slowly, somewhat hesitantly nodded. I shared that I had participated in about two productions of the Vagina Monologues and one production of the knock-off Pocketbook Monologues. "Have you heard...."

"Yes," with a quick nod and slight resigned expression.

That was the beginning of what made that May 6, 2015, one of the most epic days of my life. The remainder of the march up Seventh Avenue from 14th Street and through Times Square in the midst of early evening traffic made for an equally epic night.

All that to say that I met Eve Ensler – a writer I've been inspired by since my early twenties. A writer and activist who focused specifically on women and our connection with our bodies. The shared conversation and experience gave me the courage to ask if I could interview her for my thesis. She agreed.

So tonight, I pulled myself out of my well of sorrow to grab a bite to eat and go to Barnes & Noble to look for books by Eve Ensler so I could do proper research in order to develop questions for a woman whose work has influenced my entire adult experience.

I haven't thought about it much, but the Vagina Monologues and V-Day helped me reference my private parts without shame and embarrassment in my early twenties. It gave me reason to refer to a part of my body I knew nothing about and had no intimate connection with. A part I associated with violence and violation. Therefore, I had no understanding or appreciation for my body. It was through the V-Day movement and my time with the Women's Resource Center at the University of Wisconsin-Milwaukee that I learned to explode in anger, rather than implode silently in despair at the trauma and turmoil of being sexually violated in my youth. Eve Ensler is one of the revolutionary women I referenced in my graduate school application writing sample, titled, "Progressive Women in a Degenerating Society."

As I look back on my evening of tears and despair, perhaps it's only fitting that I would close the loop with words from Eve for the next level of my journey. Tonight, I purchased Insecure at Last: A Political Memoir and In the Body of the World: A Memoir of Cancer and Connection. I began reading In the Body of the World on the subway ride home and continued for a short time on my patio with a gentle breeze soothing me. She writes: "The absence of a body against my body created a gap, a hole, a hunger. This hunger determined my life.... The absence of a body against my body made attachment abstract. Made my own body dislocated and unable to rest or settle. A body pressed against your body is the beginning of nest. I grew up not in a home but in a kind of free fall of anger and violence that led to a life of constant movement, of leaving and falling.... For years I have been trying to find my way back to my body, and to the Earth."

I thought I had finally found myself at the expense of everyone else in my life. What if I imprisoned myself instead in an unfortunate mockery of self-actualization by self-preservation?

Meditation Verse: Song of Solomon 1:5-6
I am black and beautiful, O daughters of Jerusalem, like the tents of Kedar, like the curtains of Solomon. Do not gaze at me because I am dark, because the sun has gazed on me.

DEAR SANDRA BLAND

Dear Sandy,[21]

I don't know what really happened to you. No one, other than your murderers and God, will ever know what truly transpired during your last days and final hours here on Earth. Truthfully, and unfortunately, I don't need to know the details. The story of your arrest, imprisonment and murder are all too familiar.

You were stopped, harassed, abused, beaten and violated because Officer Brian Encinia believed he could do and say anything he wanted without repercussion. He believed he could "light you up" with electricity, drag you forcefully from your vehicle, slam your head repeatedly into the concrete ground, beat up your body and then blame you for his abuse of you. He thought he had the right to take you to jail and charge you for the effort of beating you. He knew he had support for murdering you in an isolated cell, under the watchful eye of fellow officers. He's part of a system that refuses to hold its members accountable while insisting their victims are at fault. To him, you were just another Black Woman unworthy of basic respect, your body and life available for violation. After all, society doesn't care about Black Womanhood. Black Women are unseen, unheard, unvalued and unprotected. Who'd judge him for his abusive behavior? Who'd blink twice at a Black Woman's demise in jail? Your murderer believed the history of this nation and the message of society: he could do whatever he wanted to a black body and there would be no consequential impact to his life.

Watching the assault on your body, your life, your peace, your rights, your freedom horrified me like nothing else. Indeed, it felt as if it were me being pulled over in an unfamiliar neighborhood and assaulted because I know my rights and informed the officer he was in violation. I know the fear of having a police car follow me on a remote road in a small town. In my case, I refused to pull over and called 911 to let them know I was driving alone and did not feel comfortable pulling over where I was. A short time later, the police car following me moved along.

Unfortunately, this is not a common response for us. We are taught to obey people in uniform, conform to authority, do as we're told. *Be quiet. Don't resist.* If we're good docile targets, all will go well. Indeed, all does go well for the hunter. The hunted on the other hand are aware of their fragility when their bodies are in the crosshairs and custody of those who have no respect for their life.

Your murder could have been mine and any other Black Woman in America, a country where the general public believes the word of a white man in uniform over our lifeless bodies.

Dear Sister Sandy, rest in peace. The cares of the world may no longer trouble you, but you remain a light and battle cry for those of us who remain in the darkness of apathy and injustice in this country and around the world.

Meditation Verse: Luke 23:28-31
"Daughters of Jerusalem, do not weep for me, but weep for yourselves and for your children. For the days are surely coming when they will say, 'Blessed are the barren, and the wombs that never bore, and the breasts that never nursed.' Then they will begin to say to the mountains, 'Fall on us'; and to the hills, 'Cover us.' For if they do this when the wood is green, what will happen when it is dry?"

Source: *Andy Marlette*, August 14, 2014

HOMEMADE RADICALISM

radical: very different from the usual or traditional; favoring extreme changes in existing views, habits, conditions, or institutions; associated with political views, practices, and policies of extreme change

When did your radicalization begin?
December 2014, following a series of non-indictments of police officers and white-thinking people who killed Black men and boys. The murders of Michael Brown, Eric Garner and Tamir Rice broke me open.

Where were you radicalized?
Freddie Gray. New York, NY, April 2015. On a Union Square to Times Square march route decrying the murder of Freddie Gray who was illegally pursued and arrested with force. My second march. Before then, I believed the news reports depicting protester violence. Being in a crowd of a permitted demonstration that was attacked by police before we even began marching was an eye-opener. In America's strong-hold of freedom, independence and self-expression – New York City – no less. It was astounding. And the media reported none of aggressive police tactics from that night.

How were you radicalized?
Watching police push the crowd around, listening to them curse at us. Learning that they were trying to separate people from the crowd to do harm. Knowing they were armed, and the crowd was not. Free speech didn't feel like free speech.

The right to protest didn't feel like a right. They treated it like a challenge to their authority and presence.

Do you know you're radical?
Yes, I know now. I'm learning to embrace being radical. I'm in favor of scrapping the whole country and building up again from scratch. Burn the Constitution and every law based on it. We need to start over with voices from every demographic in this country contributing to our democracy or whatever governing society we collectively agree upon. We need to stop operating from a rotten tree in order to move forward.

When did you first see yourself in the struggle?
Sandra Bland. Houston, TX, July 2015. I see myself in every part of her ending. Solo road trips. Traveling for new opportunities and fresh starts. Being followed by police cars in isolated areas. Knowing and speaking my rights. Shining a light on ignorance. Impatient with false superiority. Being a Black Woman fed up with foolishness. Being viciously attacked for my confidence and dignity. Being blamed for the harm done to me.

When did you become unapologetic?
Chikesia Clemons. Saraland, AL, 2018. She survived her attack. The way she was brutalized and violated in a public space was truly alarming. After ordering her food, she asked

for utensils. The waitress refused her request and called the police. Two male officers arrived, threw her to the ground, tossed her around like a rag doll, exposing her breasts, then flipped her face down to cuff her. Bare breasts and face to the floor. Everyone in the restaurant continued to eat as if nothing egregious was happening. That stunned me. None of those people would have ignored a white woman being similarly abused. The level of detachment it takes to ignore violence against a woman like that is truly astounding.

Chikesia was the catalyst to create a book of images of Black Women with words they use to describe how they see themselves. The project is called, *I AM WOMAN: Experiences of Black Womanhood in America*.

When did you know you wouldn't turn back?
Pamela Turner. Houston, TX, May 2019. Despite crying out for mercy for her unborn child, she was shot five times and killed by Juan Delacruz, a police officer. Whether or not she was pregnant is irrelevant. In her last moments, she attempted to appeal to a common humanity with her killer.

When did you acknowledge your trauma?
LaShawnda Jones aka **Me.** Tucson, AZ, March 2020. One of my neighbors approached an Air BnB guest of mine and told them he didn't mean them any harm, but they should leave immediately because "neighbors were discussing throwing rocks" through my windows and burning down my property. They thought I was showing off by improving my property with stone landscaping and building a log cabin in the backyard for Air BnB guests. So, they threatened to burn me out, destroy my home and business. In my mind, my

neighbors became a lynch mob. It was difficult to process how very American this interaction was. I had enough strength to get an order of protection and confirm my insurance covered bad acts of property destruction, but afterwards, with the help of quarantine, I retreated into deep hibernation. It is devastating to realize there's nowhere in this country I can go to feel safe in my own home.

When did you acknowledge your helplessness?
Walter Scott. North Charleston, SC, April 2015. He was running away when he was shot in the back by a police officer who tried to claim he feared for his life. The cop didn't realize a neighbor was video taping the whole incident from their yard. Walter Scott's killer was charged with murder and sentenced to twenty-years. Very grateful for the video.

When did you acknowledge your rage?
Eric Garner. Staten Island, NY, December 2014. When I began to understand that the media deflected from the murder of Black people by bringing up property rights during times of protest. How the fuck are property rights in the same discussion with the human right to breathe?

When did you acknowledge your grief?
George Floyd. Minneapolis, MN, May 2020. I was finally out of words. I didn't speak for several days. I didn't want to speak. I couldn't put my finger on my exact feelings, but I knew I was overwhelmed. When I was ready to communicate, my first three words were GRIEF, RAGE, TRAUMA. My rage is too much to confront and embrace directly. My trauma reaches back through centuries of

dehumanizing brutality for hundreds of millions of ancestors. My grief cries out from the first betrayal of brotherhood to the abduction and transportation by violent co-conspirators to the most racist "post-racial" society anyone could have imagined.

GRIEF RAGE TRAUMA

The cry of Black Power is at bottom a reaction to the reluctance of white power to make the kind of changes necessary to make justice a reality for the Negro. I think we've got to see that a riot is the language of the unheard. What is it that America has failed to hear? It's failed to hear that the promises of freedom and justice have not been met. It's failed to hear that large segments of white society are more concerned about tranquility and the status quo than about justice, equality and humanity.
~ Martin Luther King, Jr.

THE common refrain in response to demonstrations that turn into destruction of property is, "Why are they burning down their own neighborhoods?" This and similar questions present a disingenuous narrative. The underlining pseudo-cluelessness is infuriating! What neighborhoods do Black People own? How likely are we to burn down our own property?

When white people riot for jealousy, lost ball games and early curfews, they're allowed to incite terror with impunity. Historically, when white citizens, with the aid of state agencies, burned down majority-Black communities, murdering hundreds of Black People over the course various assaults, they were fully supported in the moment and via written history. Attacks targeting self-sufficient Black communities were not only supported by government, but Black people who attempted to stop the violence were prosecuted. Anytime we as a community have owned more than neighboring white folks were comfortable with us owning, we've been burned down or drowned out.

The Houston Riot of 1917 began with police harassing members of a Black community. An all-Black military battalion intervened to stop the violence, and they were attacked by the police force. Later the Black soldiers were put on trial; 19 were executed, 41 were sentenced to life in prison.

During the Red Summer of 1919, "race riots" broke out across the country as white Americans attacked Black Americans in their neighborhoods in twenty cities including Washington DC, Chicago, Omaha, Charleston, Longview, Knoxville and Elaine, Arkansas. (Contributors, 2021)

On Election Day in 1920, a white mob in Ocoee, FL attacked Black residents to prevent them from voting.

In 1921, Tulsa, Oklahoma became the first instance in US history that the United States military dropped bombs on American soil to kill American citizens within their community. A prosperous Black Community was annihilated because, well, what right do Black People have to prosper? Remaining survivors well into her 100's have been denied reparations repeatedly and on appeal.

In 1923, Rosewood, Florida became another self-sufficient Black Community angry white men attacked and destroyed.

There have been dozens of "race riots" across this country since colonization. They all started with white aggression against Indigenous People, African Americans (enslaved and free), Citizens, Workers, Business Owners, Homeowners, Voters in the Communities they lived in. If you didn't know about at least one of these riots, ask yourself why. Now that you know, will you ever stop hollering?

Black People, many of whom are descendants of Africans brought to this country in chains against their will, have always been trapped in a box they were never expected to escape from. When the box begins to burn from the inside, the captor's and their sympathizer's response should not be, "Oh, that poor box! What did it do to deserve being burned? The owner of that box did nothing to you! That's an ancestral box, honor it!"

∞ ∞ ∞

Trauma is the response to a deeply distressing or disturbing event that overwhelms an individual's ability to cope. It causes feelings of helplessness, diminishes their sense of self and their ability to feel their full range of emotions and experiences.

Imagine never being able to heal from a traumatic event because the same event continues to happen daily, weekly or monthly for hundreds of years all over your country.

Before camera phones and social media every Black family and community had stories of atrocities committed against them that were not addressed. That never received justice. That knowledge framed life for all the generations we've been in this land. That's trauma.

With technology, we've become unwilling witnesses to our own murders. We get to analyze the tactics used to destroy our lives and count the active and inactive accomplices standing by screaming for more blood. That's trauma.

We get to watch police officers protect their murdering comrades. Listen to prosecutors talk about investigating a clear murder as if murder is subjective. That's trauma.

Occasional arrests and indictments become tokens when there is no fear of hefty sentencing being the outcome by the perpetrators.

Trauma becomes embedded in our psyches and carried in our bodies. Have you ever wondered why Black People cry out in pain while pointing back in time to the ancestors? Each of us are a link to past suffering and brutality that never received an answer.

> And the Lord said, "What have you done? Listen; your brother's blood is crying out to me from the ground!
> ~ Genesis 4:10

The false supremacy of white America is blinded to who they are. Natural laws don't change simply because people think they are exonerated. They are not the Creator, the Savior, or the Truth. They can continually say *"move on, get over it, it happened a long time ago,"* or any banality because they are not connected to their ancestors the same way. They view their history in terms of economic gain. They view themselves as progenitors of commerce and stewards of wealth. They don't hear or see trauma because they have blinded themselves to it. But don't doubt, they, too, are traumatized. You can't hold a man down without staying down with him. You can't choke a woman without clinching your hands and breathing in her terror.

Though they are the aggressors, white people inhabit the same hell we do, they just can't see it for what it is.

Generational curses are well discussed. We don't often think about trauma being passed through the generations. But the need for justice and reparations also binds generations of African descendants to past, present and future injustices.

Generational trauma comes up as a discussion topic when the community collectively feels re-traumatized. However, since we as a people are not recognized or respected, the need for justice and reparations is dismissed for each generation. This alone tells me America is doomed. We, as a nation, need to address everything down to the roots, going back to the beginning.

Ignoring history makes people blind to the fact that the past is very much present. The past has never been able to become our history because there has not been a day in this nation's time that people of African descent have not been targeted for domination and destruction. When even the most resistant privileged Americans are willing to hear and speak truth, perhaps then we will be able to move on from where we are as a nation into a healing phase.

> *And now you are cursed from the ground, which has opened its mouth to receive your brother's blood from your hand. ~ Genesis 4:11*

Acknowledgement is needed. Amends need to be made. Reparations for hundreds of years of physical, psychological, emotional, spiritual, familial, relational, and financial harm need to be added to the federal budget for Black Americans. Nothing less than land and income is acceptable. Add in a few generations of free education with appropriate preparation. Paraphrased in the famous style of Miss Celie, "Until the United States of America does right by us, everything in this country will crumble. Everything they even attempt will fail."

America has a lot of work to do. If the country decides to be honest and compassionate, it can heal some of the trauma. But it has to do something it has never done: be honest and humane.

∞ ∞ ∞

It often feels as if we are in a constant state of grief. We barely recover from one assault before being forced to witness another. This latest murder kept me silent for days. My silence was broken by a phone call from an old friend talking their usual nonsense. The only words I got out were a somber "Good morning" and "I'm trying to understand what you're saying."

These conversations always start with the murder of Black men, women and children. Then instantly turns to what Black People did to forfeit their right to life. There must've been a reason, the friend parrots every time. Interesting how the conversation never gets to who made the random white people judge, jury and executioner? No one ever questions the white person's right to take a life when they destroy Black Lives.

That's because the system we rely on for justice is not designed to protect Black Lives. It's not intended to honor Black Lives. There are no mechanisms for humanity in the American justice system. Our system has only ever been designed and intended to protect property and uphold the right of white men to dominate or destroy everything they set their eyes on. This mentality hasn't survived for 400 years because it was only taught at the beginning. It survives because it's taught and reinforced daily.

At the start of the Civil War there were thirty-four states in the Union. Only fifteen were known as slave states, but each of the thirty-four states had slave codes (Contributors, Slave Codes, 2021). We try to act like slavery was only a Southern institution, but every corner of this country explored by white men has participated in dehumanizing people of African descent. That's why we can witness a murder in Minneapolis and respond from coast to coast with enraged pain. No matter where we are, we know that our life can be forfeit just as casually. We know that no matter the year, our murderers may never pay full consequence for taking our life. They have only to say they feared for their safety, even as they choke the breath from our lungs, to be given absolution from others who benefit from keeping Black People terrorized and traumatized.

There are too many names to mention, but this week, this month, this year we are newly seared with the murders of George Floyd, Breonna Taylor, and Ahmaud Arbery. May the known and unknown rest in peace.

IN MEMORIAM

💔 Marcellis Stinnette, October 20, 2020, Waukegan 💔 Jonathan Dwayne Price, October 3, 2020, Wolfe City 💔 Dijon Durand Kizzee, August 31, 2020, Los Angeles 💔 Rayshard Brooks, June 12, 2020, Atlanta 💔 Carlos Carson, June 6, 2020, Tulsa 💔 David McAtee, June 1, 2020 💔 Tony "Tony the Tiger" McDade, May 27, 2020, Tallahassee 💔 George Perry Floyd, May 25, 2020, Minneapolis 💔 Dreasjon "Sean" Reed, May 6, 2020, Indianapolis 💔 Michael Brent Charles Ramos, April 24, 2020, Austin 💔 Daniel T. Prude, March 30, 2020, Rochester 💔 Breonna Taylor, March 13, 2020, Louisville 💔 Manuel "Mannie" Elijah Ellis, March 3, 2020, Tacoma 💔 William Howard Green, January 27, 2020, Temple Hills 💔 John Elliot Neville, December 4, 2019, Winston-Salem 💔 Atatiana Koquice Jefferson, October 12, 2019, Fort Worth 💔 Elijah McClain, August 30, 2019, Aurora 💔 Emantic "EJ" Fitzgerald Bradford Jr., November 22, 2018, Hoover 💔 Charles "Chop" Roundtree Jr., October 17, 2018, San Antonio 💔 Chinedu Okobi, October 3, 2018, Millbrae 💔 Botham Shem Jean, September 6, 2018, Dallas 💔 Antwon Rose Jr., June 19, 2018, East Pittsburgh 💔 Saheed Vassell, April 4, 2018, Brooklyn 💔 Stephon Alonzo Clark, March 18, 2018, Sacramento 💔 Aaron Bailey, June 29, 2017, Indianapolis 💔 Charleena Chavon Lyles, June 18, 2017, Seattle 💔 Fetus of Charleena Chavon Lyles (14-15 weeks), June 18, 2017, Seattle 💔 Jordan Edwards, April 29, 2017, Balch Springs 💔 Chad Robertson, February 15, 2017, Chicago 💔 Deborah Danner, October 18, 2016, Bronx 💔 Alfred Olango, September 27, 2016, El Cajon 💔 Terence Crutcher, September 16, 2016, Tulsa 💔 Terrence LeDell Sterling, September 11, 2016, Washington, DC 💔 Korryn Gaines, August 1, 2016, Randallstown

💔 Joseph Curtis Mann, July 11, 2016, Sacramento 💔 Philando Castile, July 6, 2016, Falcon Heights 💔 Alton Sterling, July 5, 2016, Baton Rouge 💔 Bettie "Betty Boo" Jones, December 26, 2015, Chicago 💔 Quintonio LeGrier, December 26, 2015, Chicago 💔 Corey Lamar Jones, October 18, 2015, Palm Beach Gardens 💔 Jamar O'Neal Clark, November 16, 2015, Minneapolis 💔 Jeremy "Bam Bam" McDole, September 23, 2015, Wilmington 💔 India Kager, September 5, 2015, Virginia Beach 💔 Samuel Vincent DuBose, July 19, 2015, Cincinnati 💔 Sandra Bland, July 13, 2015, Waller County, Texas 💔 Brendon K. Glenn, May 5, 2015, Venice 💔 Freddie Carlos Gray Jr., April 19, 2015, Baltimore 💔 Walter Lamar Scott, April 4, 2015, North Charleston 💔 Eric Courtney Harris, April 2, 2015, Tulsa 💔 Phillip Gregory White, March 31, 2015, Vineland 💔 Mya Shawatza Hall, March 30, 2015, Fort Meade 💔 Meagan Hockaday, March 28, 2015, Oxnard 💔 Tony Terrell Robinson, Jr., March 6, 2015, Madison 💔 Janisha Fonville, February 18 2015, Charlotte 💔 Natasha McKenna, February 8, 2015, Fairfax County 💔 Jerame C. Reid, December 30, 2014, Bridgeton 💔 Rumain Brisbon, December 2, 2014, Phoenix 💔 Tamir Rice, November 22, 2014, Cleveland 💔 Akai Kareem Gurley, November 20, 2014, Brooklyn 💔 Tanisha N. Anderson, November 13, 2014, Cleveland 💔 Dante Parker, August 12, 2014, Victorville 💔 Ezell Ford, August 11, 2014, Los Angeles 💔 Michael Brown Jr., August 9, 2014, Ferguson 💔 John Crawford III, August 5, 2014, Beavercreek 💔 Eric Garner, July 17, 2014, Staten Island 💔 Dontre Hamilton, April 30, 2014, Milwaukee 💔 Victor White III, March 3, 2014, New Iberia 💔 Gabriella Monique Nevarez, March 2, 2014, Citrus Heights 💔 Yvette Smith, February 16, 2014, Bastrop County, Texas 💔 McKenzie J. Cochran, January 29, 2014, Southfield 💔 Jordan Baker, January 16, 2014, Houston 💔 Andy

Lopez, October 22, 2013, Santa Rosa 💔 Miriam Iris Carey, October 3, 2013, Washington, DC 💔 Barrington "BJ" Williams, September 17, 2013, New York City 💔 Jonathan Ferrell, September 14, 2013, Charlotte 💔 Carlos Alcis, August 15, 2013, Brooklyn 💔 Larry Eugene Jackson Jr., July 26, 2013, Austin 💔 Kyam Livingston, July 21, 2013, New York City 💔 Clinton R. Allen, March 10, 2013, Dallas 💔 Kimani "KiKi" Gray, March 9, 2013, Brooklyn 💔 Kayla Moore, February 13, 2013, Berkeley 💔 Jamaal Moore Sr., December 15, 2012, Chicago 💔 Johnnie Kamahi Warren, February 13, 2012, Dothan 💔 Shelly Marie Frey, December 6, 2012, Houston 💔 Darnisha Diana Harris, December 2, 2012, Breaux Bridge 💔 Timothy Russell, November 29, 2012, Cleveland 💔 Malissa Williams, November 29, 2012, Cleveland 💔 Noel Palanco, October 4, 2012, Queens 💔 Reynaldo Cuevas, September 7, 2012, Bronx 💔 Chavis Carter, July 28, 2012, Jonesboro 💔 Alesia Thomas, July 22, 2012, Los Angeles 💔 Shantel Davis, June 14, 2012, New York City 💔 Sharmel T. Edwards, April 21, 2012, Las Vegas 💔 Tamon Robinson, April 18, 2012, Brooklyn 💔 Ervin Lee Jefferson, III, March 24, 2012, Atlanta 💔 Kendrec McDade, March 24, 2012, Pasadena 💔 Rekia Boyd, March 21, 2012, Chicago 💔 Shereese Francis, March 15, 2012, Queens 💔 Jersey K. Green, March 12, 2012, Aurora 💔 Wendell James Allen, March 7, 2012, New Orleans 💔 Nehemiah Lazar Dillard, March 5, 2012, Gainesville 💔 Dante' Lamar Price, March 1, 2012, Dayton 💔 Raymond Luther Allen Jr., February 29, 2012, Galveston 💔 Manual Levi Loggins Jr., February 7, 2012, San Clemente 💔 Ramarley Graham, February 2, 2012, Bronx 💔 Kenneth Chamberlain Sr., November 19, 2011, White Plains 💔 Alonzo Ashley, July 18, 2011, Denver 💔 Derek Williams, July 6, 2011, Milwaukee 💔 Raheim Brown, Jr., January 22, 2011, Oakland

💔 Reginald Doucet, January 14, 2011, Los Angeles 💔 Derrick Jones, November 8, 2010, Oakland 💔 Danroy "DJ" Henry Jr., October 17, 2010, Pleasantville 💔 Aiyana Mo'Nay Stanley-Jones, May 16, 2010, Detroit 💔 Steven Eugene Washington, March 20, 2010, Los Angeles 💔 Aaron Campbell, January 29, 2010, Portland 💔 Kiwane Carrington, October 9, 2009, Champaign 💔 Victor Steen, October 3, 2009, Pensacola 💔 Shem Walker, July 11, 2009, Brooklyn 💔 Oscar Grant III, January 1, 2009, Oakland 💔 Tarika Wilson, January 4, 2008, Lima 💔 DeAunta Terrel Farrow, June 22, 2007, West Memphis 💔 Sean Bell, November 25, 2006, Queens 💔 Kathryn Johnston, November 21, 2006, Atlanta 💔 Ronald Curtis Madison, September 4, 2005, New Orleans 💔 James B. Brissette Jr., September 4, 2005, New Orleans 💔 Henry "Ace" Glover, September 2, 2005, New Orleans 💔 Timothy Stansbury, Jr., January 24, 2004, Brooklyn 💔 Ousmane Zongo, May 22, 2003, New York City 💔 Alberta Spruill, May 16, 2003, New York City 💔 Kendra Sarie James, May 5, 2003, Portland 💔 Orlando Barlow, February 28, 2003, Las Vegas 💔 Timothy DeWayne Thomas Jr., April 7, 2001, Cincinnati 💔 Ronald Beasley, June 12, 2000, Dellwood 💔 Earl Murray, June 12, 2000, Dellwood, Missouri 💔 Patrick Moses Dorismond, March 16, 2000, New York City 💔 Prince Carmen Jones Jr., September 1, 2000, Prince George's County 💔 Malcolm Ferguson, March 1, 2000, Bronx 💔 LaTanya Haggerty, June 4, 1999, Chicago 💔 Margaret LaVerne Mitchell, May 21, 1999, Los Angeles 💔 Amadou Diallo, February 4, 1999, Bronx ⚰

DON'T LEAD WITH YOUR PAIN

DON'T lead with your pain. Simple enough as thoughts go. A complex algorithm as far as implementation goes. Once upon a time, no matter where I began my life story, death had a starring role...or at least a pivotal one. During my year of intentional transformation, that most remarkable Wonder-filled Year, I tackled the challenge of trying to tell my story differently. The intention wasn't to necessarily start from scratch, but to start from a different point of reference. Reconfigure my story. Edit it to enhance the things that improved me.

The process demanded preliminary questions. What to begin with? What to leave out? How to punctuate or embellish? How to include others in the revised narrative of LaShawnda Jones' life?

At the time my company relocated its Park Avenue global headquarters from Midtown Manhattan to Tribeca, I had been sitting in the same desk with the same people surrounding me for over five years. To say I was over my cubicle and eager for a change would be an understatement. During the move, everyone was shuffled like musical chairs. In many cases, folks who had been clustered together for years were separated completely. The biggest personal benefit of the move was the opportunity to get to know new people.

My new desk was in the middle of a row of people I either knew in passing or not at all. None of this new row of colleagues knew of the many losses I had recently endured that kept my heart in a sinking pit. In fact, I began working at the company within a week of burying my younger brother Antione. Three years later, our dad, Peewee died. Almost to the day, two December's following Peewee, his mother released her hold on life as well. During yet another dreadful December three years after grandma, my maternal granddaddy left us. Essentially, my whole tenure at this company was dotted with death, darkness and compounded loss. Every day was a struggle for light and a smile.

During the first month in the new office, I made rounds to introduce myself and reconnect with colleagues in the building where I hadn't shared space with them in a while. We chatted, dined, walked and cycled. We hung out in the pantry discussing coffee and life. It was exhilarating getting to know people from *now*. From today. There was no need to add in my history of sorrows and pains. My mantra became: *Don't lead with your pain.* Don't mention Mom (dead). Don't mention siblings (dead, dead, in prison, drug addict). Don't mention dad (dead). Don't mention singleness (lonely). Don't mention friends (deserters). Don't mention hopes (disappointments). Don't mention dreams (deferred). Don't mention ambition (dust). Don't mention life (pointless).

It was a great opportunity to practice telling my story differently. Sometimes I failed miserably. The residue of pain and loss has a way of seeping into interactions – especially when people keep dying.

Three months after granddaddy passed away and a month after moving into the new office space, one of my uncles died in his sleep. He was only ten years my senior. We practically grew up together. That set my revisionist narrative back a bit. The get-to-know-you questions stung a bit deeper. *Are you married? Do you have children? Where are you from originally? Do you get back often to visit family?* Mostly my responses were level and short. Sometimes my guard was down, and my responses were raw and untempered. For example, a blank, stoic response to the news of someone I don't know losing a friend or the many stories of carnage in the news. Or alternatively, nearly breaking down when someone in the office suffered the loss of a loved one or the news highlights one person who was murdered by someone else's rage. Despite the seepage of death and darkness reentering my narrative, I kept trying to be a better representative of myself by sharing a narrative of blessings.

Often, it didn't seem as if there was anything worth talking about. Fortunately, those of us who love words are never speechless for long. I give thanks as often as I remember for the measure of joy and faith I have been blessed with. They keep me going. They propel me forward. They add purpose to my days, my years and the totality of my life.

∞ ∞ ∞

There is no pleasure like eating a good meal with good company which is revealed through good conversation. Walking in the fresh air provides peace and serenity. Cycling has become a great joy as riding balances my whole being. In sharing these activities - conversation, food, walking, cycling - I have learned to lead with my joy. I have learned to start from now. Today we are connected. Whatever comes tomorrow will come, but today I will enjoy the company and interactions I've been blessed with. These are the simple everyday joy-filled moments that nurture us back to life and light.

When we open ourselves to begin new narratives with each new person we engage with, the story we tell will change while remaining true. As our narratives change, we are better able to see how we ourselves are changing. Beginning with our perspective, focus, and goals.

My story doesn't have to be about me or my pain. Perhaps my story is the prologue to our story. What have we, as individuals, accumulated in life - physically, mentally, spiritually - to bring us to this point where we seek kinship with one another? Our individual stories flow into the multiplicity of *us*. How do *we* begin? Where to do *we* start? What are *we* leading with as we share in our togetherness?

Every living thing began with death, darkness, or a void. From our own beginnings, we know one tiny spark can cause vast emptiness to explode with abundant life. We too are creators made in the image of the Master Creator. Find a spark. Nurture it and begin rebuilding from there. After all, it is written in Genesis 1:1-3, *"In the beginning when God created the heavens and the earth, the earth was a formless void and darkness covered the face of the deep, while a wind from God swept over the face of the waters. Then God said, 'Let there be light'; and there was light.*

Meditation Verse: Ephesians 4:20-24
But you did not learn Christ in this way, if indeed you have heard Him and have been taught in Him, just as truth is in Jesus, that, in reference to your former manner of life, you lay aside the old self, which is being corrupted in accordance with the lusts of deceit, and that you be renewed in the spirit of your mind, and put on the new self, which in the likeness of God has been created in righteousness and holiness of the truth.

BE PRESENT FOR THE BATTLE

EITHER all of your words are true or your whole statement is false.

If you want me to believe you, don't use false words because I am aware that subtle deception led to the fall of mankind.

Someone who is fiercely opposed to my views regarding the innateness of human dignity and equality of every human being, no matter what our skin looks like or what faith someone claims, tagged me to a video on the Tea Party's Facebook page during the height of the Black Lives Matter marches for Michael Brown and Freddie Gray. The video was of a black male member of the United States Army who was stationed in South Korea. He was talking about how all our trust needs to be in God... and nothing should be done on our own behalf because God will do it all. To support his premise, he equated Black Lives Matter to ISIS. When he stated that people fighting for the right of human beings to simply *live* without the threat of state-sanctioned physical abuse or murder, to a group of people whose primary agenda is to destroy human life and culture wherever they go, everything else he said was tainted and suspect. Therefore, I was unable to agree with anything he said.

God says that He will fight our battles, but He also calls us to be present for the battles. Presence is the second most important element of becoming a conquering warrior. Of primary importance is trusting God. He does not send us into battle unprepared which means we will have many skirmishes to build up our spiritual strength. Every part of being requires preparation which requires showing up. We can't join the battle if we aren't there. We have to believe – have faith – that He will deliver us as victors in the battles He has placed us in. Without faith it is impossible to please God, ergo to do anything for Him (Hebrews 11:6). If we choose not to show up, not to prepare, not to believe, then we have removed ourselves from the battle and from the possibility of victory.

The difference between the young solder's instruction to do nothing and keep moving forward as we are called to do is easily identified when you know your Bible. During the exodus, when the Hebrews were trapped between the Red Sea and Pharaoh's army, Moses instructed the people to stand still and watch God save them. God corrected him immediately, ordering Moses to "Tell the people to keep going!"

> And Moses said to the people, "Do not be afraid. Stand still, and see the salvation of the Lord, which He will accomplish for you today. For the Egyptians whom you see today, you shall see again no more forever. The Lord will fight for you, and you shall hold your peace." And the Lord said to Moses, "Why do you cry to Me? Tell the children of Israel to go forward. But lift up your rod, and stretch out your hand over the sea and divide it. And the children of Israel shall go on dry ground through the midst of the sea. ... Then the Egyptians shall know that I am the Lord, when I have gained honor for Myself over Pharaoh, his chariots, and his horsemen."
> ~ Exodus 14:13-18

It's important to know what God's instructions are. His instructions inform us of His expectations for us. If people who yearn for freedom only sit home and wait for God to free them, they will never be free. They will forever be trapped in their own cage of inactivity and faithlessness.

For further illustration, look at shepherd David who had no military experience, yet he went into battle with only his sling, five stones, a shepherd's staff and his faith in God. His declaration to Goliath is one of my favorite in the Bible, it was also paraphrased by Bree Newsome when she removed the Confederate flag at the South Carolina State House on June 27, 2015, *"You come against me with hatred and oppression and violence. I come against you in the name of God. This flag comes down today!"*

In 1 Samuel 17, David declared to Goliath, "You come to me with a sword, with a spear, and with a javelin. But I come to you in the name of the Lord of hosts, the God of the armies of Israel, whom you have defied. This day the Lord will deliver you into my hand, and I will strike you and take your head from you. ... Then all this assembly shall know that the Lord does not save with sword and spear; for the battle is the Lord's, and He will give you into our hands."

The person who tagged me to the incredibly offensive video and instructed me to listen to it with my "spiritual ears" also instructed me to stay home when many in my city took to the streets to protest the non-indictments of police officers who had killed people in the public view, i.e. on camera and in front of witnesses. I don't live any part of my life without my faith, so everything I hear is filtered in the presence of the Spirit who dwells within and envelops me. May this also be true for you.

Keep going! We have work to do and battles to win!

Meditation Verse: Mark 4:23-25
Anyone with ears to hear should listen and understand." Then he added, "Pay close attention to what you hear. The closer you listen, the more understanding you will be given — and you will receive even more. To those who listen to

my teaching, more understanding will be given. But for those who are not listening, even what little understanding they have will be taken away from them."

OBSERVATIONS OF SHE WHO DIED LAUGHING

"When I die... I want my funeral to be a huge showbiz affair with lights, cameras, action.... I want Craft services, I want Paparazzi and I want publicists making a scene! I want it to be Hollywood all the way.... I want to look gorgeous, better dead than I do alive."
~ Joan Rivers

I think comedians are innately sad people. Or rather people who started their comedic journey as an effort to hide or heal themselves. You can hear in the way they express their humor which they are attempting to do. Hiders usually lash out – they have a sharp, harsh humor, most likely at someone else's expense. Healers usually attempt first to be understood – they will share their experiences as universally as possible.

I didn't know what to think about Robin Williams when his death was reported. I was certainly disconcerted hearing he had taken his own life, but I wasn't surprised. I've learned through my own trials that the loudest laughs are chortled through the deepest sorrow. It wasn't until Joan Rivers died that I understood better the nuance I couldn't quite put my finger on with Robin. He was a healer. He was a gifted comedian who created a space to bring forth genuine laughter. A true sadness about his death is in that unalterable moment, he allowed his gloom to overcome his gift.

The Friday following Joan Rivers' death I watched two hours of televised tributes to her without laughing once.

Initially, I watched out of curiosity. After a while, I was repelled by disgust. By the end of the second hour, I was quite sad for the life she had lived.

Bitter. Self-hater. Shallow. Unfulfilled. Words she used to describe her life and career.

Iconic. Legendary. Trailblazer. Words her friends, admirers and reporters used in their commentary about her. They wanted to be like her. Many interviewed for the tribute specials credited Joan with their success; they didn't think they would be where they were had she not gone before. Yet in the same specials, Joan herself rejected their praise disdainfully. You can't tell by listening to her, but she desperately wanted adulation.

In her own words, Joan wanted the end of her life to look like the excesses of Hollywood culture. It's incredibly sad and speaks volumes about what she valued most in her life.

She wanted to be seen.

She wanted to make headlines.

She wanted to be photographed and sang over by other celebrities.

I understand that she was a comedian and irreverence was her shtick, but regardless of what she did and what she believed, words have creative power. She painted a portrait of a woman who was never satisfied with who she was, what she had achieved, or what she had. She lived in fear of going broke, being rejected, and not being wanted or loved. Truthfully, if I allowed fear to ride me, those would be my top inhibitors. You may have similar fears. However, not all of us tear other people down in order to hide our insecurities.

In her autobiography, "*I Hate Everyone…Starting with Me*" Joan said, "When I die (and yes, Melissa, that day will come; and yes, Melissa, everything's in your name), I want my funeral to be a huge showbiz affair with lights, cameras, action…. I want Craft services; I want Paparazzi and I want publicists making a scene! I want it to be Hollywood all the way. I don't want some rabbi rambling on; I want Meryl Streep crying, in five different accents. I don't want a eulogy; I want Bobby Vinton to pick up my head and sing "Mr. Lonely." I want to look gorgeous, better dead than I do alive. I want to be buried in a Valentino gown and I want Harry Winston to make me a toe tag. And I want a wind machine so that even in the casket my hair is blowing just like Beyoncé's."

Joan Rivers made a career out of belittling people and calling her words "humor." In highlighting this, I wish to warn the living not to deride the departed. Joan's demons are not reserved for fame-seekers; her demons are common to all of mankind. (1 Peter 4:12). The demons, aka the enemy, insinuate themselves in our thoughts. Thoughts transform into desires and desires become plans. Suddenly we're on a path living a life we didn't really want for ourselves, but the attention and worldly benefits are misconstrued as blessings. Before long we are giving no care or concern to our spiritual health or needs. Everything becomes about the here and now and the outer image – how others see us and our trappings of success and popularity.

That is not a well-lived life. It's a very unfortunate way to choose to live and the emptiness will eventually consume you.

Not only was Joan aware of her emptiness, but she also told us about it with every joke she uttered. Her audience may have forgotten or chose to rename what she was selling but she was clear: *hate was her product*. She was a hider who hid in plain sight. She dressed her hate up in glamour and the masses ate it up.

Who idolizes someone who hates themselves and everyone else? People who also hate themselves and don't see beauty or truth in who they are.

There is another way – a fulfilling way to live and die. A way of love and self-acceptance. Begin by rejecting fear and embracing your true self. Nurture your good spots and minister to the needs-improvement areas. Practice self-care, encourage yourself and be open to those who reflect love back to you. Eventually you will create a space representative of the love you nurture.

Meditation Verse: 1 John 3:14-15
We know that we have passed from death to life because we love one another. Whoever does not love abides in death. All who hate a brother or sister are murderers, and you know that murderers do not have eternal life abiding in them.

ABOUT GRANDDADDY: DEATH & RELEASE

In *My God and Me* I wrote about my journey into finding myself, how that led to me finding God and how the deeper I drove into learning who God is the more I learned who I am. When *Desert of Solitude* was conceived, I knew the main themes would be life, death, desert and solitude as I shared valleys on my faith journey. Death has been consistent teacher. It has greatly contributed to the development of my character, my personality and my outlook, especially over the last dozen years. So much so that for years I thought the follow-up to *My God and Me: Listening, Learning and Growing on My Journey* would be *Lessons I've Learned from Death* and focus on how I processed losing loved ones. Thank God for His Breath of Life! He is our revival. Death is part of the life cycle. It does not stand alone in its own realm. Even those who die do not have to remain in death. This is a lesson we can only learn in life. Additionally, we can live in the deepest areas of our sorrow and grieve at the height of our blessings.

When my mom's dad was dying, I responded differently than I had to prior deaths in the family. We hadn't been particularly close, but he was the only granddad I've ever known. He was also the most consistent and representative father figure in my life. That's what I remember him for. He was a flawed man who always chose his family. He and Grandma married and divorced a couple of times, but he never left her or their children. After their last divorce, he moved from the house they shared in Gary, IN to live with one of their daughters across town. He was present for all the family celebrations, birthdays, holidays, feuds, sorrows and funerals. In between those times, he could usually be found simply hanging out with Grandma at the house.

I loved my grandfather, but I didn't know him, nor did he know me. Nowhere in memory could I recall spending quality relationship-building time with him. I knew about him like a story told third hand - highlights and reference points, but nothing of substance. I heard about all the good he did for his other grandchildren. I had heard the rumors of his secret wealth from working nearly every day of his life since childhood. I knew he and my grandmother loved each other but couldn't manage to live together peacefully. She had violent episodes; he had a calming effect on her... except when he was the cause of her rage. Then no one was safe. There are no stories of him ever lifting a hand to her, but like family folklore we all knew of the time she pulled her pistol and shot at him. As far as we know, he never held that against her. It was by her side that he arrived and sat when they attended my brother's funeral. Their oldest grandson. His Jim-boy. I was his Jill and up until his death my personal story about Granddaddy was premised on what he never gave me.

My family moved from Gary when I was five years old. My mom, brother and sister returned there to live for a short while before moving to Milwaukee when I was in high school. I had been sent to Milwaukee by that time and remained there. For nearly all of my life I have been a visitor among my family. When I visited, Granddaddy hugged me upon arrival and departure. Occasionally he would throw some words my way, but never anything to build or enhance a relationship with. Before he died, I had never even focused on all he had given of himself for his wife and family as a whole.

∞ ∞ ∞

When Peewee was dying, I debated going to his side because we had been estranged since my brother's funeral. Peewee had never put his wife and children first. His priorities were brothers, sister and mom – and his older brother called the shots throughout his life. When my brother, Antione, died, Peewee made decisions that hurt me and would have angered my brother in order to please his own brother and sister. After the service I angrily told him we were done. I bitterly accused him of never putting his children first. I despaired that if the death of one of his children wasn't enough for him to put us first, then nothing every would.

Luckily anger never burns long with me, unfortunately however the underlining hurt has a way of taking root. For over three years I waited for Peewee to reach out and mend the breach between us. A generic, "Shawnda, I'm doing the best I can. This is who I am," would have sufficed. In hindsight, I can appreciate that a man who didn't love and respect himself couldn't possibly love and respect what he produced. When he realized he was dying, he called his sister to come get him in Sault Ste. Marie, MI. She called their big brother in Phoenix, AZ so he could meet them in Milwaukee, WI when she returned with Peewee. Their mom called me. No one asked me to come.

The internal debate was intense. In the end, I decided not to go. At the time, my uncle and I were still in a standoff. He had been one of my childhood abusers and though we had communicated since he had been released from prison a decade earlier, he was rather hostile towards me for my active monitoring of his sex offender registration status. I concluded that Peewee had called those he wanted present at his end and that he chose to die with our relationship in a broken state.

When Peewee's mom died two years later, his sister called and told me Grandma was asking for me. By this time the two of them had moved to Phoenix to be with the estranged shot-caller oldest son/big brother. For my grandmother I would confront any adversary; it didn't' matter that I would have to deal with a hostile uncle and his family to visit with her. She and I had been close during my teens and early twenties. We had spent many quiet nights together during those years. Me reading. Grandma watching TV. Our dynamic changed when her oldest son got out of prison. Actually, the whole family changed. I had always felt like an outsider, but I was literally cast aside to make room for the two brothers upon the completion of their sentences.

Before entering the hospital, I prayed for guidance on introducing Jesus and salvation into our conversation. When I got to her bedside, I could only look at her, kiss her repeatedly and tell her over and over again that I love her. After a bit of that and concern that the attention was a bit much, I sat with her until she fell asleep. Then I took out my journal and my box of Christmas cards that had been in my bag for over a month. The first card was for her and part of my message, which I later read to her, was: *"We've never spoken of spiritual matters, but I asked God to take you in hand and hold you close. I now ask you to receive His Grace, receive His offer of Salvation, receive His Son Jesus Christ into your heart - welcome Him with your voice. I love you so very much. It's a comfort to me & it should be to you to know that God loves you so much more. He is here for you & He brought me to your side."*

Grandma didn't try to speak to me. She was on oxygen and looked weak. However, when my aunt and uncle arrived with their children later in the day, Grandma was suddenly awake and alert. In fact, my aunt went straight to her, leaned down, whispered something then started wailing. She made her way across the room to me and collapsed in my arms. Having grown up in close proximity to her dramatics, I calmly asked what was wrong. She sobbed, "Mama just told me she's ready to die." I sat her back away from me in disbelief and said, "Grandma's been peaceful and quiet all day. She hasn't said a word, but the first thing she says to you is that she's ready to die? What did you say to her?"

My aunt and I walked over to my grandma's bed, and I asked her to tell me what she had just told her daughter. She said she was ready to die. The room went into a crazy tailspin. People started crying. Aunt and uncle started calling family and friends around the country and putting the phone up to grandma's ear so she could say her goodbyes to everyone her children could possibly think of.

From the distance of time, I can appreciate that her children's over-the-top reaction is probably why she stayed silent with me. I didn't bring drama. I simply came in and sat with her.

The nurse confirmed that grandma was not on life-support, only oxygen, so no one could pull the plug. At that point, I stepped out of the room and went to the family waiting room. After a short while, the hostile uncle Akmad followed me to the room and asked to speak with me. He had avoided me for the fourteen years he had been out of prison. He served his full sentence for sexually abusing me as a child. I contributed to the avoidance game however I could.

Everything he said floored me... and made my spirit soar.

"First, thank you for loving my mother," he said.

"She's my grandmother."

"I know, but thank you for caring so much." He went on to apologize for the harm he had caused me in my youth. "Never in a million years did I ever think my actions against you all those years ago would still be impacting so many lives today – nearly thirty years later. What I did to you sickens me and there isn't a day that goes by that I'm not reminded of what I did." He confirmed he was on the sex offender's registry without me asking. I had not been able to confirm the Arizona registry when I had last checked, so his acknowledgement was comforting. He expressed his regret over having no relationship with me and asked for my forgiveness.

"You're forgiven. I forgave you a long time ago. I hope you can find it in your heart to forgive yourself. Is it okay if I hug you?"

"Yes."

We hugged. I whispered "God bless you," in his ear and he returned the words to me.

I wasn't expecting an apology from him. Shortly after he had been released from prison, my aunt thought it would be a good idea to have everyone at her house for Christmas. I arrived with my sister as my back-up with the sole goal of confronting him. I did just that and came away woefully dissatisfied. He had been defensive and dismissive at that time. When I left the gathering, I made it clear I wanted nothing else to do with him. His presence at Peewee's side when he died was the deciding factor for me to stay away. But he couldn't keep me away from my grandmother's deathbed. There was love in that relationship.

∞ ∞ ∞

Granddaddy, my mom's dad, passed three years after Peewee's mom. Unknown to me at the time, watching the way Granddaddy lived his life and tried to keep his family within reach has impacted my outlook on relationships in a silently passive way. So much so that I didn't realize how influential he had been until I loss him.

A number of years had passed since I had visited my grandparents and extended family in Gary. The last three visits were painful occasions of verbal and spiritual attacks from various family members that increased in intensity and viciousness. When I learned that Granddaddy had a stroke, I considered flying in to see him even though I wasn't keen on visiting him – or anyone – in the hospital. He had lived a relatively healthy and active life into his late eighties. When he slipped into a coma a few days later, I booked a flight without waiting for a request to come. From an uncomfortable amount of experience with death and loss, I knew his days were short. That surety drove me across the country with a determination to be present for the opportunity to touch his skin and kiss him as I told him I love him and bore witness to God's love for him. These weren't fully formed thoughts on the way to the hospital. I actually had no idea what I would say or do once I got there, but was elated to have experienced a flow of love so natural and fluid, I'm convinced he heard everything he needed to hear. Indeed, his toes were stretching and curling in response to my words.

On the drive to Gary from O'Hare International Airport, I listened to a sermon titled *You Are an Incredible Testimony of Mercy* by Pastor Carter Conlon. It calmed, centered and focused me. It confirmed what I considered to be my mission to speak life into my granddad before he left this world. I didn't know what would be required of me when I arrived at my destination, but I knew the basics: *Tell him that God loves him and bless his life.*

When I got to his floor, the enemy was standing guard at his door, intent on blocking my entry. On this side of my family, the youngest daughter was the devil's tool. She was the common denominator and instigator of the verbal and spiritual attacks against me during my last three visits to Gary. When the attacks started, she had just returned to the family after a twenty-year self-imposed exile after running away at age fourteen. Like all demons she operated in the dark murky shadows. This day she exposed herself fully. For no other reason than because she thought she had the power to stop me, she stood in my way. Her boldness was answered with disdain. As I walked pass her, I said simply, "We're done."

There was no rhyme or reason for her to try to bar me from seeing Granddaddy. We hadn't argued or fought. I disapproved of a lot of her behavior and language especially with my younger cousins, but they were all adults so I didn't get involved. I never shamed her for her choices. I only ever tried to be a sounding board and offer moral support.

Lil auntie thought she could punk her gullible Christian niece just for the heck of it. She insisted the nurse kick me out as I asked which room my grandfather was in. The nurse nervously looked between the two of us and asked for my name. She then told me I wasn't on the list of allowed visitors. I told her I had flown in from New York City to see my grandfather and that's what I was going to do. Her list didn't concern me. Lil auntie was in the background demanding the nurse call security to kick me out. There were only two rooms in that corner and one door was open. I walked to that door and saw my Granddad in the bed. After that the harping aunt and dismayed nurse were muted in my mind. I told them to do what they wanted to do and shut the door behind them as they exited to do just that.

It took half a day to get to his bedside in Merrillville, Indiana from New York City and I had only five minutes at his bedside before security walked me out of the room. It proved to be more than enough time to say what I was sent to say.

To clear the energy in the room, I began by apologizing that his daughter's negative energy was surrounding him during such a time. Then I quieted my mind and allowed the Holy Spirit to speak through me. Reaching out, I touched his arm, shoulder, forehead and feet as I prayed over him.

Granddaddy & Me, '01

"I love you, Granddaddy.

God loves you. You are highly favored. May the peace of Jesus and God's Holy Spirit comfort you. The suffering you felt in your body will not last. Where you are going, there is no more pain. No more tears. You are going to a place of love where God is waiting to embrace you. This is my prayer for you, Granddaddy. In the name of Jesus and by God's Holy Spirit. Amen."

The pulse in his neck began ticking quickly and his right foot stretched and moved. I took that as his response. Believing he heard me makes me eternally grateful for those five minutes alone with him. Towards the end, I noticed my own hand was trembling as I reached to lay it on his forehead. "Bless you Granddaddy, bless you. You are blessed and favored. May God's mercy, grace and love travel with you."

> Very truly, I tell you, unless a grain of wheat falls into the earth and dies, it remains just a single grain; but if it dies, it bears much fruit. Those who love their life lose it, and those who hate their life in this world will keep it for eternal life.
> ~ John 12:24-25

∞ ∞ ∞

My 2016 began with a funeral and honestly, it felt like an appropriate to beginning.

At any given moment, we are all dead, dying and perhaps returning to life. Death is not the end. It is the beginning. Life therefore is the end of death. This cycle is ongoing. The culture of the world fears death, but there is so much to learn from the dead, and the dying. Life is not savored at all until it is juxtaposed to death. The blessing is in recognizing the great gift of everyone who has come before and the gifts they leave behind.

It is only when we are confronted with loss that we truly appreciate what we've gained and maintained. Granddaddy closed his eyes at the end of December 2015, and we bid our collective farewell at the beginning of January 2016. It's a different take on new beginnings. Beginning the year with a burial. Beginning with death and a seed. Beginning with the celebration of a well-lived life.

In so doing, we are presented with the opportunity to release ourselves from all that's past. All that's gone. All that's dead in our lives. We can begin again in new ground fertilized with all that came before. Enriched by lessons and experiences. Emboldened by memories. Invigorated by visions of a great harvest from the seed that died and was embraced by the earth. New growth. New form. New direction.

> *Father, I thank You in the name of Jesus, Your Most Holy Son and by Your Most Amazing Spirit, Character and Nature, Love, Mercy and Faith. I thank You for every seed you've deposited in me. Everything that you've allowed to grow and prosper within me, my life, my spirit, my mind, my soul and my very being. It's truly a wonderful life even*

though I don't acknowledge it every day. I know that You've already blessed me beyond all my expectation, beyond all my hopes! So, I thank You Father, for the balance of life, in the name of Jesus, by Your Spirit. Amen.

Sermon: You Are an Incredible Testimony of Mercy
by Carter Conlon
Listen to: Smile by Nat King Cole

TO EVERYTHING THERE IS A SEASON.

FOR a number of years, I was deeply discontented with what passes for fellowship at congregation gatherings and ministry activities. Honestly, I was burnt out and disillusioned. Putting on a smiling face and making conversation with people after service, who would later avoid me like the plague, became a choir. So I stopped speaking. I stopped sharing. And I tried to stop caring. Streaming services at home became a safe and comfortable alternative.

For a couple of years streaming services provided what I needed. Distance. Freedom. Control of my time, space and interactions. It was intended to be a short reprieve but lasted much longer than I thought possible.

Though I didn't miss the people, I did miss being enveloped in song and adding my voice to the sheer volume of praise being offered to God. I missed hearing the sermons live in the space and energy they were delivered in. Over time, I began creeping back into services occasionally.

In August I got away from my life for a couple of weeks to celebrate my fortieth birthday. Traveling by planes and trains meant a lot of time for reflection, which lead to a good deal of thinking, praying and communing with my Lord and Savior. A reawakening happened during that time. Since returning home, I've been trying to drag myself out of the pit I allowed myself to sink into. I've been slowly weaning myself off of streaming the church service in lieu of attending. I actually want to be back with the congregation now.

To my surprise, the desire to return wasn't enough. Even with the best intention to get up and go, distractions kept me bound.

Distractions are interesting. Sometimes we seek them out to satisfy a sense of independence or adventure. Sometimes they are unexpected and add to frustration and anxiety. Other times they provide the change we think we need, the future we thought we sought, the opportunities we thought we were lacking. Distractions are insidious in nature, presenting as innocuous happenstances. Nothing major. Perhaps a slight detour. Nothing that can damage a life, relationship or future. But any distraction is a gateway to many more distractions.

Pain is a distraction. Anger is a distraction. Lust and romantic ideals of love are distractions. Perhaps all of life is a distraction. For what purpose are we here anyway? What assignment have we been tasked with? Few can definitively state what they believe the purpose of their life is. Yet even those few will be distracted to the point of neglecting whatever they claim their true purpose is. Through the only, the few and the many, distractions will change life's course in unimaginable ways.

> *Then many will fall away, and they will betray one another and hate one another. And many false prophets will arise and lead many astray. And because of the increase of lawlessness, the love of many will grow cold. But the one who endures to the end will be saved.*
> *~ Matthew 24:10-13*

Over a period of three weeks in the fall, an urgency came over me to get back into the church building. A need to be present during the songs and the sermons. To open myself up again. To return. To remember. To be enveloped by the healing songs of praise reverberating off the walls and ceiling of the sanctuary. To sing my *hallelujahs* and participate earnestly in corporate prayer.

On one such enriching day, I got up with the intention to go to the morning service, but an equally strong energy to clean my apartment won out. Cleaning energy is always hard to come by. The first thing I did after getting out of bed that morning was rotate my mattress and from there the cleaning spirit moved me throughout the whole apartment. Before I knew it, service was starting so I streamed it yet again. The message was titled, *"For Heaven's Sake, Hurry Up and Die"* by Pastor Carter Conlon. It was so on point, I rewound it for another listen. Afterwards, I got up and went to the afternoon service where I received another very much-needed word titled, *"Turn and Believe the Good News"* by Elder Jerry Hampton.

All this to say: God is good and He knows us better than we know ourselves. Whatever we think we need, He will allow us to pursue – for a time. Then He will call us back to Himself. The blessing in this, aside from God's overwhelming grace and mercy, is the opportunity to learn more about ourselves in a protected state – to embrace the ugliness and despair buried beneath our praise and thanksgiving. There's no fear or shame in coming to terms with everything in you that needs to die when you're wrestling with it all in the shelter of the Most High.

Know that you are blessed in the midst of your despair and uncertainty. You are loved and highly favored even as dirt clings to you during your deep cleansing and beyond.

Sermons: *For Heaven's Sake, Hurry Up and Die* by Carter Conlon
Turn and Believe the Good News by Jerry Hampton

WONDER SELF-CELEBRATION FORTY & BEYOND

CELESTIAL SKY

STORY OF MY BEGINNING

What if I told you,
Life –
A fully expressive Life –
Doesn't begin until forty?
This is a story of my beginning.

When I was thirty-eight, I was up for a significant promotion. There was a new general counsel of the global bank I worked for. My manager at the time, deputy general counsel in charge of global litigation and regulatory investigations, reported to the general counsel who in turn reported to the CEO of the corporation.

When human resources initially called to ask if I would be interested in interviewing for the incoming general counsel's executive management assistant role, they made it clear that there would be no salary increase for me. A title upgrade and extra overtime were the only offerings. My base salary was low for a senior executive assistant. The bank got me at a discount post-financial crisis in 2009. I audibly scoffed at the HR rep's arrogance and pointed out that I already had decent overtime so their offer was essentially to do the job of two people for what I was making which was less than I should be making in the first place. Further, I would risk losing what I valued about the role I was in – enjoyment of my work and my team, and a manager I truly admired. Logic told me not to mess up a good thing, however HR and my manger both suggested I at least take the interview and see how it went from there.

When I interviewed for the position, I was quite taken by the quiet, deliberate and respectful demeanor of the incoming general counsel. Immediately following that interview, I met independently with their primary executive assistant at the firm they were leaving. That meeting provided me with a horrifying look into my future.

The woman was very polite, informative and helpful as she shared the requirements and expectations of her soon-to-be former boss. She was also extremely haggard and world-worn, despite having at least one other executive assistant backing her up on a regular basis. I wouldn't have a back-up assistant to help me. After meeting and speaking with her, I devoted time to truly think about the direction my life was going in.

For approximately seven years, I had been on autopilot taking every opportunity that lead forward or upward. This was the first time I stopped and questioned what progress, success and wealth meant to me. What did any of it look like for me?

At the time I was already at my desk from 9:00am to 7:00pm most days. The next level up was around the clock availability, which meant I had to be *on* constantly. There was already no time for my life. Working around the clock would suck the little life I had left from me.

On the flip side, overtime in the Executive Management Assistant role would pay out about 75% of my current base pay which would effectively put me at an annual salary of $130,000 to $140,000 (base + OT).

The only attraction of that kind of money for this role was the ability to pay off my student loans within a few years. All in all, a weak argument in favor of pursuing a hyper-stress-inducing promotion. Fortunately, living to pay bills is not the most important thing to me.

Time is more important. Down time. Vacation time. Me time. Reproductive time – listening to my biological clock ticking away my fertility. Social time to meet and connect with a potential partner. I want to have children; time is required to allow for this process whether I do it alone or with someone.

With these considerations, selling all my waking time for a larger paycheck was not at all appealing.

Back to School

The most important question at this particular fork in the road was, *"What would I like to accomplish within the next two years?"* The first answer that came to mind was to complete my master's degree. I had put in a year of graduate study in Milwaukee prior to moving to New York City and those paid for credits were about to expire. Pursuing a degree while working 60 to 80 hours a week was not even an option. Clearly, there was a need to restructure my life to support what was important to me.

Taking the time to contemplate and evaluate what I truly wanted for my life was invaluable. Through that process, I was able to see that continuing on the corporate path would take me further away from the path I needed to get on. It took a few more years to fully comprehend and appreciate that nothing I wanted for my life was supported by the corporate structure, but in this moment, I knew enough not to jump into the hyper speed lane.

When I discussed the interview and the general focus of my hopes for the near future with my manager and HR, they assured me the role was mine if I wanted it, but if I didn't I should withdraw my name from consideration before it was officially offered to me. So, I did just that.

My decision to return to school at thirty-eight years old was a declaration of my intention to actively rebrand, remarket and reposition myself while redirecting my life through my career.

Not only did I not want a promotion, I was also no longer satisfied working as a senior executive assistant. I wanted to be able to have a larger impact, voice and contribution in my work environment. Naively, I thought obtaining a graduate degree while employed at a global bank would make me more visible and desirable for advancement opportunities within the firm.

Two weeks before I began my graduate study at The New School for Public Engagement in New York City, I had an operation to remove polyps from my uterine wall in an effort to increase my chances of becoming pregnant when the opportunity to procreate presented itself.

I was looking forward and taking aggressive action to make a way for the changes I wanted in my life.

Though my master's degree was intended to be my fortieth birthday present to myself, I decided to add a French and Italian Riviera vacation to fully celebrate the transitional accomplishment. My *Year of Wonder-Filled Living* began in January 2015. The celebration travel kicked off in May immediately following graduation, and culminated in August surrounding my birthday.

The celebrations may have been a bit pre-mature. Though, my course work was complete by graduation, I had extreme difficulty securing the required two thesis advisors for my final graduation requirement. I asked every faculty member in my department and got turned down by each one; even those whose courses I had taken during my two years at The New School. I graduated with a 3.45 GPA while working 50 hours a week in a fast-paced, high-stress corporate environment. My tuition was paid on time. I showed up for nearly all my evening classes and participated vigorously. Even so, not one professor willingly signed on and followed-through with advising me on my thesis. There was something about my intended topics of democracy being a lie, and racism being a construct we have the ability to eliminate that no one saw any value in. Mind you, the idea came from my course load and the socio-political environment the world was in with explosive protests against state violence happening around the globe. Some professors tried to tell me I was focusing on a local, domestic issue in an international program. Yet, I took a summer seminar in Poland about the Arab Spring and how modern global protests were modeled after the Civil Rights Movement in the USA. Following the seminar, I refocused my thesis on the United Nations and how the Civil Rights Movement tried to be a Human Rights cry for help from African Americans to the global community.

Graduate school in New York City made me painfully aware of the insidious nature of racism that infects everything in America.

Part of me would like to think that my topic was too controversial. From the moment I selected my topic, I was told it was too broad and I needed to narrow it. Professors were uncomfortable with it and only became open to it after the initial presentation for each course. Yet and still they would not agree to teach and guide me towards producing an acceptable paper.

My research topic began as an exploration of links between democracy, diversity, stereotypes and leadership. It ended with the goal of making a case for implementing a national human rights institute in the United States of America as mandated by the International Convention on the Elimination of All Forms of Racial Discrimination (CERD) (Jones, 2016). The Convention's oversight body, the Committee on the Elimination of Racial Discrimination, is responsible for moving member states (of which the United States is one of 177) towards implementing the requirements of the treaty throughout their jurisdictions (Jones, 2016). The USA, of course, has not done this.

At the time of my birthday trip, I was still struggling to complete my thesis paper. It turned out that the Committee on CERD was meeting at the United Nations during the time I was in France. The flight from Nice to Geneva was one hour, so I decided to spend a day there before finishing the trip in Milan and returning home. I had written in advance to ask for permission to sit in on the session. Unfortunately, I didn't get the opportunity to do that, but I did get a pass to tour the United Nations.

A year after my graduation ceremony, in pure frustration, I wrote a letter to the department chair, who had also been one of my instructors and the dean of the school. Almost immediately, the two black instructors who had agreed to advise me, but ignored me for a year and half, signed off in approval of my thesis. That's not to say I received any quality advice, guidance or the opportunity to make a presentation of my work to faculty, but finally, my graduate study was complete, and I received my paper.

GRAD SCHOOL GRADUATE

Journal: May 21, 2015

Time flies and days speed by before I can get back to finish writing down my thoughts and my praise of You, Father!

Thank You! Thank You! Thank You! Again and so many more times: Thank You!

I just came from my department graduation ceremony. It was better than I had imagined it would be. I'm very pleased I went and didn't skip it as I began to think I would while trying to log off at work this afternoon.

I haven't been feeling like a graduate or much like celebrating - but I think those feelings have changed today.

Some ladies at the office surprised me with a balloon, cards and cupcakes. It was good cheer.

Let it all go!

May 22, 2015

Today I graduated from The New School for Public Engagement with a Master of Arts degree in International Affairs with a concentration in Media and Culture. Yesterday was our first ceremony for our department. It was good to speak to a few of the other graduates and get their take on their experience and to know that my late-blooming feelings of euphoria were not the only late-blooming feelings in the class.

My thoughts are swirling around evolution – graduation... moving forward... moving on – and loneliness. I must say, I did not experience loneliness these last few days. I thought I would, and was ready for it, but that particular sadness did not weigh me down.

My co-workers provide my daily human interaction. Whatever conversations I have at work are usually the only in-person or voice-to-voice conversations I have on any given day. Social media has buoyed me up for many years, but virtual relationships have never transferred any tangible value into my daily life. Last week I deleted all my social media accounts – all the ones I could remember anyway. I had several Facebook accounts – personal, business, books, etc. Cut the cord. What a sense of freedom that provided! I've also been sleeping much better. Win-win!

That being said, there was a twinge of whimsy thinking how great it would have been to post my graduation. Fortunately, God has a way of putting people in our paths. For me, it's usually people who represent Him to me. "Him" in the sense that whatever I need in a moment, He sends someone to speak exactly that into me. Strangers spoke into my life today – on the street, in the ceremony, in the restaurant, in Central Park afterwards. "You're going far.... You're going places.... Congratulations!... This is just the beginning.... What did you do?... How did you do it?... What do you want to do?" That was powerful to me. Conversations with passers-by throughout an important day. What Facebook would have provided, only much better.

Additionally, He blesses me with a friend for the day – someone who steps in during my critical moments and allows me to lean on them. I try not to demand or expect anything, but I'm always super grateful for their willingness to show up when I need someone to do so.

That friend today was Perry. She was available. She wanted to share in my day. She brought me flowers. She took pictures. She is my best memory of my graduation.

GRAD SCHOOL GRADUATION, MAY 2015

Perry has made herself available several times in my life. I wish that she would allow me to return the favor, but she's still dependent on a lot of other people. I don't begrudge her that – it's great that she has others she can depend on, but I would like to be able to be a friend for days of need as well.

Perhaps the bigger lesson of the day is that I've been waiting... and waiting... and waiting. Today I put on my finery – crochet white dress and sequined blue shoes – and decided I am not going to wait any longer. I'm not going to bury myself in sadness or neglect myself because no one wants to do life with me. I've decided to live each moment because God will send somebody in the most bereft moments empty of companionship and camaraderie. He will place someone with me who will be His voice of love, grace, and mercy. Someone to share in His blessing.

This is my true graduation – the pivot in my evolution. Getting to inner peace and a fuller understanding of the fact I am not at all, in any way, shape, or form, alone. I can let go of the aloneness. I can let go of the sadness. I can let go of everything that will have me feeling less than, neglected, unwanted, unloved. I can CHOOSE to let it all go.

I can step outside of it and take myself home. Home to an inner space where I know without a doubt, God loves me. His Son loves me. His Holy Spirit is within me, speaking to me, holding me, loving me, keeping me. He's providing for me. He's guiding me. He's everything I need. Always has been. Always will be. In this moment. In this day. In all the days to come. Absolutely. Always. Today I became more fully knowledgeable of how well-kept I am. Praise God!

Note to Self
Adieu. May your graduation ceremonies, as you continue your spiritual journey, be everything you need them to be in the moment you are in and in the moment that they come. I pray you are able to fully live it and express it in your own company and in the company of others. May God bless you and keep you. May all your days be full of His Glory, Grace, Love and Mercy. By the name of Jesus, our dear Savior and by the magnificent Spirit of our Father God, Amen.

MONTRÉAL, QUÉBEC

Journal: May 25, 2015

Good morning, Father! This has been a great short trip and treat! I arrived in Montréal two nights ago by bus and ended up staying in my hotel room that first night. Lazed around the next morning, much more than I wanted to, but the afternoon made up for my slow start. Went to an Orientalist art exhibit at the Montréal Museum of Fine Arts. It was amazing! The paintings were magnificent even if the artists paiinted from the tainted lens of colonial racist exploitation – exposed black women vs. respectfully clothed white women, etc.

It was by far, one of the best exhibits I've ever seen.

A TANGERIAN BEAUTY BY TAPIRÓ I BARÓ

Now sitting on the top of Mont Royal in the center of Montréal. It's a gray morning but very beautiful. I can almost see myself living here – except for the winters. The French/English mix, the maneuvervility around the city, the culture, the shopping. I'm relaxed. That was my goal. Mission accomplished.

The wind just took me to an entry date: November 8 nearly two years ago. WOW!! Father, You're SO GOOD!

EXPLORING SOCIALISM

Journal: July 3, 2015

On a 6:00am flight to Chicago for the Socialism Conference. Not sure what to expect but I do expect to be inspired!

Of course, being so close to Milwaukee, I had hoped to see the man my heart and hopes have clung to for over a decade, but he graciously informed me he wasn't available.

I know I've said it many times before, but I do believe the last of whatever I thought he was for my future is gone. And I think I'm ok with that. His cavalier treatment of me has desensitized me more with each exchange. This time a chill swept through my body and took away all the excitement I was trying not to feel at the thought of seeing him. I allowed a few tears to roll because he remains the only person I truly want to see and its painful knowing he doesn't have any desire to see me.

Then I took a nap.

When I woke up, I confirmed the time and location to meet my great-aunt in South Chicago. She was having a barbeque at her house and expected some family members to stop by.

In other news, it's time to start looking for another job. I would like to leave the company but at this time I don't think I can command similar or better pay or keep my three weeks of vacation. You always provide for me, Father, so I am not worried. I know I am well taken care of.

In yet other news, I booked my 40th Birthday Celebration Trip. I will be flying in and out of Milan, Italy and making my way along the French and Italian Riviera for two weeks.

A DAY IN TORINO, PIEDMONT

Journal: August 10, 2015

Torino was a pleasant surprise. So much so, it forced me to slow down and enjoy the bit of time I had there. I arrived in an exhausted huff as night fell. From the first train station to the last, and each subway in between, I was impressed by the cleanness of the stations and the high-tech automation of the subway trains. So much so that I wondered if MTA officials in New York City were even aware of the Torino Grupo TT system, because NYC would benefit greatly from such an update.

During my compressed day in Torino, I visited only one location, but I saw a lot along the way. The National Museum of Cinema was incredibly entertaining and very interactive. I spent most of my time in the Archeology of Cinema section learning about forms of image manipulation that came before photography and motion pictures.

The actual museum portion wrapped around the interior of the building in a continuous circular walkway up four or five levels. It is quite an impressive presentation. Unfortunately, I didn't have the time or energy to cruise through the full exhibit. I had a hotel room waiting for me in Santa Margherita, a three to four-hour train ride away.

When help trips you up

August 11, 2015

Some time ago, I gave up on the notion of seeking help from others in my life. It has been my experience that true helpers assist without connection, reason, or demands. In contrast, the people I have actively sought help from helped only in situations they benefitted from or ignored the request altogether.

> "Thank you to all the people who said no."
> ~ Albert Einstein

As I write, I am sitting on a train I almost missed because someone insisted on helping me and ate up a few precious minutes I had to get to my train. I arrived at the train platform with nine minutes to spare for purchasing my ticket and boarding. The fellow "helping" me had the same problem I had, only he took a couple of minutes to admit it. I was trying to buy a ticket to Santa Margherita, Ligure. As often as Santa Margherita was entered, the options disappeared. "Helpful" Man, then started asking in Italian if I wanted to go to Santa Maria - the only option that stayed up the longest. Finally, I realized I was entering the full name for my stop when the ticket machine had the name abbreviated as S. Margherita Ligure. As soon as the light bulb went off, I tried to stop the man's frantic typing only to get shooed and shushed. "One moment," he said as he methodically typed in the full name a few more times before I urgently took over the typing. S. Margherita came up instantly. Once over that hurdle, I attempted to pay. My card was rejected - ran into the same issue the day before for my ticket to Torino. No surprise. However, as I reached for cash to insert into the machine, the "helpful" man canceled my order and started it over in Italian. I wanted to scream!

He was beaming because he finally understood what he was pushing - I originally had it on English prompts. I paid in cash and he immediately asked for money. Pointing to my change, he tapped his chest and said, "For me, please?"

"Si. Grazie. Have a good day," I said in a perturbed tone and thrust the change towards him.

I stepped out of the machine enclosure and saw that I had exactly two minutes to get to my train.

I was too anxious to decipher my ticket, so I frantically asked someone in a uniform if they could direct me. The uniformed man I approached just as frantically instructed me in Italian. I stared at him trying to translate: Two? Are saying platform two? A bystander helpfully translated: "He said hurry as fast as you can to number two!"

"Grazie!" And off I slow jogged with three heavy bags - two on wheels the other on my shoulder. I thought I was going to drop and expire right there on the platform as I ran alongside the cars looking for an open door. Suddenly a door opened and a conductor stepped off to speak to another conductor on the platform. I got a second wind and darted towards that open door. Before I could think, I tossed up my wheeled carry-on. In the space of the milliseconds it took to turn to my second bag, I thought: "What if I throw this up and the train takes off? Then I'm completely without luggage." (Yes, because things like that happen to me!) So, my bright idea solution was to hop up onto the train steps with my heaviest bag in hand. Didn't work. Took a couple of tries but eventually I was able to hoist the bag up and crawl up behind it. The train took off as I stood onboard in the door catching my breath.

In passing, I thought it would have been nice had one or both of the two conductors on the platform next to the door had helped me board, especially since they both saw me running for the train and struggling to get my luggage up. But then as I regained my calm, I suspected that additional help could have done more harm than good. After all, as "helpful" man proved, I do far better on my own!

GOOD MORNING: SANTA MARGHERITA, LIGURE

Slight Detours

August 12, 2015

For my summer vacation, I had grand plans of relaxing in the sun on various beaches along the Mediterranean Sea. Starting in Portofino, Ligure, Italy. The initial plan was three to five days along the Italian Riviera with a base in Santa Margherita.

As I write, I've just crossed the twenty-four-hour mark since arriving in Santa Margherita. However, I arrived in Italy three and a half days ago. I can't say that I wasted time, but I will say that my plans to relax were delayed and rerouted by the temptation to explore other cities along the way.

My airline ticket is in and out of Milan (Milano). Once Milano got on the itinerary, I thought it prudent to see what else struck my fancy in Northern Italy. My fight landed in Turin (Torino). A full day and night in both Milano and Torino visiting one major site each led to only one full day in Santa Margherita - my sleeping place for day trips to Portofino.

I was exhausted when I got off the train last night. The taxi ride through town livened me up a bit but there was no way I was going to begin exploring a new city after 10:00pm. So, when I woke up this morning and opened my window to the fragrant tropical-like beauty of Santa Margherita, I was pleasantly surprised. Later in the day, after enjoying breakfast with a view of the sea followed by an unexpected but much appreciated mid-morning nap I thought about riding a bike or walking to Portofino. I grabbed my camera, checked out a bike at the front desk and started on my way along the winding seaside road.

My GPS said the bike ride would take an hour. My spirit said the space I was in, Santa Margherita, had everything I wanted and asked for. There was sun. The sea and the beach were right outside the hotel's front door. Mountains dotted with colorful homes were across an expanse of water. Everything I envisioned for my stay on the Italian Riviera was where I was, yet I was still chasing Portofino, because somehow it had become the ideal.

I turned the bike around, rode back to the hotel and dropped it off before heading out again to explore Santa Margherita on foot. It's been an absolutely beautiful day!

Often, we have a goal in mind and we adhere to it so stringently that we neglect what is right in front of us. We become blind and dismissive of the blessings we have in hand. We can also go wrong by trying to do everything possible at a given time. Though I enjoyed what I experienced in Milano and Torino, my heart and mind were not interested in sight-seeing. In that regard, adding more to the itinerary took away what I needed most: rest, reflection and rejuvenation.

Most definitely, I would have enjoyed Portofino, but Santa Margherita had what I needed for the day: space to rest, a soothing environment to enjoy, and a bed for the night.

August 13, 2015

Good morning, Santa Margherita!
I'm on a train at Genova Piazza Principe en route to Nice, France.

I've been traveling for five straight days but feel as if I've been running all year and exhausted for most of that time.

I landed in Milan four days ago. Ended up falling asleep shortly after checking into my hotel room. Woke up in the evening and reviewed my travel plans. I was not well prepared for landing at all. Had no idea how far from my hotel I was from Centrale Stazione – where I got dropped off from a bus into the city from the airport. Spent far more on taxis the first couple of days because I over packed, was exhausted and had no idea where I was. I have not enjoyed the food as I wanted to because I've slept or overslept when I could which cut into exploration time and ended up eating in the touristy areas.

Milano was a blur of frustration, motion, and rushing from one point to another.

My body really couldn't move fast by the time I got to Torino on the second evening in Italy. Luckily there was a deep tub in that room. I took a sudsy milk bath and went to bed.

The next day I decided I had to see at least one landmark in Torino. It was easy to focus on the town's marketing symbol – the spire of Mole Antonelliana which housed the National Museum of Cinema. I so thoroughly enjoyed the museum and the view of Torino from the spire that I let a couple of departure times pass by with no concern. I had planned on leaving for Santa Margherita around noon. Instead I left around 6:00pm. I missed my connecting train and ended up getting to my next hotel around 10:30pm. Super late for a small town and super tired from rushing from one spot to another.

Waking up in Santa Margherita was the breath of life I needed. Truly. It was there that I regretted more than anything spending the first two days elsewhere because I would have been better served and relaxed quicker had I gone straight to Santa Margherita from Milan International Airport. I also determined there that I'd cancel some add-ons throughout the remainder of the trip. I started by cutting the rental car and road trip to Verdon Gorge in France with a stopover in Aix-en-Provence and spent the extra time in in Nice. I'm determined to get beach time in since that was the purpose of my vacation location – to spend days on Riviera beaches relaxing.

Just entered France by train from Italy. Looking forward to slowing down even more.

Father, I thank You for the opportunity to explore myself even as I explore the world You created. Blessings and honor to You always. Your daughter, LaShawnda.

Beach Morning Reflection

For several years, I've been on the lookout for a new place to live. Only two cities have made me think, "I could live here."

Montréal was the first city. I visited in May and plan on returning for another long weekend. The only major downside about moving to Montréal is the winter. I want to get out of the cold. The second city is Santa Margherita. I prefer to stay in the States for now. The commonalities between the two are the ease of mobility around town without a vehicle, access to culture and nature, and the friendliness of the people.

This morning after breakfast, I went to the beach. I don't know if any locals were on the portion of beach I was on, but there were certainly regulars, regionals and an overwhelming number of older people. I can't count how many extremely senior women were walking around in bikinis and strapless dresses on the beach and around town, as well as riding bikes. Their comfort and ease were extremely beautiful to me. They were out enjoying the water, the air, the park, the evening and the town without a care. To live in a space where women are free to be as they are with no judgmental or lascivious prying eyes felt quite liberating.

I could be a happy, carefree beach bum. Not likely, but I'm encouraged to continue seeking new and unexpected horizons.

Greeting the morning with the sea before you is a great way to envision life's endless possibilities. Explorers travel the globe to find new cultures. My explorations have yielded similar results. "Here" is not all there is. If we never move around, we will miss countless opportunities to improve countless days.

STORMY NICE, FRANCE

Life's a beach until it's not
Journal: August 14, 2015

I'm in a huge transitional period of my life and I've had no time to collect options let alone review them. My last day of work was seven days ago and today is the first day that actually feels like a vacation. Yesterday, I began the day on a beach in Santa Margherita, Ligure, Italia and realized that there was no need for me to pack anything into my days. It was then that I decided to strip down my itinerary. Today I woke up in Nice, France. I didn't plan anything for the day nor did I want to do anything. Instead, I slept off and on throughout the morning and early afternoon. Got up and started moving around 3:00pm and left the hotel around 5:00pm. Found food across from the beach and then went to enjoy the remainder of my day looking out on the most crystalline blue water I've ever seen, finally understanding why it's called the Blue Coast.

Beach Day

August 15, 2015

Today was my third beach day, but the first time I got in the water.

The first day, I just wanted to get close to the water. It was close to check out time in Santa Margherita and I couldn't see myself leaving town without stepping foot on the beach in front of the hotel. So, I went to the beach and took pictures.

Yesterday, I left the hotel in Nice with the intention of finding the beach and figuring out how best to enjoy it (there are many options on the Riviera starting with public and private). I ended the second beach day watching children frolic in the waves. Before I left, I inched towards the water but didn't go in. The beach was rocky and I didn't have flip flops or water shoes with me - both of which I traveled with. I also had items in my bag I didn't feel comfortable leaving unattended. So as I stepped away from the water, I promised myself: Tomorrow. Tomorrow, I get in the water no matter what.

Tomorrow is Today.

Today I got a late start checking out of my hotel. I had planned to get to the beach for breakfast and return for check-out. For this, I had to cancel plans to move on to the next town on my itinerary which is land locked and find a new hotel in Nice - simply because I wanted another day to enjoy this beauty.

And of course, it rained. Such is my life.

At the second hotel I relaxed by the pool while my room was prepared. It was nice, but it wasn't the Mediterranean Sea. I had promised myself a dip in the deep blue sea.

It began to rain as I sat outside. It seemed to take away any internal dilemma I was having. Soon my room was ready and I was able to take in my belongings, lie down as my phone charged and flip through brochures for activities in the area. What could I do on a rainy day?

When my phone got to 70%, I got up and started moving around. I saw the clear sunlit sky through my high window. That was all the confirmation I needed to put on a swimsuit and pack all the gear I had forgotten the day before and remove unnecessary items from my day bag.

As I almost skipped along the street towards the Promenade des Anglais and the beach, an activity list started to develop unconsciously.

As I passed a hotel that was hosting an art exhibit, I thought: I should see that before heading to the beach.

Since I hadn't had a meal all day (it was about 4:30pm), I thought, I should eat before I go to the beach.

As I passed by a knick-knack store with beach gear out front, I thought, I should stop to purchase a straw pad to lay on the rocks.

All this took time and Today, formerly known as Tomorrow, was fading away. I explored. I enjoyed. I stopped to purchase a beach pad. I stopped at the hotel to ask what time the exhibit closed, went looking for affordable and edible food, then walked back to the hotel for the exhibit. The sun was beaming. It had gotten quite warm. On my third go-round of the lobby's exhibit and gallery spaces, I noticed the atrium skylight had darkened. I looked at my clock: 6:33pm. I had at least another hour of sunlight - more than enough time for me to dip into the Mediterranean Sea that was literally across the street.

I quickstepped outside and was dismayed to see a blackened sky. There was a patch of blue sky far out over the sea, but thunderous dark grey clouds were directly overhead for the expanse of the seaside beach strip within sight. The little strip of blue sky way out over the sea gave me hope I could beat the storm.

I rushed across the street to the beach. Went to the water's edge and stripped off my dress and shoes. Pulled on my beach shoes and began to step into the water.

I played it safe. I wanted to walk in but didn't want the shock of cold water. I wanted to sit in the surf but didn't want my hair to get wet.

I waded in. I sat in the surf, and of course, a huge wave washed over me. Such is my life. My hair and everything else got completely soaked. After that, I didn't care so much about what part of the sea I didn't want to experience. Or what part was inconvenient.

I'm sure no more than five or ten minutes passed before I got out the water and walked back to my straw pad, at which point rain drops began to dance on my skin. It wasn't torrential but it cleared the beach of most of the people. I stayed with a few others, feeling lucky to be able to see and photograph such a beautiful display between sky and sea. In that time and space, luck became a blessing as evidenced by a rainbow appearing to bridge the city and water.

I thought of all the people who had run away from the storm and most likely missed this benediction.

Then I thought about all the storms in life people are unwilling to stand firm through. Running away. Hiding. They keep themselves distracted. They look for comfort and ease or look for pleasure and enjoyment. I did all those things today on the way to fulfill a promise I had made to myself. How much more focus must it take to keep our word to others?

Had I not finally dug in my heels and enjoyed what I could of the storm after getting soaked, then I wouldn't have been blessed to see the rainbow and receive this message about perseverance. And I would have missed this opportunity to reflect on the turbulences in my life I didn't have the *fortitude to move through and therefore receive the reward for.*

To live by and enjoy the sea, we must take the good with the bad. In order to truly love and enjoy people we must enter into the deep abyss of relationship and be willing to be overwhelmed by waves we weren't counting on and be willing to flow with them as their undercurrents take us where we weren't willing to go. What we find in these moments of acceptance and unity is the merging of the individual into togetherness. The expanse of our ocean crashing against another's unrelenting rocky shore can be soothing and terrifying. It could break or join the two. Sounds complicated and painful, but what is an ocean without a shore? Or a shore without an ocean? They each blend with each other to become everything they are meant to be.

CANNES, FRANCE

Journal: August 16, 2015, 12:25pm

Last night I cried myself to sleep. Damn Facebook. The sadness came while looking at an aunt's page. She had gotten a recipe from one of my cousin's and posted a photo of the results. Then she posted a whole bunch of pics with her and family. The taunting thoughts began bombarding me: they have shared memories and shared recipes. I have no shared family memories or recipes, not even with those I share a decent relationship. I remain a pariah to my relatives on both sides. Though I am grateful for the development of my self and my life, it still hurts to be without significant familial bonds.

Then one of the many female friends of the man who shall remain nameless asked him if she could go sailing with him in September when she returned to Milwaukee. Even though I had felt myself softening towards him this week, his response to her shut me down. It was immediate and he welcomed her. Which of course reminded me to my deep abiding shame of the countless times I have asked to share his presence and received no response at all. No acknowledgement. No nothing. More recently and significantly it reminded me of my request to go sailing with him while we were both in Jamaica in January. His seemingly spiteful response was to post a video of him and his travel buddy rafting on the water. It reminded me painfully that there is nothing to hold on to. That he has given me nothing. Offered me nothing. Promised me nothing. I hold on to hope I've burdened myself with. He has had no active part in the formation of my thoughts of a future together.

With that came the reminder of what I had not been focusing on because Facebook makes it possible to forget I am alone in this world. I have no loved ones sharing life with me. There are no individuals in this world interested in sharing time with me. It's for this reason that I traveled halfway around the world to celebrate my birthday: to escape the illusion that there are people who would celebrate with me. There is no such person – not one.

The whole purpose of planning this trip was to accept my singleness as a life-long probability. And enter my next forty years with the understanding that my help will not come from other people, nor will my comfort or my joy. Companionship will not be a hallmark of my life. I have offered my presence to others over and over again, but no one has offered their presence to me. I will no longer look for anyone to do so.

I listened to a sermon this morning by Pastor William Carroll titled, "When Knowing is Not Enough." It was a deep message and deeply received! I hear it. I just thought that me, my life, would mean something eventually to people – anyone, someone – here on Earth. I am repeatedly shown that I don't matter at all. People are interested only in what I can provide: attention, advice, service, care, encouragement. None are interested in me and my desire to simply connect, make a friend (be a friend, have a friend), share portions of our walks on this journey.

10:51pm:

I'm now in Cannes. It seems I've been on a film and photography theme all summer without realizing it. Arrived early evening and ended up taking a nap. Wanted to hit the beach but it was cool outside when I woke up. Walked to the beach to get an idea of my surroundings and ended up taking an hour-long trolley tour of the landmarks in Cannes. Quite beautiful. Really engaging. So happy I did it, especially because I got an idea of where to go for food. Sitting now at the New York New York restaurant across from the Cannes Film Festival building. I wasn't even looking forward to the entertainment portion of the Riviera but I'm quite excited about some of the aspects now.

Last night I saw fireworks on the Promenade des Anglais in Nice; it was a fabulous kick-off to my birthday weekend. Spending tonight in Cannes has been a wonderful continuation. I just ordered veal, mashed potatoes with mushrooms and mac n'cheese. Needed a solid meal and leaned into comfort food presented with a French flair.

This afternoon before leaving Nice, I sat and read old journal entries. Today's sadness was the same as last year's sadness and the sadness of the years before. I only had a few entries in the last year and a half, but the theme was the same. A longing for connection. Feeling adrift and abandoned by people I have loved and wanted to share life with. And just like the last time I wrote of my sadness, hurt and loneliness I was led to a passage I wrote on November 8 nearly two years ago that was full of giving thanks and gratitude for everything Father God was doing in my life. I reaffirmed my thanks and gratitude as I read and cried.

Reminder to Give Thanks in All Things
November 8, 2013, 9:15am

Good morning, Father! Thank You for Your message this morning: "Last year at this time, none of this," while standing in the middle of my beautiful new home You've provided for me and admiring the beautiful furniture You've allowed me to acquire and pay off in a less than a year. Thank You. I took Your message to mean next year at this time (or a little later) I will be looking back in even more amazed gratitude. Thank you, Father. Oh, the amazing wonders You can do with things that seem impossible to me. I'm in awe. I'm in tears. I'm in wonder. I'm so amazed and humbled.

Thank You, Father God.

Father, thank You for making all things new. Thank You for reviving me. Thank You for bringing me from the brink. Thank You for holding on to me during the blackest, darkest night. A night when I was set aside and abandoned by friends, family, and most painful of all, the man my heart and soul loves. I truly didn't see any way back to myself. No way back to loving people. No way back to wanting any relationship with anyone. But You kept me from falling into complete despair. You minister to me in my brokenness. Your presence assured me better days were ahead, all I had to do was hold on. So, I held on, even with no interest and no strength. The flame of hope was still burning low, and love was still my foundation but it was faith that kept me moving. Faith and trust that You did not bring me this far to have me die in a barren state (emotionally, spiritually, physically) while still in the desert (wasteland). Unproductive all around.

You've invested Your life into me. Your character, Your nature, Your hopes, Your plans, Your good thoughts, all that You Are – Your Spirit, Your Son, Your Love. Such a rich investment can do nothing but yield a surplus. Thank You, Father God, for all that You Are. Thank You for making me all that I am. Because You Are, I am. I thank You for allowing me to see the connection. I praise You. I honor You. I love You with everything You have invested in me. Amen. Amen. Amen.

Thank You. Thank You. Thank You, Abba Father God. My Good Thing. My Wisdom. My Understanding. My Love. My Joy. My Patience. My Hope. My Kindness. My Strength. My Peace, Shelter, Hiding Place, Protector, Provider, Mate, Partner, Friend, Lover, Husband, Master. My Everything. Thank You.

Throughout October, the hurt and anger was processed and witnessed out of me. I can't say what was the first or second step, although it may be safe to say that closing on my home released a lot of negative energy that was bound up in me (fear, anxiety, stress, worry – Will I actually get this home? Was it a pipe dream? What next? What if this doesn't go through? etc.). Once I let all that go, I think Love, Hope and Faith had more room to maneuver in me. Forgiveness wasn't a difficult consideration anymore. On October 20th I attended the Gospel Explosion at Circle of Sisters. I heard a song that literally changed my life in that moment, "It's not over (when God is in it)." It's not over| It's not finished | It's not ending, it's just beginning. |When God is in it, all things are new.

[....] Thank You, Father God for the revelation, the understanding and the prayer You put in my heart today. Thank You. May I live up to your plans for me. Amen. Amen. Amen.

Becoming enough for me

What if I wake up the morning after this most wonderful year has ended and I have only myself and God to greet, as has been the norm for many years now? Would this year have lost its designation? Would it have ceased to be a wonderful year in my life? No longer wonderful because I am still single and without children or close friends? Because there remains no one special to share an ordinary or a special day with?

No. This year will still be remembered as wonderful. For I grew more into the woman I am becoming. I am finally ready to embrace myself in solitude without props of hope for others to remove me from myself. Or make me "more" somehow than who I am at my lowest and loneliest moments.

I see now, and I accept, that I have to be enough for me. In my sadness and in my joy, I have to know and appreciate that my griefs and my celebrations are for me to encounter, embrace, endure and experience. If I am alone then I am alone. If love visits me in the form of a person, then at that time I will enjoy love's visit. Until then I will be the love I have been waiting for and I will honor my life with my presence and all my good intentions.

> Sermon: *When Knowing is Not Enough* by William Carroll
> Listen to: *It's Not Over* by Israel Houghton & New Breed

GRASSE, FRANCE

Journal: August 17, 2015

Aujourd'hui c'est mon anniversaire!

J'ai quarante ans!! Ooh la la! Bon anniversaire, ma chérie belle! Bon Anniversaire! C'est le début du reste de votre vie.

Mom didn't make it to 40. She died at 36.

Lil bro, Antione, didn't make it to 40. He died at 30.

I couldn't see my life beyond the length of time my mother had. The last few years have been so dark, I had very little hope for a future. But turning 40 gives me hope. Forty is such a significant number in the Bible. God cleansed the world with forty days and nights of rainfall. Moses began his outward assignment at forty. The Jews spent forty years in the desert weeding out the generations that kept corrupting The Promise. Jesus spent forty days and nights in the desert wrestling against the enemy's temptations and, in the process, demonstrated how we can also win.

They are all good company to be in.

6:38pm

It's been a great day! Took my time getting up and going. Went to Grasse to tour the Fragonard perfume factory and museum. It was a refreshingly pleasant afternoon.

360 ○ IN GENEVA, SWITZERLAND

Journal: August 19, 2015

I arrived in Geneva, Switzerland early this morning. Took a train to the United Nations to see it before my scheduled tour tomorrow.

The symbolism of the UN is overwhelming and depressing. The idea that nations have come together to monitor, support, aid and sanction each other in an effort to make the world better for all of humanity is such a beautiful thing. Yet having an awareness that none of the signed and ratified treaties the UN has orchestrated throughout its seventy-year history have curbed the state violence against Black and Brown bodies in America or the inhumanity of mass incarceration for profit is extremely depressing. If a united international body can't control its strongest member, how can it police or keep peace effectively?

My tumultuous thoughts made me feel like a rebel as I stood at the gates of the United Nations. The thoughts didn't abate after I hopped on the trolley to return to the center of town where I caught a bus to Mont Salève.

> Prepare your work outside, get everything ready for you in the field; and after that build your house.
> ~ Proverbs 24:27

Mont Salève was listed as one of the best destinations for a day in Geneva and it's fabulous! The bus ride through the city and countryside was beautiful. The cable car ride up the mountain was a replay of the bus ride from the air. When I got to the top of the mountain everything made sense.

When I got back to the ground, what made sense was clarified. When I got back to town to look at the mountain in the distance what was clarified was confirmed.

The long and the short of it is: we all want to be on top of the mountain. No one enjoys the hard work of the climb, and the journey to the mountain can be the most off-putting part of the effort. Mountain tops are desirable because they appear insurmountable. Therefore, if one can conquer a mountain, wouldn't they also acquire a cloak of insurmountable resolve; the persona of an overcomer?

What I've come away with from my afternoon admiring Mont Salève from various angles is that if we view our biggest problems as mountains, we have only to change our perspective to make our problems manageable. With a changed perspective anything is possible. I approached Mont Salève in turmoil and came away with clarity. That's not to say that I received solutions for any of the evils in the world. However, I do know a solution exists and change is possible. I know that what appears huge today may fit on the tip of my fingernail tomorrow. The problems may not change, but their impact definitely will.

HOMEWARD BOUND

Me Time
August 21, 2015

Back in Milano, on the plane about to take off for home.

This has been one of the best trips of my life. Seriously. In reflecting on why, I've concluded that it's simply because it was all about me. Just me. I wasn't meeting up with anyone and therefore focused on other people's needs, wants, or preferences. It wasn't for school, work or church and therefore learning and performance priorities were not paramount. There was no hope or expectation of seeing anyone and therefore the disappointment of someone not wanting to see me wasn't an issue.

I was free to think about what I wanted most to do, see and experience. Although I came prepared to log into my work email a few times, I never did – work wasn't a priority during my personal time. I wrote some blogs while traveling, but never got around to posting. Again, not a priority.

Sleep was had, trains were missed, I darted here, hurried there, lazed around, and explored impulsively. It was phenomenal! Each day had pivotal moments and motivations that were in service of me; reminders of my deep, eternal connection to my Maker.

A life spent running around for everyone else, stressing over other people's priorities narrowed my ability to see beyond the moment and the false urgencies scattered throughout each day. My world view had become myopic. Overall exhaustion prevented me from projecting my larger vision before me as impetus for continual pursuit of purpose.

We don't need more.
August 22, 2015

Society - parents, teachers, churches, media, other people - teaches that we need more, and more is always external and in addition to who we are.

For the last fifteen years or so I've hoped and expected a man would come my way and bless my life with his presence and partnership. For the last twenty-five years I've envisioned that at some point I would have children whom I would be able to nurture with all the love overflowing in my being. For most of my life, I've pined for others in order to experience love. None of those others have shown up. To compensate, I then spent years pouring into everyone else within my social and work circles.

What I so desperately needed was for someone to pour into me.

The primary determinant for a celebratory fortieth birthday trip was to pour into myself all the love and attention I was waiting for someone else to give me. To focus my energy on my own comfort and well-being. Though I don't neglect necessities or general self-care, quality "me time" is rare. It's important to acknowledge that even when we take care of ourselves, we can still overlook core needs.

What if I am enough as I am?

Home. At once, I'm blissful and at peace.

It's wonderful to be content with who I am, where I am and what I have. Existing in my own space and enjoying it.

Arrived home last night around 6:30pm New York time (1:30am Milan). No hassle. God provided an attentive and responsive taxi driver for me to share my ecstatic excitement with on the forty-five minute ride from JFK International to my East Harlem apartment. I'm extremely appreciative for being so well covered.

Last night, I finally opened the bottle of Bordeaux I purchased in France for my birthday evening.

Note to self: must put wine opener in travel case.

Fell asleep on the sofa. Woke up disoriented and dragged myself to my very comfortable and appreciated bed.

This morning, I woke up and headed straight for my patio. Uncovered the table and bench. Put on hot water for tea and carried a breakfast tray outside to enjoy the beautiful late summer morning. It's here in my extended personal space in the grandness of New York City, that I sit, write and reflect.

Thank You.

Thank You, Father God for Your provision for me – Your care for me – Your concern for me. Thank You, Father for showing me yet again that I am worthy of Your creative power; that there is a purpose in this life You have given me; and showing me what is right before me is so much more than I can see at any given moment.

The Universe, and everything beyond, is right before me and all I see is my patio, my neighbors, and the surrounding buildings. I need to remember that the wall before me isn't the end of anything in my life – it's the beginning of a new perspective. Thank You for enriching me in wisdom. Glory to Your Name! All honor, majesty, power and love to You. In the name of Jesus, Your Son and Offering, my Savior and Example, and by Your most perfect Holy Spirit. AMEN!

REALITY SUCKS

MOUNTAIN CLIMBING DURING MONSOON

TODAY

*When we expect to see our greatness
by how others appreciate and represent us,
we set ourselves up for disappointment.*

Okay, today I'm going to admit that I am not happy.
I try so hard not to think about happiness. *What is it anyway?* I try to focus on maintaining and increasing the measure of joy I've been given. Joy, I understand. Joy, I have. Joy, I can always come back to. I can have a horrible day but enjoy good moments throughout. It could be raining on my head, but my soul still smiles. But, happiness? That has remained elusive. Does it even exist?

STORK DELIVERY: UNINVITED AND MISGUIDED 22-YEAR-OLD

Have you ever had someone crash land into your life with all the force that nature can provide and immediately know that your life as you know and appreciate it is about to change?

A couple of summers ago, some misguided and unrepentant stork dropped a twenty-two year-old prima donna aspiring hardcore rap superstar into my quiet solitary life. She's the daughter of a cousin from a branch of the family that has done me no good and therefore we've had nothing to do with each other most of my life. Be that as it may, apparently my living in New York City became a benefit to them so the homing device on the stork was set to me and I became the most unsuspecting and unprepared recipient of a post-teen, fully attitudinal, unemployed, broke dreamer with extremely anti-reality-based expectations. Additionally, she acted like she knew everything, didn't have to learn anything, shared nothing, took whatever and answered to no one. She expected to live off of others yet had no understanding of respect, grace or hospitality. She was also traveling with a male friend who shared all her unfortunate qualities.

In the beginning, I referred to her as Lil' Cuz. That soon became Lil' Girl which was usually accompanied by *Father, have mercy!* In the end, she was referred to as Youngin' which became a verbal cue for me to patiently respond to the child and not the adult she thought she was.

The way Youngin' got to me was through a frantic text from her mother, my older cousin by eight months. Big Cuz and I were truly close as children. We were each other's confidants and protectors until our thirteenth year when I moved across the country.

During a rather humdrum summer morning at work, I received a text from Big Cuz stating, "My daughter's in New York and I'm worried about her. I gave her your number so I won't go crazy." Fifteen minutes later Lil Cuz called me (for the first time ever). She had been in NYC for two weeks and had run out of money. Or so her story went. She came so she could attend an eight week acting class. One of her best friends was traveling with her to help her, but he wasn't working and didn't have any money either, so he hadn't proven to be much help. He wasn't her boyfriend, but they started the grand NYC adventure as good friends. By the time they showed up at my job that afternoon, they could barely look at each other. They both shared that they had been fighting and bickering from the stress of the City for the last week. I allowed them both to come home with me to decompress and think about their next steps.

They ended up asking if they could stay for two weeks. The goal was to look for work and then they would set off for an affordable hostel for the remainder of their time in NYC. I agreed to two weeks rent free, but they had to get out of the house each day to look for work (day jobs at least) or otherwise find something to do in the City. I made it clear that they were not allowed or welcome to lay up in my house while I was at work supporting myself.

Towards the end of two weeks (with one day to go), Lil Cuz's friend, whom security at my job nicknamed Rico Suave, lost it and snapped, "I don't need to put up with this," as he stormed out of my home. I had come home early and found him dancing around my apartment with loud music blasting. He hadn't left the house all day but lied to my face swearing that he had.

Liz Cuz on the other hand asked if she could impose (my word, she has no understanding of what an imposition is) on me for two more weeks. She effectively stayed for a month without contributing to her expenses but offering slick remarks and major attitude – as well as disrupting my sleep, peace, equilibrium and summer. Her end came when she told me in effect that she was grown, living her life and could handle her money (after getting her first pay check). This was in response to me asking follow-up questions about her new job and plans. Whatever I responded, she came back with, I'll get out of your house tonight. I replied with a simple okay.

I think they both expected me to chase them down and beg them to stay. If so, they were both disappointed. The first night they arrived in my home, I told them both I would hold them to their word. I stayed true to mine…. Except for when I told Lil Cuz we were done after her outburst. She moved out but she did not lose my number. She's been working me like some sort of guerilla warfare strategist from the beginning.

Lil Cuz left NYC at the end of the summer. She returned to celebrate New Year's Eve in Brooklyn. I asked no questions, wanted no details. She texted me to let me know how fly she was to be flying in for the New Year and to ask if I could go to Brooklyn on a Friday afternoon to check her into her bed and breakfast room because she was landing after the office closes. All via text. I don't know how long it took I looked at my phone with my head tilted to the side. Finally, I responded that the only place I was going to be on a Friday afternoon was at my desk at work. To which she blithely responded, "Oh, yeah, I forgot about work." That one statement pretty much sums up Lil Cuz and her grasp of the real world.

The following spring, during another blissfully normal day at work, Youngin' texted to say she was back in NYC and asked if she could stay with me for two weeks. She offered to pay $150 per week. I told her that was a discussion, not a text. We spoke during my lunch hour and she ended up meeting me at my apartment after work. A few days before her two weeks were up, without contributing a dime to her upkeep (again), despite setting her own terms, she texted me again at work to say she had gotten a job and asked if she could stay another two weeks. I congratulated her on the job and ignored the remainder. It was the day before Good Friday and I was intent on enjoying my three-day weekend with a pure faith-focus – no distractions or frustrating conversations.

The day after Resurrection Sunday, I wrote talking points for a discussion with Youngin'. It came to a full single-space page. I also drew up a weekly roommate rental agreement that represented half of my monthly housing expenses. The revelation I had while doing that was that in opening my home to this little imp she decided that I was easy pickings for being taken advantage of. Youngin' was the first one to mention money during her first stay the prior summer. I believe her expectation was that by offering me $100 for her last week, she's be allowed to do whatever she wanted to do in my home. I quickly disabused her of that notion. When she offered to pay, I told her it was up to her, but whatever she decided, I would hold her to it. My reasoning then was: she's a young woman taking a big step to build a life in NYC and though she hadn't planned for the cost of an extended stay in NYC, she was still responsible for the decisions and agreements she made. It also provided me an opportunity to evaluate how she valued her word.

What I learned is that I will never again allow anyone to enter my home with the idea that their terms are ruling my roost. My hospitality was too broad. It always has been. I offered her the same hospitality I've provided to friends who have known me for years. However, she was not a friend nor did know each other. Neither was she a good guest. Another lesson I had to learn. As a consequence, the more she took my generosity and hospitality for granted, the less I offered.

I reined myself in when I reined her in. The haphazard way she lived her life was a disruption to mine. I'm twenty years her senior and have been working and contributing to households since I was sixteen. I didn't understand her – the way she thought, the way she acted or her complete lack of responsibility and honor. She was incomprehensible to me.

When she first contacted me, I thought it extremely possible that she would be a pure blessing to my life. An opportunity for me to love someone and share some of the bounty and provision God has blessed me with in New York City. By the time she left that first summer, I was disappointed and disillusioned by yet another contact that didn't have to go as sour as it did. I was no longer interested in even sharing time with her.

This second time around I was reluctant to open my home to her again. Luckily for Youngin', I admire the passion it takes to pursue one's dreams. I also believe I should do what I can to help those who ask for assistance. Two weeks didn't sound so bad. It sounded like an opportunity to try building a relationship with Youngin' again. An opportunity to provide guidance and support for her transition to New York City. We're now nearing the end of four weeks, her scheduled departure is two days away, and I can't wait to shut my door behind her.

Occasionally, she was pleasant company. Quite honestly, it was nice to have someone to talk to at the end of the day. We had a few good conversations. Red herrings for the most part. Overall, I have a sense that she was misrepresenting herself, her interests and her intent – that she was essentially not being honest. One of her philosophies that she chose to share with me, was, "You either crap on people or get crapped on" (language edited). She had shared the message on Instagram in a video. After seeing it, I asked her if she was crapping on me or was I crapping on her. She tried to insist that neither was the case while also insisting that her followers understood what she meant. I was well aware that she thought she was getting over on me. Her blatant post was simply a crude confirmation. Afterward, she continued to post messages that have confirmed her character, true outlook on life and the type of human interactions she thrives on. However, her behavior and her explicit lack of interest in spending time in my presence (i.e. getting to know me) has led to me enjoying her presence less and less which directly corresponded to my eagerness for her departure.

So the blessings I had hoped for from the interactions with Youngin' did not manifest. Nevertheless, I did receive blessings in the form of closure and revelation.

Meditation Verse: Deuteronomy 28:1-6

If you will only obey the Lord your God, by diligently observing all his commandments that I am commanding you today, the Lord your God will set you high above all the nations of the earth; all these blessings shall come upon you and overtake you, if you obey the Lord your God:
Blessed shall you be in the city,
and blessed shall you be in the field.

> *Blessed shall be the fruit of your womb,*
> *the fruit of your ground, and the fruit of your livestock,*
> *both the increase of your cattle and the issue of your flock.*
> *Blessed shall be your basket and your kneading bowl.*
> *Blessed shall you be when you come in,*
> *and blessed shall you be when you go out.*

She was uninvited and misguided.

> We must no longer be children, tossed to-and-fro and blown about by every wind of doctrine, by people's trickery, by their craftiness in deceitful scheming. But speaking the truth in love, we must grow up in every way into Him who is the head, into Christ, from whom the whole body, joined and knit together by every ligament with which it is equipped, as each part is working properly, promotes the body's growth in building itself up in love.
> Ephesians 4:14-16

When the stork delivered the ill-tempered twenty-two-year-old relative and her tag-along-friend, I was happy for the company. After our discussion the first night, I was looking forward to sharing some quintessential New York moments with a couple of out-of-towners. I'm sad to report that my gratitude for their company and hopeful outlook didn't last long. Mostly because my house guests were exhausting. They weren't gracious. They were dismissive of me, my time and the largesse of my hospitality (i.e. opening my home to two people I didn't know). In short, they were not good guests. Still, I didn't regret inviting them in. From the first day, I felt I was being tested in some way. That was the true source of my giddiness. I was looking forward to the test. Eager to embrace blessings. Not so eager to embrace the disappointment that quickly arrived to overshadow my small spot of light.

Youngin' comes from a very vicious degenerate family. Her grandmother, the wife of Peewee's older brother, used to use words against me that left no doubt that she thought me ugly, unappealing and practically worthless – usually as compared to her daughter, Big Cuz, Youngin's mother, who was deemed everything I was not and superior to me in every way. I never held any of this against Big Cuz because her mother brainwashed her in other ways and essentially thwarted her growth, development and life. I eventually forgave Big Cuz's mother because I had witnessed how much she deluded herself, and through her self-delusion spread damage and hate throughout her immediate and extended families. Big Cuz's mom was devoted to an emotionally and physically abusive husband who turned out to be an amazingly adept liar and destroyer himself. Unfortunately, her devotion and delusion stemmed from her own mother-father-daughter issues. Overall, her issues from her primary relationships were magnified and poured into her only surviving daughter – the cousin whom I have remained available to for the length of our lives. Even though we hadn't spent time with one another since Youngin' was around two years old, except for a brief visit when our grandmother was dying a few years prior. That was the last time Big Cuz and I exchanged numbers "to keep in touch."

There remains some resentment and mistrust on my end because experience has taught me to be on guard when interacting with anyone from this branch of the family. However, I've never been comfortable applying all the malice and wrongdoing of her parents to Big Cuz. By the same token, I did not burden Youngin' with the history I have with her mother and grandparents. My word to her was that she'd be judged by her own interactions with me. I've always hoped Big Cuz had survived her childhood whole and intact, if not spiritually, then perhaps emotionally. Unfortunately, time and very limited exposure tells a different story. Being around her daughter for a cumulative two months tells the remainder of what I need to know about the type of women Big Cuz and her daughter became.

Within a couple of days with Youngin', I was thanking God for not giving me situations in life I had no preparation or wisdom for. I could see how the things her mother hadn't been taught were glaring absent lessons in Youngin's interactions with me. I could see how she mimicked an emotional hardness she had no true understanding of, a street persona she had no experience of, and a world-weary nonchalance she couldn't quite pull off. I hoped to reverse some of that. People I spoke with encouraged me to simply live my life and allow her to see an alternative way to live. Honestly, that's all I can do and therefore all I had been doing. Unfortunately, she closed herself to me before we ever got started. She actually admitted to shutting herself down and just trying to get through the days I had agreed to share my home with her. As if dropping in on me and pleading for shelter without notice or grace was more of an inconvenient hardship for her than me.

At the end of her third week, during her second stay, she posted on Instagram an exchange with her grandmother, Big Cuz's mom, in which she was inviting her "Grammy" to NYC in July to celebrate her mixed tape (CD) release party. She then went on to invite her whole family to the City and the party. Now as far as I know, she's broke. That's the premise on which she asked to stay with me. She had started a minimum wage job a

week prior and had plans to move out the following weekend into a weekly rental in New Jersey. By no stretch of the imagination, based on the information she had given me, could she afford to produce a CD recording and host a release party in New York City within the next two months.

I didn't mention the Instagram post to her. She mentioned her plans to me a couple of days later. I asked no questions. She would not be in my home in July. She had been insisting that she was independent and was getting by in NYC on her own. However this venture works out, it's her experience; she has to own it and figure it out. What I know for sure is that her grandmother will not step foot in my home. At all. Ever. If asked, I would meet her in a public place but I would not bring that unfiltered dark energy into my private space.

So essentially, Youngin's decision to post her plans and invitation aligned her firmly with an attacker on my life and existence. The characteristics I had not been willing to fully apply to Youngin' became undeniably obvious.

During her last week in my home, I sat Youngin' down twice to discuss the way she chose to communicate with me. Both conversations were the result of text messages. The first text we discussed was one in which she asked to stay for another two weeks after she started working. I responded a few days later with the sit-down and a typed weekly rental contract. The second text was her snarky response to a paper note I left next to a dirty can on the counter, "rinse before recycle" on my way out the door to work. In both sit-downs she applied negative characteristics to my personality.

During the first sit-down, she said that she didn't want to talk to me, in general, because I would "go left" (go off on her) and she didn't want to deal with that. She had no examples of me "going left." There are none. When I asked for further clarification, she told me I was a dictator. I asked her if she knew what "dictator" meant. She asked for a definition. I said simply, "someone who controls you and tells you what to do." She double-downed and said, "Yeah, you're a dictator." I told her I had never been called that before and asked for examples. She cited the fact that she can't come and go as she pleases. "This is my home. You had fuller access when you first came. You messed that up. Next." She then said that my telling her that she needed a job made her anxious and she felt like she needed to please me by accepting anything.

At that point, I realized she was intent on talking out the side of her mouth.

At the beginning of her second week with me, she had an orientation for a sales job and a second interview for a hostess post at Rockefeller Center's Top of the Rock. She had made it sound like she was working in a restaurant there, so I told her that would be a good place for her to work. She would see and perhaps interact with a lot of entertainment folks. She could start building a network for her music. She got a call for a second interview at the Rock on the same day she had an orientation for a sales job she couldn't even describe the product or service for. She asked me what she should do. I responded that a bird in the hand is better than two in the bush. She asked for clarification. I said, an orientation is better than an interview. She asked me, "What would you do?" The orientation was 9:00am-3:00pm and the second interview was at 2:00pm. I told her I would go to the orientation and ask for an early release. If they refused, I would decide by lunch time on whether or not I wanted the job. If it wasn't for me, I would head to the second interview. She did what I said I would do and she got offered the job at Rockefeller Center. She started the following week.

So… as she sat at my dining table and told me I was a dictator whom she didn't want to talk to about her concerns because I might "go left" on her when all I've done is attempt to encourage her towards actual independence in New York City, I became disheartened by her very amateur character assignation attempt.

I had started that first sit-down by telling her that my struggle was staying true to myself and my faith practices while not condemning her for her choices and preferences – though I hoped she would grow out of some of her preferences. I told her that she was bringing things into my home that I had purposefully expelled from my life years ago. Though they may seem like small things, small openings make a way for larger intrusions.

She asked for an example, I gave her three.

One night during her first week, she spoke about how much she depends on horoscopes. She doesn't begin her day with them, but she ends her day with them because she likes to see how they can explain her emotions and the content of her day to her. I told her I stopped reading horoscopes years ago and no longer paid any attention to them. I shared that I depended on God for everything and He has been extremely good to me. She responded that she had never needed to depend on God for anything because she had her parents. I wanted to point out that the fact that she was in my house proved her statement a lie. It was only by God's grace that I opened myself and my home to her at all, but I held my tongue.

A couple of days before Good Friday, Youngin' asked me to look at some lyrics she had written that day. The first two lines were a refrain, "God is good. Amen n-g-a." After my eyes registered that she wrote that twice, I tossed her phone back to her. "That's extremely disrespectful. Why would you approach God like that?"

"I'm not calling God a n-g-a!" She laughed as she said this.

"But you're calling someone He created one while referencing Him. We are to approach God with reverence and respect."

"We communicate with God in different ways, Shawnda. He understands me and knows what I mean."

I ignored that foolishness. Maybe I went back to watching TV. She was writing for commercial gain and shock value. Her words were not meant to be an actual communication with or about God. It was blasphemy.

This exchange was one of the reasons she said she didn't like talking to me. Apparently, my rejection of her blasphemy hurt her feelings.

I no longer actively listen to popular music (radio, cd, parties, clubs, etc.). I mentioned that her choice of music – with words that were offensive to women and Black people was nothing that I wanted to hear in my home. She had taken to playing her iPhone on speaker while in the bathroom. Music that raised my eyebrows and hackles in the morning, was her motivation to get going. When I told her I didn't want to hear that mess in my space, I also told her what she feeds her ears and mind will flow through her life. She rolled her eyes and agreed to keep her ear buds in going forward.

My third example was about a pork-riddled dinner she had cooked the week prior. I had stopped eating pork about five years before she arrived on my door step. The first year was a pork fast to see if I could do it. I did it and I haven't gone back – for the most part. During the second year I spent two weeks in

Poland and couldn't see myself staying in Poland and not having any polish sausage. I ate so much sausage during my stay that I was completely over it before the trip ended. I haven't craved pork since.

One night, Youngin' made dinner. She made baked spaghetti, home fries and salmon patties. I was out of the house when she came from the store and started cooking but I saw that she put sausage in the pasta. I asked her what kind of sausage she had used. She said pork. I said okay. She then asked if I eat pork. I said no. She apologized for cooking with pork. I told her not to worry about it. When I saw how much pasta she had cooked – an overflowing 13x9 inch pan – I felt bad for not eating any. I thanked her for cooking dinner and told her everything smelled great. She looked really disappointed, so I gave in and told her maybe I could eat a little of the pasta. She cheered up and said please do! I fixed my plate with all of her options. I picked out noticeable pieces of sausage and I thought I was doing good. So good in fact that when I packed up the pasta to freeze for her I nibbled quite a bit more.

That night I woke up vomiting in bed. I have no way of knowing if it was from the first mercy bite or the last greedy bite, but I know that my body rejected it all. The next morning, I told her what happened and told her that I knew better and I shouldn't have agreed to eat the pork dish when I knew my body couldn't handle it.

The pork incident wrapped up the list of expelled things Youngin' had brought back into my life. I was a breath away from mentioning her grandmother as the main thing I've exorcised that felt as if it was seeking a foot hold to climb back in, but I have no kind words for her grandmother. Though long forgiven, I have no fond memories of her, so I don't mention her.

"When you have a faith practice, or a life practice for that matter, it is imperative that you protect what is important to you. For years now, I had been removing things from my life on purpose. There was a time when I was trying to write my own horoscope charts. A time when I went to clubs and danced to the raps songs. I used to LOVE pork! Now, I'm done with those things. There's a twenty-year age difference between us. I don't expect you to be where I am. I got here by living and making choices for myself. You will do the same. There are some things that I will say "no" to from now on and some things that just aren't welcome in my home."

She apologized for those instances. I assured her I didn't think she had done any of those things with malicious intent. By the same token, I know that many people are not aware of how they are being used by the enemy. I was very much under attack. The instrument being used against me simply didn't know she was a tool. I told Youngin' I wanted her to be who she was, but by the same token I needed to be true to myself and protect the work that has been done in my life.

A few days later during her text rebuttal of a simple instruction that didn't require a response, she asked "Where is all this animosity coming from?" When I sat her down later that day, I began with, "This is the second time in a week that you've applied negative characteristics to me that have nothing to do with me. Where are your preconceived notions coming from?" Of course I knew. I thought she'd want to come clean as a sneak-attack-agent-sent-by-the-enemy.

"I don't have any preconceived notions. That's not how I treat people."

"No, you do have preconceived notions about me. Have I ever "gone left" on you?"

"No, but I haven't given you a reason to."

I restrained from rolling my eyes. Even though I wanted to believe she was unaware of her negative impact, she was hitting former soft spots with no way of knowing these were former vulnerabilities of mine. "I don't need a reason to go left. Have I gone left on you?"

"No."

"Yet last week you said that you thought that I would. That's a preconceived notion. You had no basis for that comment or belief. I am not a dictator and I have no animosity in me. I am a very consistent person. I can tell you without a doubt that you could ask people about me from different time periods of my life, who have never met each other, and you will pretty much get the same description of me as a person. I know how I come across to people, because they tell me and they tell other people. I hear the same things over and over again."

She uttered some feeble defense that made no sense. Then began talking about how uncomfortable, yet comfortable, she was in my home.

That actually hit me in the heart. I take pleasure in my hospitality and how well it's received. I had told her during our last sit-down that her haphazard way of living put me at a disadvantage. She skeptically asked how. I responded that the two times she showed up on my doorstep asking for shelter left me unable to prepare myself or my home for her. My home is a clutter fest with piles of personal papers, documents, writing projects, photo prints and supplies covering every surface. My life was exposed to a person I knew nothing about, who had not given me notice or time to put my home in order before they entered.

A person's mess is an intimate thing – as is their home. The only thing that made me feel less exposed was her obtuseness – her utter lack of awareness of how exposed I really was. Her complete lack of care was to my advantage in this area. My apartment had two rooms. I could close the door to my bedroom but the rest of the space was open (kitchen, dining and living area). "You're uncomfortable here?"

"Yes."

"No one has ever told me they've felt uncomfortable in my home." I paused. "I don't think I've ever stayed anywhere I was not comfortable." I was completely taken aback. She was sitting curled up in the curved arm of my cozy velvet sofa, feet tucked to the side with my faux fur throw laid across her lap. I wanted to ask her why she was still in my house. Perhaps the expression on my face conveyed my thoughts.

She tried to backtrack and said, "Well, that's why I said I'm comfortable, but uncomfortable. I feel safe here, but we don't have the same interests and that makes me uncomfortable. We like different music and different TV shows. I don't know what to talk to you about. Each week I've been here, I've tried to adjust to how I think you want me to be. I've tried to stay out your way. I know you're used to living alone so I've tried to give you your space. When you're on the sofa, I sit at the table. I figure it would be awkward to sit on the sofa with you while you're watching TV and I'm on my phone. I don't want you to feel uncomfortable in your home."

"Are you serious?" I was incredulous. "You don't have to worry about me feeling uncomfortable in my home. That's not going to happen. If I want to do something and you're in my way, I will let you know. Trying to act like you're not here, doesn't make it so. Do you think I don't know you're here when you're sitting behind me at the table? Yes, I like living alone, but you're here, so be here. You don't get to know people by avoiding interacting with them. How are we going to learn anything about each other if you're constantly changing based on what you think I want? Just be yourself. It shouldn't be so hard to be who you are." Famous last words....

"I tried being myself. You don't like horoscopes. You don't like my music or my creativity. I'm not like you."

"So... you can't talk about anything other than horoscopes? The first two lines of your song is a summary of everything you've ever written?"

"No!"

"Then there must be more to talk about. You keep talking about how different we are. We both write. There's a great deal to talk about with writing." She mumbled an agreement.

I was pretty amazed by the ridiculous words she sprouted. I spoke only enough to refute what she was saying. By the second sit-down I had already resolved that the agreed upon day would be her last day in my house. She would not be welcomed back a third time. I even debated blocking her number so she couldn't reach me, but I decided I would rather know how she was getting on in the City than not.

She seemed to have gotten more comfortable showing more attitude with time. I could hear in her various ramblings that she was choosing the wrong words, but even with follow-up questions and providing definitions she insisted she was saying what she wanted to say. When she first arrived to my home, I told her I would hold her to her words. Words carry weight with me. Though I don't believe she believes the ridiculous accusations she hurled at my character, I do believe her intent was to inflict harm any way she could. That exposed her character and what I saw was not pleasant.

> *A good tree cannot bear bad fruit, nor can a bad tree bear good fruit. Every tree that does not bear good fruit is cut down and thrown into the fire. Thus you will know them by their fruits.*
> *~ Matthew 7:18-20*

I ruminated on Youngin's words and actions for perhaps a month after her departure. I thought about the two sit-down conversations I had initiated to clarify expectations and understandings for both of us during her four weeks in my home. After our second sit-down, I couldn't stop thinking how much she was like her grandmother, who is the hateful aunt from my youth. Fortunately for me, I remember my lessons well. I learned how to deal with my aunt by marriage as a child. I remember how she claimed to be such a good friend of my mother's (their husbands were brothers). I remember how my mother saw her as a friend and sister. Yet when I saw that "aunt" for the first time in a decade months after my mother died, all she did was desecrate my mother's memory, her beauty and her marriage. Before I completely lost my cool, I reminded her that my mother loved her like a sister and had never spoke an ill word against her – even when she spoke ill to me. As I got up to leave, I said, "I'm not going to sit here and listen to you disrespect my mother whom I just buried." I may have referred to her own abusive marriage and how she was projecting her flaws onto my mother. In fact, I'm sure I did. She called me out my name and it was pretty much about to go down from there. Lucky for her, her sister stepped in and kicked me out.

My grief over losing my mother had weakened and overwhelmed me to the point that I had foolishly accepted an invitation from Big Cuz to move to Arizona to be close to her family for emotional support. Big Cuz had come to Milwaukee, where I lived at the time, in an effort to provide moral support. Or so she said. However, she couldn't handle the cold and couldn't manage life without her super large extended family in close proximity. Her effort for me made me want to try for her. So I packed up and moved across the country ill-prepared, with the short-sighted intention of depending on people who had only ever been destructive towards me.

In hindsight, I see the aunt's attack as a targeted attack. I was already doing well in life… for my roots. I was twenty-one with no children, working on my bachelor's degree and supporting myself as an assistant restaurant manager. That wasn't supposed to be my life. I was the no-good, too-black, too-ugly, too-skinny, too-stupid, can't-talk-right niece that would never amount to anything. Nothing like her perfect, light-skinned, beautiful, well-formed, super smart daughter, Big Cuz, who had dropped out of high school and had two kids by this time, no steady employment and was only focused on men, drinking and the next party.

Without any spiritual understanding at the time, this aunt provided my first spiritual lesson on the power of our words. As a teen I referenced her as a person who only spoke evil into me, yet every word she spoke against me manifested in her daughter's life. That's probably the main reason I have compassion for my cousin. Big Cuz has lived her mother's words, self-hatred, and repression all her life and perhaps remain unaware of how profoundly she's been impacted by her mother's bitterness. This is also why I do my best not to speak ill of anyone. I have no desire for my words to ricochet off of them and enter the generations that birth from me. The one thing I have been the most purposeful about has been breaking the chains of bondage, or generational curses, attached to my bloodline and life. There are things that occur in families that people assume are natural or just the way things are. I've looked at thought patterns, actions and behaviors within my family networks and sourced them to symptoms, root causes, conditioning and training.

Everything begins with the way we think. Yet it is not practical to attack other people's thoughts. However, we can confront and attack our own way of thinking. In that way we can prune our own lives at the root. Our thinking projects our reality and from that we perceive what is possible for us in our lives. We can cultivate fantastic lives just by cultivating our thoughts.

We can hold our thoughts up to a greater truth. For me today, that Truth is the Word of God. In my youth, that truth was what I thought of myself – or who I knew myself to be.

The way I began changing my life was by holding the painful destructive things up to who I knew I was in that moment and who I saw myself becoming. If someone's words about me did not align with what I knew to be true about me, I rejected it. When I began to study the Bible in my thirties, I dove deeper and began pulling up things festering under the surface of self. The things I pulled up were held up to the light and sat next to the things the Word of God said about me. Everything I pulled from the darkness inside me burned up in the light. There was no substance to it. No truth. The footholds began to fall away from my life.

On the surface, the interactions I had with Youngin' may appear to be small and inconsequential, however, the test is always in the spirit.

What I know to be true of myself and where I was in the moment Youngin' arrived on my doorstep, was a downward spiral of deepening apathy. I was over everything. Nothing held any interest for me. I was tired of living alone and tired of being alone. Completely exhausted and discouraged with my solitary existence. Yet I was channeling all my remaining energy into changing my whole life so I could be better positioned to receive a partner and a family.

> *See to it that no one takes you captive through philosophy and empty deceit, according to human tradition, according to the elemental spirits of the universe, and not according to Christ. For in Him the whole fullness of deity dwells bodily, and you have come to fullness in Him, who is the head of every ruler and authority.*
> *~ Colossians 2:8-10*

Life transformation is a slow-moving wheel. My accumulated disappointments fermented into depression. I had stopped nurturing my job. I no longer enjoyed my home in New York City. Traveling, the longest, most constant love of my life, had become a boring chore. How did all this happen? Everything that had been a source of passion and excitement in my life had dried up. My thinking began to change. I can't pinpoint any particular thought moment, but going to church was no longer a priority. Listening to sermons I missed no longer interested me. I stopped checking on the people who stopped checking on me. I stopped caring about things I had no control over or was not impacted by. I didn't want to want anything. Life had become a big *blah* and I felt like a wisp floating on the wind waiting to land in my final resting spot. *Can't I be done now, Father? I'm so over all of this.*

Then a twenty-two-year-old relative catapulted into my life and sparked all the dormant instincts and urges I had come to believe would disappear from the earth with no one benefiting from them. The most prominent was my need to love. Instantly, even as I protested the no-warning drop-in, I thanked God for finally sending me someone to love. I had been telling Him for years that I would welcome whomever He sent to my door. The table He provided for me would be their table. That prayer began when I purchased my apartment and furnished it with the largest dining table I could fit in the space with very comfortable seating. At the time, my prayer was for a husband and Bible study group to share the space with. A few years later, a disrespectful young relative showed up. I was ready to embrace her flaws and all. I was willing to wrestle with her and nurture her into the light.

Until I noticed how she was actually inching me further away from the bit of light I was clinging to. Oddly, one of her regular complaints about me was that I kept challenging her. An interesting word choice since she was the adversary in my home opposing my life. Perhaps what she really wanted to know was, "Why was I resisting her?"

During our first sit-down conversation to discuss expectations and understanding, I decided I had to be vocal about the love I have for myself, my God and the work He has performed in my life. I had to actively protect my blessings and declare them off limits for encroachment. From the seat of my truth, I could see how Youngin' was running from wisdom and the Word when she avoided me and attacked my character. It was clear she was not interested in building or having a relationship with me. She vehemently and viciously took advantage of, then rejected, me, my love, my hospitality and my lifestyle.

This realization did not hurt. The act of dealing with Youngin' shocked me into revival. When confronted with her departure, my shoulders gently shrugged upwards and eased down again. I let go – mentally, emotionally and spiritually.

Trying to hold on to her while she was holding on to everything I've already let go of, would've kept all that baggage in my life. I've come too far to turn back now. I will not risk my true life for someone who doesn't know enough to recognize love when she's sitting in the midst of it.

Youngin', like her grandmother, was one of the best and most effective haters in my life. The lessons they provided on the nature of people and the spirit in the world are not things that can be fully appreciated via Bible text. They are best received as on-the-job-training. For being such excellent trainers throughout my spiritual journey, I remain grateful to them both.

Meditation Verse: Ephesians 6:10-12

Finally, be strong in the Lord and in the strength of his power. Put on the whole armor of God, so that you may be able to stand against the wiles of the devil. For our struggle is not against enemies of blood and flesh, but against the rulers, against the authorities, against the cosmic powers of this present darkness, against the spiritual forces of evil in the heavenly places.

IF, IN LEAVING A PLACE...

If, in leaving a place,
Those you leave behind
Sigh in relief and
Give thanks to God
For your departure
Then you can trust that
You offered no good
Provided nothing of substance
Added no value
To the space you vacated.
If, in leaving a place,
Your absence
Brings relief and praise
Then your presence must
Lend towards darkness.
Hate, malice, venom –
These are choices.
You choose to do wrong.
Plot to go out of your way
To cause harm.
You speak death even as
You're wrapped in the embrace of life.
I have no sympathy for your wayward travels.
I spoke caution for the danger
You're rushing towards
Offered respite from the
Consequences of your choices.
Warm shelter and full belly
In the midst of a concrete jungle.
You took what you wanted
Wasted the remainder unnecessarily

Misused, overused and abused my hospitality.
You left with no understanding of the
Safe harbor you cast aside in
Favor of lies and misrepresentations
There was no acknowledgement of grace
No thank you
No gratitude
Not even a: ♪♯ *Dear John, by the time*
you read this line, I'll be gone... ♭♪
No, instead you left a petition
for an order of protection
claiming harassment and abuse.
As if I were the one who
Showed up on your doorstep
Without warning or invitation
You asked for a restraining order
As if I were the one
Sleeping in your home with ill intent
Plotting against your peace
And dreaming of your downfall.

Entitled complaints all.
As if you have a right
To my life.
My property, my income,
My provision, my inheritance
Simply because you showed up
And lusted for the fruit of my
Praise, hard work and perseverance.
My struggle.
I have no curses to hurl at you
There's no need.
You aren't worth my frustration.
When I opened my home to you,
I made available to you everything
God has made available to me.

You have no idea how blessed you were
sitting in the shelter of the grace that covers me.
You rejected that when you attacked me.

A character like yours
doesn't require strong sight to see.
Your stench permeates around you
It turns the edges of the space you inhabit.
You are your own worst enemy,
But you think you're a boss
Making boss moves.
High-rise self-aggrandizement
In a borrowed Top Ramen reality.
Check yourself.
Check yourself.
Check yourself,
'Cause you're
Wr-wr-wr-wreckin' yourself.

If, in leaving a place,
Those you leave behind
Are filled with satisfaction and joy,
Then your boss move –
Your departure –
Was actually an
Answered prayer.

Thank you for testing
My faith and resolve.
Thank you for dropping in.
Thanks so much more for leaving.

FAMILY DILEMMA

At a church in Tucson, I sat in on a three-part series titled Family Matters presented by Denisha Workizer, Ryan Kramer, and Gary Barteau. This series was very powerful for me. Like many, I've struggled painfully, and mightily, with my relatives through every stage of life. Unlike many, after a while, at each stage I have consistently chosen separation and distance in order to preserve my life. Self-preservation has been both a blessing and curse. The instinct to cut off my arm, my foot, even my heart in order to breathe and live another day with a bit less pain has been my status quo since adolescence. But now, as I approach my middle years, after living the last fifteen years alone without family input or interaction in my daily life, it feels as if I've over-preserved myself. I've processed out the salt and flavor of life, the meat of existence, the joy of being. I've grown stale.

The Tug-of-War of Returning

The aunt who knows me best and had a hand in mothering me during a portion of my teen years, dropped me in my twenties. No rhyme or reason I'm aware of. She simply stopped communicating and interacting with me.

She had a very controlling stranglehold on many people. The hold she had on me was through constant reminders of how she stepped in to help my mom when no one else would. Her idea of being paid back was me owing her my life and being willing to give her whatever she wanted whenever she asked for it. Preferably before she asked for it. When I moved away at the age of thirty, my main intent was to get away from the yoke she kept trying to attach to me. My insight into my aunt's character was very limited then. Fortunately, I see her much clearer now.

After I moved to New York City, the only time my aunt and I communicated during the first ten years of my self-exile, was surrounding the death of family members.

When my aunt became ill a couple of years ago, she began sporadically reaching out in earnest. Meaning her speech was earnest but her follow-through was not. I listen to her with a very skeptical ear, in an attempt to discern truth and need from hyperbole. Despite not being able to trust her, I do find that I would still like to have a good relationship with her. What I'm coming to terms with is that such is not possible.

My return to Arizona was not meant to be shared with relatives in the state. There was no intention of interacting with people who have no goodwill towards me. However, I am very talkative, my aunt is very nosy... and I've never been a deflector or a liar. She knows this. When I don't want to answer a question, she'll keep at me until my guard lowers, and I overshare throughout the course of the conversation. She is also good at inserting herself without invitation. Long story short, I eventually shared my intention to move to Tucson and she began planning my life. First, she wanted to visit me in New York City before I leave for good. She wanted to join me in various endeavors when I arrive in my new home and insisted I pick her up and drop her off in Mesa (suburb of Phoenix about 1.5-hour drive away from me) so she can do so. Her suggestions exasperated me. Each time I impatiently cut her off. *"I've been in New York for twelve years, if you haven't visited by now, I'm not holding my breath for a visit before my final exit. I'm not driving to Phoenix on a regular to pick you up and drop you off in order to participate in an activity with me. No. No. No. Then... Okay, do you want to spend Christmas with me? In March, I'll be in Phoenix for an event and will stop by* to visit. *When do you want to come to New York? I'll see what I can do."*

Love is very simple. So is relationship. Love embodies the desire to provide and accommodate. That is the essence, the true core, of relationship. My aunt no longer manipulates me from the angle of owing her anything. She targets my loneliness by revealing her own. She tries to identify with me being on my own by claiming to be the same. In addition to being "on her own," she's ill, she's dying, and unemployed. What she doesn't like mentioning is that she has three children, several grandchildren, a brother, nieces and nephews in the same city. She claims no one's checking on her or looking out for her. She's not eating. She can't go shopping. No one cares. So yeah, I finally gave in and agreed to visit her. I told her two weeks in advance when I would come.

When I called to tell her I was in Phoenix and leaving the event I had attended, she passed the phone to one of her grandsons who was visiting. She called a few minutes later, as I was heading to the highway to get across town to frantically tell me her brother and his wife also "dropped by." I could hear her anxiety through the phone. I wasn't prepared for a visit with her, her brother and his wife – far too much ridiculous energy in one space. I told her as much and told her I was fine staying on the highway and returning to Tucson directly. She said her visitors wouldn't be there long and asked me to come by as I intended. By the time I arrived at her complex, I had to use the restroom, so I called and told her I would bite the bullet and deal with her brother and sister-in-law because I needed a bathroom. She calmly replied, "Can you go to McDonald's down the street? I'll send my grandson down to take you there."

"I just passed McDonald's. I can get there just fine." This was my first visit since my grandmother, her mother, died four years prior. Yet, she refused me entry for a time in preference for her brother whom she later shared lives around the corner.

I drove to McDonald's and ordered food while I was there. Then I drove to another location to journal. I was gone for close to two hours, during which she called three times. My internal debate was should I get back on the road and drive back home to Tucson or should I follow-through on the visit I said I would make? I suspected she had set me up. She had always tried to force me into interacting with her brothers even when I have been direct about not wanting contact. Though that wasn't the case this time. I had already tried scheduling time with her brother. That seemed to surprise her. Against my better judgement, I completed my journal entry and went to visit my aunt. When I arrived, I was surprised to see her son – who had according to him, been living with her for four years. His girlfriend shared his room with him.

The lonely aunt whom no one was checking on, literally had a full house.

My aunt has always made destructive choices. She has never chosen love for the sake of love. Not for her children, not for her husband, not for her mother. Nor for me. I have always given her the benefit of the doubt, but her actions have always been honest expressions of her priorities. She always says I'm like a daughter to her. Yet she did not drop out of contact with her children for ten years.

I view my aunt now as a gateway drug or disease. She chooses everyone and everything I don't want in my life. Even my willingness to accommodate her for love's sake is not a good reason to open the door of my life to her when I know she will continue to pull undesirable people and elements in.

Ultimatums

I have nieces of my own whom I have no contact or relationship with. My brothers' daughters were kept away from his family since he died eleven years ago. The girls were still sweet then. And I did what I could in all my broken exiled loneliness to maintain a semblance of a relationship with their mother, thereby staying within their world. I reached out to cultivate relationships. I called, I visited, and I sent care-packages. Their mother instigated and participated in his murder. The police refused to investigate so she was never charged. She and I had a couple of conversations about what witnesses shared with me and my family. To my recollection she never denied her part. She didn't want me connecting with her daughters and when she gave up trying to manipulate me through them, she shut down access altogether.

Several years ago, I connected with one niece on Facebook. I was quite excited to be able to see her and her sisters virtually and perhaps hear about them online. My excitement died a pitifully quick death. They were playing a short game they thought was a long con. Be borderline courteous for a couple of short emails or texts. Hit me up for money. When I refuse, tell me to go kill myself or that I'm not a real auntie because I'm not paying for the privilege. This cycle happens every few years. It's been three years since the last time.

Last week, my middle niece texted me from an unknown number. Cue borderline courteous brief texts. She said she has a lot of questions and asked to speak to me. I suggested the following evening. When I got on the phone with her, she began with a disclaimer. "I don't mean to come off as rude, but on the other hand, I am very angry, and I just want some answers. Why are you not interested in having a relationship with your deceased brother's children? Why don't you ever come around or call? Why didn't you reach out when your grandfather died? I know you were in Gary, why didn't you stop by?"

Sometimes, people create their own alternate realities. She's eighteen now. She was fifteen when she told me I am not her aunt because I don't "act like" the aunts she acknowledges. For example, her mother's sister is accessible and available for everything. I reminded her of this exchange. And because I know her mother used to text awful things to me then pass the phone to her so she could add her own awfulness, I offered, "Perhaps your mother had your phone when that text was sent."

"No that was me. That's how I felt because you've never been around, and I don't understand why you don't want a relationship with me."

This is where my heart would've broken if it hadn't been targeted and trampled under-foot for so many years.

I told her, "Your mother would be better able to answer why I haven't been around. I have never not wanted a relationship with you. However, if you're asking if I want to work on a relationship with you where you have all these expectations about who and what I should be and how I should perform in a role, then no, I am not interested in that. But if you're interested in getting to know me and allowing me to get to know you, then yes, absolutely. I would absolutely love to build a relationship with you.

It's an odd thing when you can be hurt by someone, move to protect yourself from their fiery barbs and still ache because of the pain they're experiencing. It's not lost on me that this girl is reaching out with the same hand she's lashing me with. Even as she's seeking love and knowledge, she's attempting to punish and destroy. She wants a connection, yet she keeps burning the bridge we're meeting on. I see it. I get it. I'm just not here for it. I'm over all this foolishness in my life.

I'm a self- preservationist who has never had the luxury of sharing my pain with anyone connected to the source of the pain despite having a host of pain points.... Because of my history, I am not interested in coddling, thereby further enabling, an abusive personality. Also because of my own seeking and longing, I will continue to re-open the door the tiniest bit as the simplest invitation I can manage.

Even if I took her at her word and dismissed her methods as learned behavior from having fed on breasts of malice and destruction, then I'm still blurry as to her true intent.

Before the end of the call, she said, "It would have been nice to have had you or someone from my dad's side of the family at my graduation."

"It would've been nice to have been invited. When was your graduation?"

"It's this Friday."

"Yeah, an invitation would've been nice. Have you decided on a college?"

"Yes, I leave in August for Atlanta."

We talked a bit about college. I'm quite happy for her and wish her all the best in all she does. However, it wasn't lost on me that the timing and the purpose of her call speaks more to her expectation for a financial acknowledgement of her accomplishments than to an interest in getting to know me.

Reconciling Past, Present and Future

Both my aunt and my niece represent the current state of my familial relationships. More importantly, my aunt's solidly entrenched in the past. Everything I have worked to extricate from my life would return to roost in my home and life should she be allowed access to either. I know it. I see it. I don't want it.

My niece also represents a future hope. She and her sisters could have filled the void of the children I never had and I would have joyfully showered them with everything I had. She also represents a future destruction as a reminder that the enemy is roaming the earth seeking people to devour. From that perspective, just being able to build and maintain a path to healthy communication would be a blessing to cherish.

COMPLAINING IS CONTAGIOUS

Negative energy surrounds us. Sometimes we get so enveloped in it that we forget negativity is not our natural state. I make a conscious effort to correct people when they speak negatively into my life. Some think I'm defensive for doing that and I think they are destroyers for planting corrupted seeds into my life. Save yourself. Step away from complainers and those who have nothing good to say. Most importantly, reject their words.

Lessons from negative speak:
- Complaining is contagious.
- Even when it's not directed towards you or is about you, it will still impact your life.
- Negativity seeps into your consciousness. It's an infection that weakens you without detection or bench marks.
- A negative outlook is a way of life. It's the dominant attitude with which you interact with the world.
- A negative complaining nature stems from an entitled nature with a superiority complex. If you take a moment analyze (not really listen, but review) the complaints of someone in your circle, you'll hear it's all about them with no concern for others involved.
- Complainers think there would be no problems if they were in charge.
    - Your listening ear and time are your only valuable offerings. Wouldn't you rather invest your time and lend your ears to something productive and edifying?

LITTLE TYRANTS

Seven years into my tenure as an executive assistant at one of the top financial corporations in the world, I took a leap into a different role. The title was Program Analyst in O&T Communications. It was supposed to be my way out of the dead-end road I was on as an admin. I needed something different. Though I am consistent by nature, change is my constant.

Something different looked like:
1. not being anyone's assistant
2. positioning myself for a managerial role upon graduation from grad school
3. learning and using other skills. Unfortunately, my something different was in direct opposition to the status quo.

My big career transition took place in the summer following the departure of my dear Boss Lady, whom I had worked with for five years. When Boss Lady hired me, she was clear about her desire to have a partner in the office. She wanted a delegate to take care of the things she didn't have time to think about. I never considered how autonomous I was in that role. I only answered to one person. If I needed something to do my job, it wasn't a matter of asking permission as much as just sending her an invoice or request for approval with instructions on who to reply to with her approval.

That's what I was used to. Doing my job by managing my manager and her office.

Boss Lady left the company in late spring to pursue private practice. I became a ship without mooring. For five years, she had been the one human constant in a life that had no one else showing up in it. As I told her then, she was my longest relationship. However, I thought the break would be good because change is sometimes good.

She asked me to follow her to her new company but I thought it was the perfect opportunity for me to explore "something different".

"I didn't owe you a conversation."
The program analyst role was a pit-stop along the road of my corporate career.

I began that role with a great deal of hope and expectation for a bright transformative future. Within two weeks, I knew it was not a good fit. I transferred out by week five. The team manager managed to micro-manage me through remedial tasks supplied by other team members while remaining completely hands off. She rarely communicated with me, but when she did she insisted she wanted me to be able to do her job. It felt very disingenuous since she entrusted my training to someone she said I wouldn't be working with. None of it made any sense.

One day we had an exchange following a request I put in for a free e-shipping application I had access to in my prior role with Boss Lady. I assumed I lost it in the transfer, so I put in an order for it. She responded that she revoked my access to the application along with other applications I didn't need for my role in her group. I told her that I had repeatedly told her, my trainer and the HR recruiter that I was closing out items from my prior role. All she had to do was have a simple conversation with me before she revoked accesses I've had for years and still needed for a few more weeks.

"I didn't owe you that conversation," she told me curtly. "I spoke to the manager you reported to and she didn't mention any leftover work you were doing. If she needs your time for something, that's a conversation she needs to have with me."

I can toss out everything else she said in a half hour of trying to talk down to me about policy, but the statement that she doesn't owe me a conversation about my workload and the beneficiaries of my work product within the company we both worked for told me everything I needed to know about her as a manager. Or rather, it was confirmation of what her lack of engagement with me told me.

This chick thought she owned me and my labor.

Everything she said, and the manner in which she said it, pointed to the fact that she thought she was my de facto master.

What I know for sure is that no one owns me. I provide labor for an income. As does she. I report up a chain of command. As does she.

1. Owe: she assumed that everything she needed to know about me she could learn from quick updates from other people. Therefore, it wasn't worth her time to communicate directly with me.
2. Conversation: She preferred to limit my productivity than to ask me if I needed anything before she revoked my access to software which she didn't have access to or authority to reinstate. I badgered the help desk for three weeks because I thought they were responsible for items that dropped from my tech profile.
3. I/you: This came across in such a haughty way. How dare I suggest she should have talked to me before she made a decision she had every right to make that impacted my performance and my follow-through on my word.

If I got fired or quit, another company would pay me for my labor. They will not pay her for my labor. She receives no income for the services I provide for the company or people within the company. Though she was my manager, she was also a co-worker in that we were both employed by the same firm

She did not sour me on female managers. I have been fortunate to work for powerful women for most of my work life. They aren't running the world, but they are certainly running their lives and are sought-after leaders in their professions. I didn't get along with some and others were difficult to acclimate to. There were even some rocky patches with the women with whom I formed very good work relationships. Every woman I have ever worked for has been opinionated, outspoken, ambitious, direct and unapologetically herself. That is what I love and respect about each of them. The ones I didn't get along with were the ones who didn't respect me as an individual with thoughts independent from theirs. The ones I worked well with, were the ones who not only respected my individuality but also respected my counsel.

When you stand in the presence of greatness – any form of greatness – you learn to be a greater version of yourself and when you're in the presence of a fool, you have no trouble identifying them as such.

INTRUSION, VIOLATION & DESTRUCTION

Trust in the Lord with all your heart, and do not rely on your own insight. In all your ways acknowledge Him, and He will make straight your paths.
~ Proverbs 3:5-6

When I returned home from my fortieth birthday trip, I found that my patio had been vandalized and my home had been entered without my permission and without notifying me. The trespasser had jumped over my patio fence. The three flourishing potted plants were tomato, watermelon and zucchini. The intruder picked nearly all of my budding watermelons and smashed them, leaving two evenly cut and scooped out halves on top of the fence. The intruder had also broken my water valve. The outdoor knob was turned off but water was still pouring out. In my apartment several things were knocked over and out of place. All of the items were on a path to the internal water valve and the patio door.

I bent myself into a pretzel trying to make the situation seem less hateful and malicious. Then I unbent myself and got pissed.

For a span of years, I was seemingly surrounded by people who assumed I don't know what I was talking about when I expressed grievances. They went out of their way to explain how a phantom "other" certainly meant no harm (even when a perpetrator hadn't been identified). Initially, I was astounded and flabbergasted when people I confided in or lodged a complaint with defended the behavior of people who caused me harm. Now I get angry. Now I perceive that there's an underlining bias that instantly disregards, and attempts to invalidate, any grievance I voice.

During the same span of time, I also noticed when non-black women make complaints (even of the most insignificant nature) they have no shortage of people to commiserate with and to soothe them. The most emotionally and psychologically debilitating realization I've had while observing the world from New York City, is that a black woman's pain has no value in in the world. Generally speaking, American society doesn't even acknowledge Black Women are capable of experiencing hurt or pain. Therefore, there's no compassion, empathy or sympathy for any of our trials and struggles. Our basic need for safety and security is ignored by those in authority positions (i.e. educators, employers, doctors, landlords, police, courts, politicians, etc.) and we receive no support or understanding to overcome what we lack. The consequence of this dismissively callous treatment is that Black Women, by and large, become out-spoken, independent, strong, self-sufficient, no-nonsense doers. We are the backbone of families, communities and society. We represent ourselves.

The only other two people who had a key to my apartment were the super and the porter. Before I left for my vacation, I had pushed all my container plants against the perimeter of my fence and asked the porter if he could water the pots over the fence. He agreed.

The day after my return, I spoke to the porter over my patio fence. I asked him if he had watered my plants at all. He said he hadn't gotten to it because his daughter had been sick and had he hadn't been to work the first week I was away and was now catching up. I told him about the broken water valve and destroyed fruit. He claimed to know nothing about it... then hopped over my fence in one leap to look at the damaged water valve.

A few days later, he stopped me in the hall and asked, "How long are your watermelons going to take to grow?"

"You mean the watermelon that was cut and left on the fence?"

"No. I saw that you have more watermelons growing. How long are they going to take to mature? A year? Longer?"

His observation flabbergasted me. When I was sitting across from the plant I couldn't see the low hanging fruit hidden behind the leaves of the neighboring tomato plant. It took me standing over it to see the small balls of fruit within the leaves. It would have been impossible for him to see the budding fruit the other side of my fence or even from the water valve twelve feet away.

A couple of days later, while getting my mail in the lobby, the super stopped me to say nonchalantly, "Oh, by the way, I had to turn off the water on your patio last week because it was spraying all over the place."

"Excuse me?"

He repeated himself and added, "When you need something done, ask me. I'll do it. Don't ask the other guy. He doesn't know what he's doing."

The machismo in that statement with his puffed out chest, slapped me in the face. I told him there was no way my water was spraying last week because I had turned my water off from within my apartment. Additionally, I had already been gone for a week by that time, so the only way the water would have been on was if someone had entered my apartment to turn it on. "Did you enter my apartment to turn on the water?"

"I did not go into your apartment."

"I had asked the porter to water my plants from over my fence. He told me he was out sick the first week I was away. Perhaps he thought it would be easier to water my plants from within my patio when he returned and jumped the fence. Maybe he tried to turn on the water outside and stripped the valve then entered my apartment to check the main valve."

"No one entered your apartment."

"Someone did enter my apartment and someone has damaged my property. If it wasn't you or him, it was certainly someone in this building." My patio is enclosed by a large terrace accessible only by building residents through our building which is secured.

"Your water valve was probably sun-damaged."

"Seriously? You're claiming the sun melted covered metal without damaging the metal cover?" At this point I ended the conversation and went into my apartment. It crossed my mind that he had seen the porter doing what I asked him to do and took over the task without getting the information I had provided.

Honestly, I would have been fine if they had entered my apartment in an attempt to correct what they broke. My fault for asking for help. I was not okay with them lying to me. When I went to the board and management and asked for the video footage facing the front and back of my apartment, they stonewalled me for five months. Then they boldly told me I needed a court order for the footage, which required a police report. Since nothing was stolen, the police would not write up a report. Five months after the incident there was no evidence of trespass.

The whole situation sucked the wind out of me. It embittered me and ruined my experience of my home as a safe space. I changed the locks and refused to share the key with management. Then I installed my own security alarm and cameras.

Sometimes I think it doesn't take much to make me feel completely insignificant. Then upon closer analysis, I always come to the same root – a demonstrated lack of care and concern for my personhood; a violation of my sense of safety and security.

The arrogance of men is such that:
1) They violate women then ask us about it like their intrusion is not an issue.
2) They speak of their act of violation in a revisionist manner in order to suggest:
    (a) no wrong doing on their part
    (b) a woman doesn't know what she's talking about
3) Their destruction extends beyond the physical and corrupts the psyche, spirit and soul

∞ ∞ ∞

Spiritual attacks manifest in the body

Throughout the weekend following my return home, I struggled with a very painful, temple-stabbing headache. Any kind of headache is rare for me. So is illness. There was a huge welt on my collar bone, possibly from an insect bite which could have also been the source of a 12-hour fever I was struggling through as well. My left arm and elbow had been tender and achy for weeks and the last of several sores received from kneeling in a thorn bush a month and a half prior still hadn't fully healed. My foot had been a swollen, throbbing red slab for a nearly two months. It was so bad that I was sent to the emergency room by the nurse at work. I was prescribed drugs for four weeks and didn't see any real change while taking the pills.

Normally, I heal quickly so all these little things added up to a big scare. While on vacation, towards the end of my refill, I began rubbing coconut oil and Cortisone cream unto my swollen foot. The swelling went down and stayed down. When I got back home, I stopped paying attention to my foot. A week later, a slight swelling returned. During my fever I rubbed Cortisone on the insect bite, the thorn sores and my swollen foot. The foot went down and the last sore finally began closing over.

I don't know what poisons were in my body, but I know there was poison in me. All the small and not-so-small ailments worked as a warning that I'd left myself open and unprotected for attacks. In the absence of relationships to attack, my physical health and mental sense of well-being became targets.

Due to the accumulation of physical issues, I didn't have the energy or mindset to recover gracefully from the violation of my personal space. I wallowed in anger and animosity for much longer than I should have.

> *I have said this to you, so that in me you may have peace. In the world you face persecution. But take courage; I have conquered the world!"*
> *~ John 16:33*

Tainted Garden

Serpents and gardens became a theme for the season after I purchased my East Harlem co-op. Taint and corrosion joined in. Paradise and sanctuary tried to reclaim the space. Malice and lies darkened it all. Truth and love hovered above. Bitterness and resentment laid me down.

It was hard to process the extreme sense of violation and how unsafe I felt in my home. The thought that someone believed they had the right to enter my home whenever they wanted to without explanation made me think of the road to tyranny. Many people are only an opportunity away from destroying someone. Men do not stop doing what they think they can get away with. Meaning, the super and porter having a key to my home was no longer an option. Letting them know I was not an easy target was paramount.

Regaining my equilibrium has been extremely slow. I'm not sure if I've completely recovered. My home became a place I closed myself up in. I have not enjoyed my outdoor space. I certainly no longer trust my neighbors to assist me on any level. That was the last summer I enjoyed sitting in my patio garden. It was also the last time my garden flourished. It dried up that summer due to the lost water source and my lack of interest in nurturing it. Even though I went through the steps and planted seeds the next two years, nothing grew successfully. Everything died or was overtaken by weeds.

It's a struggle not to give in to the lies the serpents tell about their superiority, their sly cunning, their knowledge, their right to infringe increasingly on your rights. The propaganda about my own worthlessness and conquerability, my invisibleness and insignificance. The biggest deception they propagate is that there is no violation, no trespass, no destruction because they are simply doing what they want to do. They have a right to my space, my life my peace.

It's imperative to push back and say, "No. You don't." Even when fear tries to consume you. When we confront the devil, he will flee.

The work of the enemy is to steal, kill and destroy. Knowing this doesn't negate the trauma when the enemy appears and does just that. One benefit of spiritual warfare is that the Believer becomes increasingly more adept at recognizing the attacks, attackers, targets, and weapons being used as well as the battleground. When you've survived the first couple of skirmishes, you learn to see the enemy for who he is *in* everyone who comes against you. That doesn't necessarily make you want to excuse the people being used... but that too becomes part of the battle – learning to forgive people for behavior that is intended to hurt you.

ADVERSARIAL FELLOWSHIP

What fellowship does light have with the darkness?
I thought it was safe to come out. Safe to reach out and invite people in. Instead, I've continued to bump my head against walls of unbelief, false teachings, worldly judgment and adversarial aggression thinly cloaked under a veil of fellowship.

For nearly a dozen years, one of my primary desires was for faith-based fellowship. It proved to be quite the elusive desire.

Conversions within the faith

My biggest and most painful disappointments with fellowship have taken place within the congregations I have participated in.

In each of the three congregations I have been part of since 2006, there has been a strong and perverse element of control exerted over groups by group leaders. Group leaders, who by virtue of our shared proclaimed belief were brothers and sisters in Christ, deemed it their right – indeed, their duty - to tell me and others how to believe, how to interact, what to do, when to do it and how to do it in order to live our faith daily.

I understand and appreciate the need for organization, leadership and management. I do not agree or believe that someone's position in a congregation gives them the authority to rule or direct my faith walk, ministry contributions, life practice or schedule.

There have been many instances where I have collided with leaders within the congregation because they were teaching something or acting or treating people in ways contrary to my understanding of the Word of God or in opposition to my experience of the Holy Spirit's operation in my life. It has always been after my attempt to explain my understanding based on scripture that the battle emerged from the shadows in a very aggressive and usually hateful way. I don't recall my scriptural evidence being argued against with their scriptural evidence, unless it was with a verse that they quoted to claim their authority over my personhood. Usually, they responded by stating policy and rules or preferences of their leadership. Quoting policy when confronted with violating God's Word is confirmation of wrong doing.

Shortly after moving into my building, one of my neighbors, whom I was excited to be building a relationship with, invited me to her worship hall. We had spoken often of our faith walk and life experiences. I thought there was a genuine connection. She was actually a dinner guest in my home when she issued her invitation. I accepted and agree to accompany her the next day to service. I had never been to a Jehovah's Witness meeting. I can't say that I have ever done any reading on what Jehovah's Witnesses believe. However, I have known and worked with Jehovah Witnesses, so I was familiar with some espoused practices.

I attended the service and appreciated the family-focused message. What came after the message threw me for a loop. After the speaker delivered their message, the congregation read and analyzed a Watchtower article and its accompanying images. On our walk home, my neighbor asked me what I thought. I took special care to frame my words gently. She asked me if I would return for another service. I responded with a firm "no," at which point I sensed she shut and down and put me on her blacklist. She asked a couple of additional questions, but she didn't appear to interested in my answers. In an effort to get a better understanding of what I had witnessed in the meeting hall, I asked her about terminology. The terminology question lead to a discussion of our beliefs about life after death. I told her I hadn't really studied scripture on life after death but I took comfort in a couple of scriptures that alluded to renewed life, specifically Matthew 22:23-33 and 1 Thessalonians 4:13-16. She ignored my scripture references, and as we had gotten to our apartment building by this point, she abruptly told me to have a nice day.

> Jesus answered them, "You are wrong, because you know neither the Scriptures nor the power of God. For in the resurrection they neither marry nor are given in marriage, but are like angels in heaven. And as for the resurrection of the dead, have you not read what was said to you by God: 'I am the God of Abraham, and the God of Isaac, and the God of Jacob'? He is not God of the dead, but of the living."
> ~ Matthew 22:29-30

This neighbor was the person to sit for me for a photography project focusing on women in their own spaces. I had explained the project to her as well as my intentions to show and possible exhibit the finished images. She sounded very supportive and interested in the project. By the time I joined her at her meeting hall, I had already edited a couple of my favorite images in an Impressionists painting software I was learning. Her finished images were lovely, colorful and vibrant. When I called her to review the photos and asked for her signed photo release to show the images publicly, she told me she was uncomfortable with the word "spirit" in my business name, Spirit Harvest, and didn't want to be associated with it.

I was stunned and thrown. Then I got angry.

I hadn't asked her to convert me.

Spirit Harvest is my primary distribution channel for everything that has been seeded in my spirit and life. As such, it is a direct representation of my life. From my point of view, if she wasn't comfortable with the word "spirit" then she wasn't comfortable with me. There is no place I am willing to go and no one I am willing to deal with without the presence of the Holy Spirit housed within me.

I reasoned that the only way she could be hurt or angry with my lack of interest in practicing my faith the way she practices hers, was if she had somehow invested in getting me to think like her. I am not lost. I am not looking for something to believe in. In all our interactions, I had been very clear about the solidness of my faith. I shared about my faith-based writings and how I wanted my photography to be an expression of everything God has put in me. When I accepted her invitation, I told her that I enjoy visiting different churches when I travel and had sat in a lot of different denominational meetings, but I hadn't been to a Jehovah Witness Hall yet. I was not asking to become a subscriber to her publication or her message.

I have invited people to events and services with my various non-denominational congregations. Some wanted to talk about their experience, some did not. One, a professed non-believer, has attended several church events with me. Other people's attendance or lack of interest in returning to my congregational meetings have never been a basis of terminating interaction with them. Our interactions were not predicated on my need for them to think or experience a service or practice a belief like I do.

I am not a converter. I am a sharer.

I do not believe it's my job to get other people to believe and live as I do. I believe it's my job to live my best life according to my belief and faith. By living my best life, I am able to share the best fruit of my life with those willing to partake of my offerings. That's it. That's all.

Meditation Verse: 1 Thessalonians 4:13-16

But we do not want you to be uninformed, brothers and sisters, about those who have died, so that you may not grieve as others do who have no hope. For since we believe that Jesus died and rose again, even so, through Jesus, God will bring with him those who have died. For this we declare to you by the word of the Lord, that we who are alive, who are left until the coming of the Lord, will by no means precede those who have died. For the Lord himself, with a cry of command, with the archangel's call and with the sound of God's trumpet, will descend from heaven, and the dead in Christ will rise first.

RETHINKING LIFE

Have you ever thought about what you've been taught to think?

During the last few years, I've been struggling a great deal with "*the way things are supposed to be.*"

When I was in high school, we were taught that a college degree would lead to a good job and a comfortable life. Higher education became my own personal albatross. The first degree I completed was an associate degree no one acknowledged. It rolled into a seven year pursuit of a four year degree that also went largely unacknowledged. Fifteen years after acquiring my bachelors I completed my Masters in International Affairs while working for a global firm. When I began that program, my manager at the time, rejected my quest for tuition reimbursement, which was stated to be provided at manager's discretion. Her reason was that my current role as her executive assistant (she was a global head of a department) would not receive any benefit from anything I could learn in a graduate program.

Fast forward four years to a follow-up conversation with another manager about career opportunities. I had spoken with a few managing directors (all division heads with global reach) about recently acquiring my M.A. and wanting to transition out of the admin role into a project or program management role. I told my manager I had hit a wall. I had reached out to the MD's I had some history with (I had been with the company for over ten years and working with executives for over eight years) and they had begun avoiding me. I told my manager, who actually had a job posted that was a match for my skills, refused to answer my questions about what he was looking for to fill the role.

My manager coolly said, "Your initiative and confidence are admirable, but in this case you've over-stepped yourself." This is a woman I openly admired. I had asked her to mentor me when she hired me. I had been completely honest about my career and life goals. She told me to come to her if I needed help. This meeting was me asking for help after six months of getting nowhere.

"You may not want to hear this," she continued, "but if you want a different career, you're going to have to start over."

"Start over for what?" Was my incredulous response. "My ten years with this firm don't mean anything? Or because my advanced education was a waste of money? You're telling me that my experience and education are worthless?

"No, not quite worthless, just not worth as much as you think."

"Really? I've been working for over twenty years and you're saying I need to compete with college graduates with no real world experience??

"If you want to change careers. You don't have the experience in the area you want to transition to."

"I'm a quick learner and most of my work is project based. I'm not reaching here. I'm seeking opportunities that align with my skillset and interests, which I am more than qualified for."

"That's not the point. This firm does not have a corporate structure to supports training people. We hire people who know what they need to do."

"My learning curve in any new role in this company would be much shorter than anyone coming from outside. No matter who is hired for a role, they are going to have to learn their new job."

"That may be true, but that's not how it's done. I'm not trying to be mean here."

"Go on."

I had reached out to one of her colleagues before he began with the firm. He was in a newly created hybrid role overseeing government affairs based in Washington DC. I emailed him to introduce myself and asked if he had considered creating a project role in his new org and if so, if he would consider me for the role. I mentioned my tenure in the department, my good working relationship with the executive offices across the company, my flexibility to travel between DC and NYC as needed, and the projects I had been responsible for in a related group of the department. He never responded. But he had obviously spoken to my manager, his peer but a senior in the department. When I spoke to her about his lack of reply, she became scathing.

"I wouldn't hire you for that role."

Completely taken aback, I stiffly asked, "Why not?"

"Because you don't have any experience on the Hill. In a role like that someone with two to three years' experience in DC would be more practical. They would already know how to get around.

"So an outside person with two to three years' work experience beats my internal ten years? My skills and experience are completely transferable for this."

"Yes."

Moral of the story: as long as I was okay being led by the nose in circles, life was good from the outside. When I confronted the bias and idiotic excuses, all I could see was the outline of the matrix and the cube I was stuck in.

Career mobility was not intended for me. Non-support roles in the executive office were not intended for me. My "superiors" would decide which opportunities I would or would not have access to. It was not for me to impose my career objectives on them.

I was relatively content as an executive assistant until I realized management had decided that's all I would ever be.

∞ ∞ ∞

When your adulation yields nothing for you, is it really worth it? Throughout my life, I've adored several men. Those men adored being adored but none adored me. Nor were they interested in doing anything for me.

A stark comparison would be the years I spent adoring four precious children in my first brownstone apartment. Every time their eyes touched on me in greeting they became screeching jumping beans. Their excitement was palpable. They brought me so much joy, I can't even articulate it. Our adulation was completely reciprocal. They jumped, I jumped. They screeched, I screeched. They were a balm for so many wounds. Their pureness was joy.

My admiration of my managers, colleagues and company got me nowhere. My availability, interest, eagerness, planning, preparation – none of that was worthy of promotional opportunities. Working long hours, logging in on vacation, being ready and available for whatever were expectations of the role I had and salary I received. None of that translated to being seen, respected, appreciated, honored or promoted.

I received occasional treats and pats on the head. I was the recipient of the occasional "thank you" and "you're the best" and quite honestly I was paid extremely well to do a job that kept me seated in front of a computer most of the day. But none of that was fulfilling for any amount of time.

I wasn't growing. I was on a hamster wheel running in place. For the first six years I thought I was working towards something. I had no idea I had plateaued out in year two. When I finally saw that I was running in circles on a hamster wheel inside a cube placed in a larger matrix, I decided to step off the wheel, crawl out the box and escape the matrix.

∞ ∞ ∞

One would think that running in circles within a confined space would make one dizzy. In fact, it's when one comes to a full stop that confusion sets in. While doing what one is supposed to do – what is expected of us – there is a system in place to support those expectations. There is a system in place to suppress a mind that wants to think, a consciousness that wants to wake, a heart that wants to love, a soul that wants to spark life and lungs that want to breathe.

Once you step out the system, your sense are overwhelmed. Restrictive structures become comfortable after a while. You don't have to think beyond your confinement. Repetition is easy. Stepping into a space where one step in front of the other changes your perspective is a shock to your internal systems. Jump starting yourself and your life requires the full expansion and use of your lungs – for every breath. I had been a shallow breather for most of my life. Shallow breaths rarely made noise or moved the body. You can blend into the background with shallow breathing.

Learning to breathe deeply was a chore. I started with counting deep breaths in yoga. Then I started self-regulating with deep breathing. Eventually, experiencing life flowing through me fully and deeply made me a bit arrogant. I started breathing in as much as I wanted for as long as I wanted. You can't do that on a spinning wheel. Only short raspy breaths are possible on a never-ending wheel

∞ ∞ ∞

Disconnecting from New York and its worldly bounties was the beginning of rethinking my life. I did well in the city, but I didn't feel well. I felt like I was losing myself. As if I was disappearing more into nothingness as time passed. Shortly before that fateful conversation with my manager, I had printed out a BitMoji image of me sitting cross-legged in the desert with the words "Vision Quest" arched overheard. I placed it under my keyboard. I knew I was already seeking, but didn't know what I was seeking. The desert was calling.

My mission became finding my true self and creating a life I wanted to nurture my evolving self into. This process required a rethinking of everything. Did I really want what I wanted? Did I truly need what I though were necessities Where id want to live? Why did I want to live there? Where did I want to go and for how long? What did I wan to do while moving about examining myself? As much as I thought I knew myself, I was clueless.

PROVING GROUND

Prove me, O Lord, and try me; test my heart and mind. For your steadfast love is before my eyes, and I walk in faithfulness to you.
~ Psalm 26:2-3

proving ground
an environment that serves to demonstrate whether something, such as a theory or product, really works.

What do you believe about your belief?
- Do you believe you have power over your decisions?
- Do you believe you are enough for your life?
- Do you believe you are capable of doing what needs to be done today?

I have a friend who is going through a tumultuous season with her teenage son. She's a believer who has struggled, like all of us, with understanding how to apply the Word to her life. And how to be the Word in her life. Her focus is selective with an attempt at literal application. Over the years, she has repeatedly missed the same mark. A mark that appears to me to be an easy goal. Simple to achieve. No hardship at all. Her test has been love. Love is her proving ground. Truthfully speaking, love is the proving ground for all of us.

What do you know or understand about love?
- I know if I allow love to have its way in my life, I am *de facto* relinquishing control over where love leads me.

- I know love has nothing to do with romance, lust or physical desires, yet everything to do with one's heart and spirit.
- I know love has nothing to do with me in and of myself while at the same time I am both fully a product and a conduit of love.

I know God is Love. I know that He created a human version of Himself to live among the rest of His creation here on Earth in order to minister to us in our sin, our sorrow, our disappointments, our madness, our bondage, our sickness, and even in our death. Love is so much more powerful than obedience, preferences, plans, lifestyle, ideals, gender, sexuality and doctrine.

Love covers a multitude of sins because love is not diminished by sin. But perhaps love is proved by sin.

Do you love me?
No.
Why not?
Because you hurt me.
Then you never loved me at all.

Hatred stirs up strife, but love covers all offenses.
~ Proverbs 10:12

People who sin against you, violate your trust, hurt your heart, betray your relationship - whatever the trespass may be - are still precious to the Lord. God has not stopped loving the person you turned your back on because they do not live the way you want them to live. He is actually proving to that person that you had no understanding of love at all. You who may have been this person's light and source of love took action to drive them further into darkness instead.

How do you respond when your interpretation of the Bible is challenged by a situation within your own family or friend circles? Do you respond in love, with your heart and spirit projecting the love God gave the world when He offered His Son for His Creation?

Or do you respond in ego, in self, with pride?

Ego
a person's sense of self-esteem or self-importance.

Self
a person or thing referred to with respect to complete individuality; a person's nature, character; personal interest.

Pride
a high or inordinate opinion of one's own dignity, importance, merit, or superiority.

If we believe God IS who He says He Is, then we know His Word is performative. He didn't just tell us about love being gentle, long-suffering, kind, selfless and faithful. He gave us His Spirit of Love from the beginning when He breathed His Life into our lungs. And again, in the middle when He sacrificed His Son, Jesus, to show both obedience to the responsibility of Love and the extreme performance of Love. No one on Earth is worthy to be the Lamb. Not one person. There has never been an alternative to Jesus. No person created has been a potential stand-in cross-bearer for His assignment. Yet Jesus chose to die for us all. Not because we deserve His death, His blood, His concern, or His sacrifice. We didn't then and we don't now. He didn't want to die. Certainly not for a sinning, dying populace. But Jesus too is a product and conduit of Love. He is the Word Love personified. And even He said that those who come after Him will perform greater deeds than He did. Those who believe in Him, will perform Love better than His example. Imagine that!

As you consider Love, evaluate your relationships, especially the strained, difficult ones. In your interactions with the people dear to you, do you represent Love? Are you taking the responsibility of gentleness, kindness, patience, care, sacrifice and faithfulness seriously? Or are you focused only on self - your beliefs, your concerns, your perspective? The bumps and boulders in the road are your tests. Your relationships and daily interactions are your proving ground. If you are alive, it's not too late to take on the responsibility of love and prove yourself the perfect conduit within your circles.

Meditation Verse: John 14:11-12

Believe me that I am in the Father and the Father is in me; but if you do not, then believe me because of the works themselves. Very truly, I tell you, the one who believes in me will also do the works that I do and, in fact, will do greater works than these, because I am going to the Father.

LESSONS FROM LANCE ARMSTRONG[22]

1. Everything done in the dark will eventually come to the light
2. Greed will finish you off more completely than cancer, aging or broken relationships
3. Glory and money can be more seductive than integrity and honor, but they certainly don't last longer.
4. A man is only as good as his word.
5. A man whose word is no good is no good to the world.
6. Image is everything. If a tarnished image is all you have, you don't have much and what you have isn't worth having.
7. People are eager for idols. Some people prefer to hold up one person rather than pull themselves up by the strength of their own dreams.
8. People feel betrayed when their idols fall and break. They would rather glue the idol back together instead of exploring their unreasonable need to aspire to an image created by someone else for someone else.
9. People can only be manipulated to the extent that they want to believe the lie.
10. A man who becomes a brand is not to be trusted. The brand will become bigger than the man. The brand can be bought and sold. Which means the interests of buyers and investors will eventually outweigh the interests of the man. The bottom line for investors and buyers is always money – how much they're putting out and how much they're getting back. It's never character.
11. Don't sell yourself short. You're worth more than ten years in the limelight; ten years of pandering; and ten years of praise. You're worth more than any price you can put on yourself.

Seek God. He will bring you to a greatness that far outshines anything the world has to offer.
12. Without integrity, there is no way to be graceful under fire.

What does it profit a man to gain the world and lose his soul? True question. Real world issue.

PRAYER & A SONG

Waking up with a song in my heart and spirit is the most encouraging things I've experienced in my faith walk.

One late summer night, on the way to my weekly prayer service, I turned left after exiting my office building. Left is the most direct route to the Hudson River Greenway and is opposite my subway train home. I grabbed a CitiBike from the rack in front of the building and began a sunset ride. A mile or two along the Greenway, I pulled over to sit on a park bench to contemplate the setting sun and my barren life. My spirits were low. My heart was heavy. My mind and my body were extremely tired. Eventually, due to the limited time I had the bike share for, I pulled myself from the bench and continued riding until I got to prayer service at church. I was an hour late but just on time for the message: *Ask God to move me beyond freedom into my full purpose in His service.*

Throughout the corporate prayer following the message, communion and praise team wrapping up the evening, I became extremely open and vulnerable. After leaving the church, I walked to Columbus Circle to reflect on the city, people, lights, night, and my life. All I wanted to do was cry.

I dragged myself home and prepped myself for a nice, retching cry to sleep. It didn't come. I was asleep before my head hit the pillow. When I awoke the next morning, the words, *"You are my strength, strength like no other, strength like no other reaches to me"* were flowing through my spirit and humming in my throat. All I could do was give thanks for the song.

I searched the song and was rewarded with William Murphy beginning his recording by encouraging listeners to speak life into themselves. "Say this tonight: *You are my strength. Strength* like no other. Strength like no other. Now lay your hands on yourself and say: *Reaches to me.* The strength of God is reaching for you tonight. [....] Thank you for being so gracious. Thank you for being so kind."

During the prayer service the night before, Pastor Conlon asked "What's keeping you from going that full distance with God? What is it you're afraid of? Are you afraid provision won't be there? Are you afraid your message will be rejected when it's spoken? What causes you to draw back and say, 'Lord use me for your glory... except for this... or that... or this...but for anything else, God, just use me for your glory?'"

"The problem is you want to come out of something, but you don't necessarily want to go *in to* what God has for you. You stop halfway and say, 'I was set free' for the rest of your life, but you don't want to be used of God to set others free."

Meditation Verse: Psalm 18:1-6
I love you, O Lord, my strength. The Lord is my rock, my fortress, and my deliverer, my God, my rock in whom I take refuge, my shield, and the horn of my salvation, my stronghold. I call upon the Lord, who is worthy to be praised, so I shall be saved from my enemies. The cords of death encompassed me; the torrents of perdition assailed me; the cords of Sheol entangled me; the snares of death confronted me. In my distress I called upon the Lord; to my God I cried for help. From His temple He heard my voice, and my cry to Him reached His ears

Sermon: Thoughts on prayer by Pastor Carter Conlon
Listen to: You Are My Strength by William Murphy

GRACE MOUNTAINTOP

THE JOURNEY

The journey is hard and long.
It doesn't get easier
or shorter
by staying where you are.
Get up.
Keep moving.
You'll be glad you did.

HOW DO YOU HANDLE CONTENTMENT?

For a while, I struggled with being content in my blessed state (overflowing cup of grace). I'm used to having *just one more* hurdle, *yet another* obstacle, and *some more* unforeseen challenges to get through before I can breathe easy about a plan, an opportunity or change. Essentially, I'm used to the prize being visible but out of reach or learning to appreciate what I get when I don't get what I want. How would I act if I got what I wanted; if my most earnest prayer was answered? Would I remember that I had asked to be blessed and embrace the responsibility of receiving God's favor and grace with wisdom and gratitude? Or would I lose sight of the blessing and treat God's favor as a common unremarkable thing?

I would like to say without a doubt that recognizing my blessings and receiving them with great appreciation is natural for me. Sadly, I've come to realize my seasons of abundance are when contentment requires as much hard work and focus as perseverance in hardship. It's easy to lose sight of a blessing after it's received. Life doesn't pause in a sunny patch for any length of time. New challenges are steps away.

On the other hand, who can forget the weight of the world when it's weighing them down? No one. Focusing on our difficulties comes naturally. Unfortunately, when we allow ourselves to be consumed by our troubles, we keep ourselves of appreciation and gratitude.

One thought that helps me recalibrate my mindset is: *What would I do if this blessed situation was a difficult problem?*

Immediately, strategic plans for fixing the problem come to mind. There is always something to *do* to eliminate a problem.

But what can be done with a blessing? The most obvious answer is: *Enjoy and share it.* My mind insists there is more to do.

I don't have an established behavioral pattern for when things go really well in my life. The closest situation I can think of is event planning. For many years, I was responsible for planning a conference for my department. Each year, I received praise for excellent execution. Each pat on the back received a smile and, "Thanks… until next time!" While the conference was happening I was taking notes for the next year – what could be changed or improved?

The tendency to immediately jump to the next thing dominated every area of my life until I forced myself to stop, rest and soak in a job well done. The inability or unwillingness to do so signified a deficit of gratitude and thanksgiving in my heart and spirit. Appreciating and honoring completion should be a natural step of a well-executed plan. There should be an engaged experience of something coming to fruition in my life. It is not appropriate to fruit bearing process as an afterthought. The journey is too hard a long not to rest before moving on to the next challenge.

It's nonsensical to labor over a plant and ignore it when it blooms. Yet, in many instances, I had been ignoring my blooms. Growing forward and living an enriched life requires the ability to enjoy the fruit or your labor.

ONCE & FOR ALL

The song *Once and for All* by Laura Daigle cracked open the floodgates to my heart the first time I heard it. From the opening verse... *God I give you what I can today | These scattered ashes that I hid away | I lay it all at Your feet.* to the refrain... *Oh, let this be | Where I die | My Lord with Thee | Crucified |Be lifted high | As my kingdoms fall | Once and for all |Once and for all...* this song enraptures me and puts my spirit into a state of instant praise and prayer.

Father, let me die in You. Pour over me. Don't let me go. Don't leave me to my own devices... my habits of self-destruction. Continue to cleanse me. Purify my heart, My Dear Father. Let this be where I die - with You, crucified and lifted high. Survivor of the world; glorified by Your refining fires.

Pour over me... Let this be where I die... let this moment be the end of me. Help me to release every thought and hope I've held tightly to. Cleanse me of every idea of righteousness and right living. Scrub me of the compromises made from my understanding of who I am in this world. Lead me to my full surrender into your embrace and everything I am becoming.

God I give you what I can today... You know I don't have much - only my hopes, dreams and visions - but I do believe if I give them all back to you they will not remain fruitless dead things. With me, they've turned to ashes without ever taking flight... but You said Your Word does not return to You void. You will flesh out everything I've given back to you. This I do believe.

From the corners of my deepest shame, the empty places where I've worn your name... I tried to be everything I thought I was meant to be only to become no one of value in this world. No one of value to anyone anywhere. What keeps me is my knowledge of You. I'm not so down that I neglect to value who I am in You. I honor who You are in me.

Breathe Your Life into me. Let this be where I come alive.

Amen.

Listen to: *Once & For All* by Lauren Daigle

GETTING BACK UP AGAIN

When I started cycling as a hobby, I didn't have any awareness of the different types of recreational cycling. Riding a bike was pretty much just riding a bike. After a few rides with other cyclists, I learned that my pace is very leisurely – and I like it that way. A couple of riding buddies dropped me quickly because they were literally riding circles around me. They were in it for the speed. I was in for the joy of experiencing the world from a different perspective.

During my first cycling season, I signed up for three touring events. The first one was the forty mile Five Boro Bike Tour in early May. This ride begins in Lower Manhattan near Battery Park, winds uptown through Harlem, cuts across into the Bronx for a quick peek before looping into Queens. From an exploration of several Queens's neighborhoods the cyclists roll *en masse* into Brooklyn passing Borough Hall, cruising along the Navy Yards to the coastline of Bay Ridge on the way to the Verrazano Bridge to cross into Staten Island for the finish line. I fell in love with how much of the City I saw on that first ride. Far more than I had seen at any other point before or since. In mid-September I rode in my second ride, the New York Century. I had signed up for the fifty-five-mile route which was similar to the Five Boro route. Didn't think I would finish but I did. In late September, I rode in my third and final event for that season, Escape New York. The Escape started uptown in Morningside Heights at Sakura Park for a direct line north to the George Washington Bridge for crossing into New Jersey. It was a beautiful day. I got a late start but was confident that I would be able to finish the fifty-mile course I had registered for.

My mom died riding her bike. I had just turned twenty-one and was still having fun with friends that summer. The night she died, I was driving back home to Milwaukee from Great America in Gurnee, Illinois. She was trying to get to a path along Lake Michigan. She thought she was approaching a bridge to the lake front., but instead she rode off of a steep staircase into the night. As her wheels left the ground, she flew off her bike and hit her head when she landed at the bottom of the stairs. She died shortly after at the hospital, before any of the family was notified.

As I rode through New Jersey in the early miles of Escape New York, I had a conversation with God. I haven't really delved into the things I said to Him that day, but I believe I said some horrible things. Oh, how I railed at Him during those early miles!

I thought I was ready to die. I thought I was done with life. I wanted to know why He had taken everybody in the world who had ever loved me and left me here alone. It wasn't right. It wasn't fair. Why was I being punished? This could not be His grand plan for me. What was I missing? A lone woman without a mother, brother, sister, husband or children. A woman with no one to love. What type of life is that? I asked Him to take me.

Then the oddest thing happened around mile eight. I felt a peace come over me. I can't articulate what I received in my spirit, but it was an answer that confirmed life. The Great Comforter was comforting me. I was being embraced and held close. I was receiving all the love I had claimed was absent from my life during my brief broken tirade.

For three miles, I seemed to be chasing sun beams as they danced through the leaves overhead and dazzled houses. I was still enraptured with the twinkling light when an SUV cut in front of me for a right turn at the bottom of downhill slope. There was no room for me to maneuver. Due to my late start, I was the only rider on the street at that moment. For a split second I thought about hopping the curb, but there was a sign post in my way. Running headfirst into a pole seemed less appealing than being ran over by a sports utility vehicle. I stayed my course and in the next second I was rolling full length along the side of the SUV listening to the crunch of my bike as it was ran over and dragged a few feet along the pavement. After rolling off the back of the SUV, I landed on my back without slamming my head on the ground. There was a man tending to his lawn across the street. He witnessed the whole incident, but never moved from his lawn.

The female driver got out her car frantically squealing that she hadn't seen me. Even though she rode up from behind me to cut me off. I managed to sit up and take inventory of my body. I was still alive and nothing seemed to be broken. Two of the event marshals were at my side within a couple of minutes. Their first questions were: "Can you get up?" and "Can you finish the ride?"

It felt as if the peace I had felt for the three miles prior to getting hit had disappeared. The frantic woman pissed me off. The marshals with their cavalier questions irritated me. The unconcerned man watching the scene from his lawn disgusted me. These roiling emotions perhaps provided the fuel I needed to move. Instantly, I was back in my flesh and frustrated over what I didn't have. A great part of me wanted to lay there prone in the street until someone came to lift me up and carry me home. But that's not the type of care or service I receive in life. I'm a big woman and I've noticed throughout life that people expect me to take a lickin' and keep on tickin'. When you're always treated in such a way, you learn to do exactly that. So, I got up.

The police arrived to take a report. They took my bike to their station since I was headed to the hospital via ambulance. I received a clean bill of health with a warning that my body would soon be in excruciating pain. That proved to be very true. After checking out of the Emergency Room, the event service vehicle picked me up, took me to get my bike from the police station, then dropped me off on the New Jersey side of the George Washington Bridge. Apparently, they couldn't ride over the bridge and cross over into New York from New Jersey. So, like a good big girl, I unloaded my bike and rode across the George Washington Bridge into New York City to finish the last five miles of the Escape New York ride upright and peddling. When I got to the finish festival, I lurched over to a bench and sat on it for over two hours. That the last half mile to get home through busy City streets was too difficult to contemplate. By the time I made it home, my body had stiffened to the point that my movements were all jerky. I nearly fell off my bike as I dismounted because I couldn't bend my knee.

That was a day that the deep abiding anger and resentment resurfaced to roost in my soul. I've tried often to get rid of it, but it clings to me in the most unexpected ways.

No one came to see about me. Not my landlord or his wife who lived upstairs. My landlord saw me struggling to dismount and asked what had happened. I told him as I made my way into my apartment and blessed sleep. I posted on Facebook what had happened while I was still at the hospital. On acquaintance sent a text. That represented the extent of my circle.

It seemed my conversation with God had gone full circle that day. I was back to being angry and inconsolable about being alone. Or rather, now I was hurt to realize that I *could have* died and it wouldn't have made any difference to anyone. Everyone I interacted with in my daily life turned out to be the man on his lawn observing my trouble and pain with no real interest.

Folks at work congratulated me for getting up and showing up for work. They were impressed by my fortitude. Which stung me even more, because it implied I could have chosen to wait for someone to come and rescue me. Like, all I had to do was wait for a helping hand to reach down to me. Again, that's not the type of care and concern I receive in life from people. Had I chosen to remain prone in the middle of that New Jersey Street, I would still be there. No one was coming for me. That was abundantly clear when I got home. There was no one to claim me or speak for me in my infirmity. That's a harsh and hard reality I had to come face to face with...and yet, here I am.

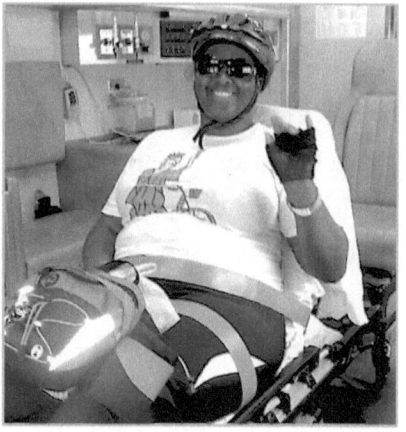

Despite these harsh feelings, the one photo I have from that day is of me strapped on a gurney in the back of the ambulance with a wide smile on my face and a gentle wave at my fingertips. I was amazed when I saw that photo afterwards. Looking at it reminds me the peace I thought had left me when the SUV hit me, was actually still with me.

Our true strength comes from within - from the indwelling Spirit of Christ sustaining us. What you cannot do for yourself, the Holy Spirit will guide and carry you through. This was by far one of the loneliest physical moments of my life, yet I had never been surer of God's presence being with me. In that regard, it was far and away one of the most enlightening moments of my life.

It took a few years to get back on my bike after that. I attempted to hop back on right away, but the trauma was too much for me to overcome immediately. The experience was more debilitating than I could understand or process on my own. There were many false starts to return to cycling. Many of those ended with me sitting on my sofa and staring at my bike with sadness and trepidation. A couple of times I made it out the house.

A couple of years after I got hit, registered for the Five Boro Bike Tour, made to registration on the day of the event and rode twenty-six miles before stopping and heading home. That particular May day, I was actually freezing. Despite having rode twenty-six miles, my knees were locking and my hands were ice-cubes. I hadn't trained that season so my body was not prepared for a long ride. It shut down. I thought I would rest up at the Brooklyn rest stop and hop back on to finish the last fourteen miles. This rest stop was next to a pier directly across from Manhattan.

I walked my bike over to the edge of the pier for a selfie with Manhattan as background. Soon my eyes were tearing up. I don't remember what was going through my mind at that moment, but I remember feeling hopeless, worthless, and unfit for the challenge I had set for myself. I was shaking, shivering. Perhaps I was in shock from forcing my body to ride for miles with locking joints.

While standing on the Brooklyn pier, I was bombarded with the memory of overwhelming feelings. Memory was the true trauma. Remembering my fragility and vulnerability in the harsh callousness of the world. Remembering my solitude. Remembering the onslaught of peace and fearing it wasn't real. That brought the anguish.

If I could overcome all my pain, perhaps I would begin to believe I didn't need anyone at all. Sadly, I wanted to need people. I didn't want to be an island. Yet there I stood looking across the East River at one of the greatest islands in the world. Manhattan. A global center of finance, fashion, entertainment, real estate, culture and fear. Manhattan. An island festering with all its vices, exporting its overflow and importing more daring troubles. Seeing myself as Manhattan didn't bring joy; it added to my trauma.

I went home and sat on the sofa for another couple of years.

∞ ∞ ∞

Two years after freezing up on the Five Boro, I decided I was done wimping out on the sidelines. At the time my office was in Midtown East and I lived in East Harlem. The distance between office and home was an easy four miles. No problem. I hyped myself up and believed the hype. One beautiful autumn morning, I walked into the bike room and pulled down my bike. Pumped my tires and hopped on for a revitalizing commute to work.

When I had walked across town with my neighbor to her prayer hall, I noticed a bike lane on Second Avenue, three avenues to the east of my apartment building off of Park Avenue. My office was on Park Avenue, so in theory the bike ride should be a straight shot downtown with only a little bit of cross town action. What's wrong with theories? They aren't fact.

That commute turned out to be devastating and traumatic. The bike lane I had seen was less than a mile long after I got on it. From there I zigzagged across avenues and weaved through narrow barricaded lanes while also leap frogging busses. Construction of the Second Avenue subway was in progress and to say that drivers were irate would be an understatement. I didn't feel safe. There was no space for cyclists to ride alongside cars in the construction zone. I headed west towards Central Park in an effort to ride around the construction zone. I was deterred by steep hills and long buildings straddling blocks. Circled back to Lexington Avenue, a high-traffic street for pedestrians, cars, busses and subway stops. Essentially getting to work that day was a challenge beyond anything I expected. But I made it. I was reluctant to ride home but more adamant about not giving in the fear again. I modified the route home and rode up through Central Park. That ride was soothing enough to relieve me of the morning's anxiety.

Still it took another few weeks before I got on my bike again. This time for a Black Girls Do Bike group ride. It took place on a crisp, clear day in early December. *Black Girls Do Bike* (BGDB) is an organization of women cyclists who ride at the pace of their slowest rider with the idea that no woman is left behind. The group ride was amazing, invigorating and freeing! We rode from Midtown Manhattan to Brooklyn for a book event. What a great way to combine two of my loves!

During the ride, I learned that BGDB was participating in the American Diabetes Association Tour de Cure Atlanta. The event was scheduled for the coming June. I immediately signed up to ride in the event, which also turned out to be my first fund-raising event.

This was the spark and the goal I needed to keep getting back on my bike and to keep moving forward.

A month or so after riding with BGDB, my company moved down to Tribeca. My four-mile commute turned into an eight mile ride. At this point, it had been over four years, or four full cycling seasons, since I had gotten hit by the SUV and became a stranger to my bike.

Thank God for His sparks!

After settling into the new office, I kick started my physical fitness goals by signing up with a personal trainer at the company gym. I was five months into my fortieth year and my life was nothing like what I would have envisioned if I were able to envision myself beyond forty. My weight was abysmal and depressing. My skin hadn't been clear since I moved to New York City and it wasn't likely to snap back at this point.

All my life, I've been criticized for my height, weight and general size. As a result, since I developed body consciousness, I've been attempting to alter my body. I began dieting in earnest at the age of seventeen. At the time, I was nothing but muscle on bone with some fatty tissue on top and in the back. I was worrying the scale because I wanted to join the Navy. According to the recruiter, I was overweight. I needed to lose ten pounds. In high school I participated in sports year round. My primaries were basketball and track and field. I also played tennis and softball. During the sports seasons, I worked out five days a week on average. It was at the peak of this youthful fitness that I was first told that I was overweight.

It was hard for me to reconcile that concept, but I tried. I stopped eating in an effort to lose those elusive ten pounds. When I cheated on my no-food diet, I tried eating grapefruits only. When I got sick of the grapefruits, I tried bagels only. I didn't care for bagels at the time, so that was the last straw. I gave up on joining the Navy and decided to attend DePaul University instead.

My current weight is nearly one hundred and twenty pounds more than my first overweight diagnosis. I didn't begin feeling overweight until about fifty pounds ago. I wonder how I would have handled my body differently had I not been infected by other people's opinions about my weight. Perhaps I wouldn't have been in denial about my weight gain for so long. Or perhaps I would look at my current round lushness with more appreciation. Who knows? The sad truth is now, I finally see a bit of what the recruiter, the doctors, the not-so-loving relatives who have called me fat or looked at me with discuss while on the scale, saw. Although I don't look at myself as some blob of fat, as a couple of doctor's looks have suggested thoughts along that line, I do see an overly generous form that could stand to lose some pounds. At the same time, I also see my best body to come inside of the frame I'm walking around in now. More often than not, I look at myself with curiosity... and wonder. *Is this as big as I'm going to allow myself to get? How did I get this large, round and wide? What would it take for me to get motivated to get moving on a consistent basis? Have I had enough of not feeling like myself?*

There have been some good excuses over the years for not keeping to an active schedule. That autumn morning when I battled traffic and leaped frogged busses to get to work was the beginning of a renaissance. It wasn't instant and it hasn't remained constant, but the spark is there. There's a light flickering in me, urging me not to give up on myself. Waiting for me to expel all my fear and ignite into an explosion of light and life.

During the initial consultation with the personal trainer, Xuan, she asked about my eating habits and workout routine. I didn't mind sharing. I had been cleaning up my food intake for years, though I continue to have an incorrigible sweet tooth. I had also been sporadically active over the years so working towards a goal wasn't a problem. In response to her question, I said, "I used to be an athlete. It's just a matter of getting back into a routine."

To her credit, Xuan didn't look doubtful. She said only, "We'll schedule an assessment for next week. I would like to see how your body moves."

The morning of my physical assessment Xuan, I surprised myself by waking up before my alarm and getting out of bed an hour earlier than my norm. I got ready in record time. Even better, I remembered to pack work clothes *and* grabbed a water bottle. I made the 8:00AM appointment on time – with energy. The biggest shock was that I wasn't dragging.

I used to be a morning person, too. New York City has a way of beating you down. Not on purpose. Indirectly, under the guise of "the good life." There's so much stimuli in the City that it's hard for a brain to stop calculating life variables and simply relax. In addition to that, there's so much to do, that one's down time, i.e. after work hours, usually becomes a speed race to do as much as possible on the home front or simply zone out on the sofa. You're either at full speed or no speed.

Unfortunately for me, I've been at no speed for a while. Over the last couple of years, it has become harder and harder to drag myself out of bed in the morning no matter how much sleep I managed the night before. My days offered very little to look forward to. Until I had a personal training appointment.

Xuan lit a fire in me. She recognized and connected with something in me that very few people see and acknowledge. "You've proved that you used to be an athlete," she said at the end of the first session, "I can see it in your form and the way you move."

Another thing I've received all my life are compliments on my form and posture, so I didn't take her words as false flattery at all. I responded, "Luckily for me, the body remembers. Yay, muscle memory! I just have to get myself moving."

"Yes, muscle memory. The body does remember. Working out is just like riding a bike too."

Halfway through the assessment, Xuan observed, "You need a sergeant. Someone to push you. You are capable of so much more than you think. I'm really impressed with you."

Cue warm fuzzy feelings

Her physical assessment was a full body workout for me which included: various lunges and squats with and without weights, deadlifts (from bar only to 20 lbs. then 50 lbs. added), push-ups, sit-ups, planks and deep stretches. I'm not a profuse sweater, but she had my forearms and forehead dripping in the thirty-five minutes I was with her. She actually impressed me.

My overall goal for jump-starting my fitness was so I could return to cycling with a prepared body. A body that was conditioned and trained for vigorous activity. Finally, there was determination to conquer the beast and ride it into the sun. In order to do so, it was necessary to set aside the fear and anxiety of sharing the road with motorists and put myself back into the flow of traffic. I added a layer by commuting to work a couple of days a week that spring.

After riding a mile and a half across town in heavy traffic, I hit the Hudson River Greenway. By this point, I refused to be intimidated by traffic, aggressive drivers and huge buses. The payoff for my effort was seven miles of car-free joy along the tree-lined Hudson River, from Harlem to Tribeca, to the back door of my office building. For the weekends, I invited co-workers and neighbors to ride North on the Greenway to explore hidden treats in that direction. I mapped out cycling events for the year and signed up for most of them.

Eventually, my momentum and enthusiasm waned. I didn't beat myself up because I had gotten off my butt and rocked out for most of the year. I had taken the time to focus on my body, my health, my energy and stress levels. I reengaged with myself. I wooed myself. Challenged myself. Exposed the hidden things and kicked them out of myself. Then I moved on.

∞ ∞ ∞

By the time I got gun-ho about cycling, I had missed the registration period for the Five Boro Bike Tour. The forty-mile route is a car-free scenic tour though all of New York City – Manhattan, the Bronx, Brooklyn, Queens and Staten Island. Not to be deterred, I signed up for the first NYC ride event of the season, *Bike the Boros: Staten Island*. It was a mid-April ride which allowed two months' recovery time before the *Tour de Cure Atlanta* I had already signed up for.

Bike the Boros: Staten Island ride offered two routes – 35 and 50-mile loops around Staten Island. Since I hadn't been training, 35 miles was the safest option. It also sounded like a great replacement for the Five Boro ride I had missed. Unfortunately for me, I had never explored Staten Island, so I was unaware of its very hilly landscape. I kept an event journal during the ride so I could look back on how I handled my return to cycling.

> **7:00-9:00 AM** *Today is the day. I got up, got prepped and got out. The ferry ride to Staten Island was uneventful. Now waiting for the day to unfold and see how I handle the 35-mile route.*
>
> **9:40 AM** *Made it to registration before they closed down at 9:30. Hit the road at 9:40.*
> **11:00-11:25 AM** *First rest area at 12miles. Already exceeded my expectations!! I was ready to exit the route by mile 3. Staten Island is hilly! Who knew?!?!?*

I am super proud of myself for pushing through the hills and making it to the first rest stop. Making it to the first rest stop usually means you can make it to the second. And once you make it to the second rest stop you're pretty much done. #crossingmyfingers

12:30-1:00 PM Second rest stop @ mile 24. Made it. I was seriously looking for the exit 4 miles back. This hill was literally the last straw! Then I looked at my route sheet and saw that I was only 4 miles away from the rest stop. I sat on a retaining wall for a while catching my breath and gathering my strength to tackle an extremely steep hill. Ended up walking my bike up it instead. Then got back on. It's important to always get back on.

The downhill on the other side of the steep uphill was a mix of reward and terror. Like: a little bit of "Oh yay! Downhill!" and a whole lot of "Oh shit! This is treacherous!" It was a steep, winding downhill road with no shoulder to speak of, two-way traffic with a lot of pot holes, a couple of stop signs peppering the decline and a couple of hairpin sharp turns coming off the hill thrown in for good measure. Not for the faint of heart! Who knew that was coming!?

2:23 PM Finish line! I did it.

Pretty much from the beginning of the ride, I was ready to give up. Even before the ride. I had to talk myself into showing up. I didn't prep the night before as I should have. Prepping in the morning delayed my departure. I almost missed registration and the opportunity to ride with any group of riders. Getting to the start line required a forty-minute subway ride, a mile and a half of cycling across town and a half hour ferry ride.

The commitment is certainly in the start, perhaps that's why it's so hard to begin something. By starting and not giving up when the course proved to be harder than I expected, or had trained for, I achieved my first goal of the ride: make it to the first rest stop.

At no point before I started, did I plan on or expect that I would finish the 35 miles I signed up for. Even at the first rest stop, I was telling myself I could stop at 20 miles and I would be okay with that. I was about to throw my hat in when I saw the crazy hill. Then I looked at my cue sheet. The second rest stop was only four miles away. *I can do four more miles!*

The rest stops are where cyclists are able to get off their bikes, breathe, use the restroom, refill on water, eat (usually fresh fruit, bagels, and granola; sometimes PBJ sandwiches and other goodies or bagged lunches). Rest stops are crucial for necessary refueling. When riders return to the course, they are better than fresh – they have a tempered second wind and fluid, warmed-up muscles and tendons.

As I got up from my breather at the bottom of that monster hill I was ready to call a taxi. In fact, I saw people turning back and getting into cars. What helped me was finding out how close I was to a rest stop. I knew if I made the second rest stop, I could finish the course. I didn't see the end until I was close to it. Focusing on the step in front of me is what got me through the whole challenge. I think this is true for most things in life.

GIVE THANKS FOR WHAT YOU'VE BEEN DELIVERED FROM

Give thanks for what you have been delivered from because none of us know the depth of our capacity for depravity. This is good because the burden of knowing would be too great. I've been seasoned and scorched by touches of evil within my own family. So much so, that even before I began my walk with God, I petitioned Him constantly to release me from the generational bondage, sins, oppressions, chains, curses – whatever you want to call the things that seem embedded in family DNA. I prayed and begged to be released. I prayed that the children He would allow me to bare would never be touched by what degenerated generations of relatives and ancestors before them.

In the beginning, my prayers weren't elaborate. They weren't long or scripture based. After all, I began praying before I read or understood anything in the Bible. I simply prayed for deliverance from what I knew. I was a product of a family steeped in sexual violence – rape and child molestation, physical and emotional abuse of partners and children. I witnessed nonchalance and inaction by those not directly attacked as they berated victims for not "getting over" being violated. Through a season of homelessness with my immediate family, I was confronted with hopelessness, carelessness, hatefulness, neglect and misery. I also knew how all the negatives were hidden from as many as possible behind charm, smiles, laughter, nice clothes and clean houses. I knew that silence – not talking about any of the horrible abuses – protected the abusers. But I also knew enough to pray for protection from God, whom I instinctively believed to be larger than my troubles and circumstances.

I knew I wanted to be delivered from it all. I wanted to be saved. I wanted to live free from fear.

My continual prayer is one of thanksgiving for being delivered from what I knew and everything I had (and have) no knowledge of. I am eternally grateful for the care and provision my life has been blessed with. I am extremely grateful for my awareness of God's glory, grace and mercy – and so amazed that He saw fit to not just hear me, but to answer me and take me beyond my request.

Many people see injustice and abuse and choose to not to confront the abuser. Bystanders have many excuses, chief among them is "it's not my business." The bottom line is bystanders are cowards. They are selfish and lack compassion. This statement covers equally those who watch violence unfold in their homes and stay quiet. As well as those bear witness of populations of people being oppressed and hold their heads down. No one can save the world, but each of us can chip in to make a portion of the world we inhabit a little bit better.

To God be the glory, honor and power forever.

THANK YOU, LORD.

Thank You, Lord
For bringing me to this point today.
Thank You for not leaving me where You last placed me.
Thank You for keeping me and loving me.
Thank You for peace.
Thank You for the storms.
Thank You for the fire and cleansing.
Thank You for pain and healing.
Thank You for my assignment.
Thank You for the many battles in this warring world.
Thank You for rest.
Thank You for victory,
Amen.

HARVEST LESSON: LOVE ANYWAY

1. People's judgment of me is not my issue.
2. Rejection has never broken me, nor will it ever.
3. The world's example of love is not the love I live by.
4. Grace is not an excuse for wrong behavior.
5. Mercy is not a free ticket to take people for granted.
6. When God dwells within, not only are you unbreakable, you're also unstoppable.
7. My heart may lead me wrong, but God will not. He always brings me back to where I need to be.
8. I may not always be right, but with my heart set on God, I know He'll work everything out for my good.
9. Faith, hope, and love remain. Love is the greatest, but each is co-dependent.
10. I am a blessing to everyone I encounter. You too are a blessing. We may not realize it or act like it, but it is a fact.
11. When God pruned and weeded people out of my life, the desire to chase after them disappeared. I've learned to allow Him to perform His Word.
12. I believe in God. I am not God. My response to being mistreated may not resemble your idea of love, grace or mercy, but God has tempered me.
13. My walk with God is unlike anyone else's. It's okay if other people don't understand me or my process, they are a similar mystery to me.
14. Solitude and loneliness have strengthened me in ways I never imagined.

15. In my solitude, I've been eagerly willing to obey God. In my quietness, I've my faith has increased, my joy has spread, and my self-awareness has deepened.
16. Being alone is hard, but it's also the best way to hear God clearly and intimately.
17. A pure heart is better than good intentions.
18. Intentions without action aren't worth talking about.
19. When I grow up... wait... I am grown, and still growing.
20. Those who hide themselves will entice you to live in the shadows with them. Hug tightly to the light.
21. The brighter your light shines, the more opposition you attract. Resist hiding your light. Your opposition will disappear.
22. People will resent your light. Shine anyway.
23. Once you commit to being your best self, you'll attract people eager to provoke the worst out of you. Commit to being better anyway. Resisting adversaries will strengthen you.
24. The most destructive adversaries are those closest to us. Resist the darkness within your circles and yourself.
25. Friends and family will attempt to sabotage your walk. Keep moving forward; they will fall to the wayside eventually.
26. Abusers will cry loudest about your lack of charity when their abusiveness is confronted. Confront them anyway.
27. Every attack of the enemy is intended to destroy your faith. Resist. Stand firm. Then continue moving forward.
28. A jerk by any other name is still a jerk... even when they claim Jesus and quote scripture.

29. When your faith flounders and doubt overwhelm you, hold on to whatever you can until you get through. You will be refreshed.
30. People will ridicule your faith. Build your faith anyway.
31. I may not be better than my haters, but their envy is confirmation that I make better choices.
32. People will hate you. Let them. They cannot deny your greatness.
33. The biggest challenges in your life are all the same lesson presented in various degrees, dimensions and perspectives. Get knowledge. Get understanding. Evolve.
34. Wanting the best for someone isn't as important as them wanting the best for themselves.
35. We are all free to live as we want. Make sure your free will doesn't contradict or shame your faith.
36. It's essential to let God do His crippling work in your heart and spirit. His processes will disable the power of sin in your life.
37. People will take advantage of your kindness. Be kind anyway.
38. Anger, exhaustion and disappointment are part of the journey. So are rest and recovery.
39. The last person standing has no one to lean on. Don't worry. God has you.
40. When you can encourage yourself, the lack of encouragement from others is not devastating.
41. Bitterness may occasionally overwhelm you. Immerse yourself in sweetness

42. Living for Christ is a process I hope to get right one step at a time.
43. You will grow exceedingly weary. Rest as needed.
44. God sacrificed His Firstborn Son. He understands pain and struggle.
45. I am a creation of the Most High. He is my shield.
46. Jesus wept. He understands sorrow.
47. Jesus loved. He understands longing.
48. Joy-stealers will remark on your fallen countenance. Keep radiating joy and shame the thieves.
49. Your joy will be attacked. Rejoice anyway.
50. Your love will often be rejected. Love anyway.

WHERE CAN I DO THE MOST GOOD?

Over time, receiving little to nothing in response to my giving and openness has led to a distancing of my heart from the giving and services I offer. During the Christmas holiday shortly before my Granddad died, I received a request to help a young mother who had also just lost her mother. I sent a check without really thinking about it. The outpouring of gratitude from the young woman for something that didn't take much effort on my part stung my sleeping, giving heart.

I responded in gratitude to her gratitude and that series of exchanges warmed the coldness that had taken up residence in my heart.

During the exchange, my emotional prayerful response was to say and write, "Where can I do the most good, Father? Lead me there, Lord, please."

My thoughts were consumed at the time with a grander gesture I had made a few days prior – a day of travel for a few minutes at my granddaddy's sickbed that was harshly attacked and ridiculed by his youngest daughter, my aunt. I wasn't actually trying to make a grand gesture – my heart was set on speaking life over his departure. However, when weighed next to mailing a check to an unknown recipient, there is obviously more effort in the former act. Yet, it was the latter that received the most gracious response. It was the graciousness of the response that humbled me. My heart has not been fully committed to my giving endeavors for quite some time. To be able to see two different scales of giving in both personal and impersonal situations provided a space to learn and evaluate my heart as well as how it's impacted by the response to the fruit it bears.

I fully and thankfully receive the Christ in the call, the message and the process. Humbly, I submit to you to consider giving where your gift(s) may make the most difference. A small consideration for you may impact another's life greatly. In this process and cycle of giving and receiving, both parties experience God's abundant supply.

Meditation Verse: 1 Chronicles 29:14-18
"These things did not really come from me and my people.
Everything comes from You;
we have given You back what You gave us.
We are like foreigners and strangers, as our ancestors were.
Our time on earth is like a shadow. There is no hope.
Lord our God, we have gathered all this to build your
Temple for worship to You. But everything has come from
You; everything belongs to You. I know, my God, that You
test people's hearts. You are happy when people do what is
right. I was happy to give all these things, and I gave with an
honest heart. Your people gathered here are happy to give
to You, and I rejoice to see their giving. Lord, You are the
God of our ancestors, the God of Abraham, Isaac, and
Jacob. Make Your people want to serve You always, and
make them want to obey You.

Listen to: I Surrender by Psalmist Raine

MY CENTER

Thank you for continually
bringing me back
in a world without
permanence
or true connection.
I am constantly returned
to my center,
to You, My Father,
My Mother, My Creator
My Being.

I'M 41, WTF

I'm 41 – what the *bleep*! Officially, my *Turning 40, A Year of Wonder-filled Living* has come to an end. Unofficially, I'm still exploring the idea of wonder-filled living.

As I write, I'm standing at the top of Frederick Douglass Circle which is basically the entry into West Harlem from the Upper West Side. Some folks have been referring to this area are South Harlem but prefer just Harlem. The namesake of the circle is Frederick Douglass and his contribution to the American story is represented with a lovely statue in a round-about at Central Park North at Eighth Avenue. It's a nice cross section to enjoy the pace of the City.

I don't' know what I want to talk about, but I know I'm feeling good.

I'm in transition. This year was transition. This year was a celebration of where I was, where I'm going and just *being*. Being who I am. Experiencing the moment, experiencing life. Being content with who I am, where I am and how I am. It's been quite a year full of processes. Full of life. **Yay** for turning 40! *Rah! Rah! Rah!*

BALANCE OF LIFE

My 41st birthday was also spent alone. It was planned to be so, but even if that hadn't been the case, it probably would've still been so. That's the route my life has taken. It was quite a pleasant day. There were no expectations of anyone showing up or providing entertainment or sustenance or anything. Therefore, there was no disappointment. There was only relaxation and satisfaction in my own company. That was a great boon. It was also a great way for me to acknowledge that this is essentially my life. It's something I need to embrace and stop trying to avoid and change.

For example, the weekend following my birthday, I planned on riding in *Summer Streets*, an annual biking event that closes Park Avenue to traffic from 72nd Street to City Hall for three Saturday mornings in August. The streets are available for recreational use from 7:00am-1:00pm during those days. It is one of my favorite events in the City. I invited someone to share the ride with me. I missed the whole event trying to accommodate her. She didn't want to get up early so she asked if we could meet at 10:00. Then 11:00am. At that point, I knew it wasn't likely that she'd show up, so I told her I would meet her at 53rd and Park where a lot of activities were set up. I waited in the area for her for over an hour because she kept saying she was on her way. Then it started down pouring. By the time the rain slowed down a bit, the streets were being opened again. That was the last Saturday of the event and the only one I had been able to make and I missed it because I was hoping to share it with someone. During the time I spent waiting for her I could have ridden the full course and been on my return uptown. Essentially, inviting someone into my favorite pastime, led to me missing out on it.

This has been a common occurrence in my life. People generally don't say they don't want to or they aren't interested. They prefer to lead you on and waste your time.

It has taken a long time to accept that it's always better when I spend time by myself and do things that I enjoy by myself. I no longer wait for people. I keep moving and let them know where they can intersect with me.

That being said, my fortieth year was a wonderful. I never thought I'd turn forty as a single woman with no children. Despite that area of sadness in my life, there's bounty. I have a well-paying job that covers my housing, food and hobbies – cycling, photography and travel. It's a good life. This is what I have. This is the life I'm the steward of. These are the blessings I've been given to walk in and I will continue to do so.

Maybe occasionally, due to loneliness, I may forget how good God has provides for me, but like clockwork, folks remind me why I enjoy my solitude when they enter my space.

I'm grateful to be able to see them out and rebalance my energy.

PAINT & PRAISE: YOUR BLESSINGS REQUIRE WORK!

This last year has consisted of several transitions. All big deals. One transition is moving from New York City to Tucson, AZ. I began the process nearly two years ago and I'm now approaching the final curtain call on my time in NYC. For the last week I've been painting and prepping my Harlem apartment for viewing and sale.

The year has been extremely busy. Who knew "leaving New York" a year ago wouldn't be the end of my time in New York? Flying back and forth between New York and Arizona every few weeks – closing out one life and starting up another left me frazzled. I was so consumed with getting things done, I spent little time sitting at Jesus's feet or otherwise soaking in the Word.

The year was full of running here and there, doing this and that, thinking through scenarios, trying new things, letting go of everything that doesn't work, quitting my job in NYC, moving across the country, looking for work in Tucson, returning to NYC to manage issues, taking a summer temp job in NYC, starting a national call for submissions for a new book project (*I AM WOMAN: Expressions of Black Womanhood in America*), launching a pro photographer career, etc. Just stuff. But this week, enclosed in the four walls of my East Harlem apartment, painting and prepping it for sale, the transition became a concrete change. This process was near completion. There's very little else to do on my end. The to-do lists have stopped clamoring in my head. It was just me, the walls, and gospel music.

And God. He just came on in.

I've been assuring people there's nothing I will miss about NYC once I left. Leaving my apartment hasn't been particularly sentimental as I didn't think I had any special memories in it. I didn't want to return. In fact, I was quite despondent for a few weeks when I got back to the City. The peace of the desert was simply glorious.

Over the last few days, God has reminded me why my time in New York City has been sacred. I've long considered it to be on-the-job-training for whatever God has in store for me. This is the place He chose to bring me to an understanding of *Who HE IS* and *Who I AM in HIM*. He's been romancing me this week. Gently walking me down memory lane. What a wonderful blessing this place has been!

Sometimes all we remember are the hardships or the sour taste difficulties leave in our mouth. I know I'm blessed, but I rarely think on the many ways God has blessed my life. I remember the many hardships. I recall how He's brought me through each of them. I praise Him for all that. But the intricacies and intimacies are forgotten. He reminded me that He doesn't only perform His Word when I call on Him. His Word is performing in my life every moment of every day. He is present always. He wanted this time with me. He wanted to end this season the way we began - with me looking to Him, focusing on Him and His Word. Seeking His guidance and instruction every morning into the evening.

The last few days have been sprinkled with spontaneous worship and deeply moving intercessory prayer. I didn't see any of it coming. But I know it has all been by His design.

∞ ∞ ∞

Two nights prior, I was sitting on the futon in the empty apartment. I sat there and looked at the whole apartment from the vantage point where I could see every single room in the unit. I sat there and tears came to my eyes. God was reminding me of His all-consuming goodness.

I cried out: "My God! My God! Your promises have carried me such a long way! You've stayed with me. You've blessed me. Absolutely everything You have done for me – every challenge, every obstacle, every blessing, every overflowing goodness, you brought my way – You have been there with me through it all! You have held me up. You have guided me. You took me into places I never even imagined going, never even thought I would even want, and you brought me out of those same places when I realized those were not the things that I needed. They weren't the blessings I was looking for!" You didn't leave me. You didn't punish me. You let me figure it out and escorted me out. Thank You, Father God, in the name of Jesus!"

Throughout the week, I tackled the task of painting my whole apartment from the floor to the nine-foot ceilings and across the ceiling in each room. It was such a huge undertaking! Luckily, it's a job done well, if I do say so myself!

It did cross my mind to pay for help, however the price was prohibitive. It didn't make sense to pay an arm and a leg for something I could technically do and had the time to do.

God is so good; He preps me for everything before I know what's coming.

While I was painting last night, *Trust In You* by Anthong Brown and Group Therapy came on. The song broke me open. I broke down and started praising and worshipping God. The praise break lasted for a couple of songs. That moment was on my mind the next morning.

I had to begin painting with the song. Following that urging, the Spirit moved me to share: *Every single blessing God brings your way requires work. Your labor investment secures your bounty.*

We are not blessed in vacuums, where we're sucking things in and giving nothing back.

Our blessings are more than a checkmark on something God has done for us.

God is in the business of working everything for our good according to His purposes. As He continually performs His Word, He keeps moving us forward.

As I worked my back to clean, paint, and prepare my apartment, it was with the sure knowledge that I'm entering a new stage of life. Nothing I've ever done has been in vain.

As I prepare my final exit from New York City as a resident, the thought top of mind is how much work blessings require.

God has called us to work upon this earth, to do good things in his name. I'm not saying property is a good thing. However, He blesses us with things to improve our lives, to improve our walks, to improve our journey. It is incumbent upon us to obey and to observe what he's doing to us, for us, in us, and all around us!

Knowing this, the human in me stood in that apartment, telling God He gave me too much work. Or he blessed me too much! Why did I have to perform hard physical labor to walk into my next thing?

The rebel in me considered hiring help again.

Then He reminded me of our intimacy, of our history. I arrived in New York with only God. He brought me full circle; showed me the end of this cycle was leaving with Him as well.

God has imbued me with so much confidence in His presence in my life, I can step to every challenge with absolute certainly He will carry me through.

Yes, I'm doing good work, but I'm not getting by on my skill or knowledge or education. It's all by God's goodness, grace and mercy!

Our blessings require work! Find the work in your blessing. Produce something good. Our prosperity may not look like what we think it should. It may not feel the way we want it to feel. But we can rest assured God will bless us with everything life needs.

BOUNTY IN THE DESERT

New York has not been a desert that has completely killed my hope, but it has killed a lot of things in my life. It has processed me through letting go of a lot of unnecessary things. The process was necessary, as was the letting go. How appropriate that this portion of my journey ends in the verdant forest near the top of a desert mountain, viewing a valley below and reflecting on the lowest point of my life... which was also the most productive part of my life. Spiritually productive. Financially productive. Physically productive. Intellectually productive. I have grown so much in New York City. I have learned how to fight spiritually. I have learned how to stand spiritually. I have learned how to pray spiritually. I've learned how to think, live, exist. I have explored my spirit fully in New York City. Even though Tucson is technically in a desert, it represents abundant opportunity to live more freely and fully as myself. It is where I believe I am being lead to next. It is where I will continue to prosper in all things God brings into my life. It's amazing that He would bring me to the top of a mountain in the desert and there's nothing but greenery. There's nothing but lushness. There's nothing but beauty. There's nothing but His creative glory. This is so amazing to me, so very amazing. I hope you understand my words are not enough to do justice to the paradox of nature.

In the same frame of sight, I see the dry desert at the foot of the mountain and lush forest above. There's a sky lodge near the top of Mount Lemmon, Ski Valley. It is the southernmost sky lodge in the United States and receives about 180 inches of snow annually. Tucson's average annual temperature 70.9 degrees. I didn't know that skiing was possible so far south in Arizona. It gets really cold at 8000 feet. In fact, it was about thirty degrees cooler at that elevation when I drove up than it was in town. As much as I love the dry heat of the desert, I love my seasons. Witnessing the spectacular color change of trees in autumn is like a visual symphony. Knowing that I will be a short drive away from enjoying everything I love about seasonal change in the Midwest and Northwest without leaving home for more than a few hours is evidence of the gentle way my Heavenly Father curates my life. I've always loved having snow for the holidays and He has picked a city for me to move to that has access to everything I love about nature.

Father God, I thank You for Your gentle unfolding of next steps.

MOUNTAINTOP PERSPECTIVE

While in Geneva, Switzerland during my fortieth birthday celebration, I visited Mont Salève, aptly called the balcony of Geneva, even though it is technically in France. The 4524 feet mountain in the French Pre-Alps range provides an amazing panoramic view of Lake Geneva and its surrounding city. I knew none of this when I arrived in Geneva. I was simply looking for something to do on a free afternoon. After visiting the United Nations Headquarters, seeing Geneva from above seemed like the best use of my time. I arrived at the bottom of the mountain shortly before the cable car service ended, with enough time to get up the mountain and make a video message expounding on the transformative power of God's mercy and grace from whatever perspective we are viewing our life from. From below or from up high, the problem may not change, but how you tackle it will.

Unfortunately, the audio on the video I made at the top of Mont Salève was ruined. I had an amazing word come through me that was powerful and received by me also. It was a study on perspective.

Over a year later, near the top of another mountain in Tucson, Arizona that message returned to me.

I abruptly decided to visit Tucson to scout as my next hometown. One of the days, I drove up Mount Lemmon which is about 9000 feet high. I must say that I have a consternation for heights. I don't like the idea of being afraid of anything, so for heights, I'll simply say, I'm not fond of them. In this instance, I was determined to drive up the mountain for the message I knew was waiting for me.

Perspective. Looking at the valley below, I saw many dark shadowy spots. Each one covered blocks or miles. Looking up, I saw many fluffy white clouds floating overhead. In the natural, soft and fluffy shouldn't translate to dark and shadowy. From the ground, clouds simply provide shade. You know this, even though you can't pinpoint which cloud is providing what. However, from above, you can see that clouds don't cover much and you can literally connect a cloud in the sky to a shape on the ground. That's pretty amazing and very interesting. Our imagery, use and understanding of something changes with our perspective and experience of it.

When I was flying through the clouds on the flight from New York City to Tucson, I was able to also see that when I was flying through the clouds, I saw the clouds make dots on the landscape below. That too was a beautiful sight to see. I'm stunned by the majesty and interconnectedness of everything. I'm enthralled by God's grace, His creativity and His mercy. His beauty. His provision. Such a lushness in the desert. How amazing is that? Such a lush green valley in the middle of the Sonoran Desert in Southern Arizona. Think on that. What won't He do for you? He will hydrate your dry places. Feed your hunger. Light your darkness. Cover you from over exposure.

God's provision is beyond our understanding, but not beyond our ability to accept what He provides for us. All we have to do is be willing, be open and be receptive. Willingness, openness and receptiveness will allow so much blessing to pour into our lives. We will have more than we need, more than we ever thought we could receive, more than our greatest imaginings. God's provision grants all that. Wow.

BEAUTIFY YOUR DESERT

I am at an elevation of 8,000 feet, near the top of Mount Lemmon in Tucson, Arizona. At 9,157 feet, Mount Lemmon has the tallest peak in the Catalina Mountain range, one of five ranges ringing Tucson, nestled in the valley below.

I am amazed. I had read about the different climates and different vegetation going up the mountain, but seeing provides a whole different level of believing, understanding and appreciating. As I traveled up the mountain, the lower part is what you would expect to see in a desert – sparse and dry vegetation, mostly cacti dotting the foothills. At the top of the mountain, the traveler is greeted with the lush, vibrant populous beauty of evergreen pine trees – an actual forest of alpines and aspens. It brought to mind a conversation with an old friend a couple years ago when she was thinking about making major life changes. She lamented on how difficult it is to move the mountains in her life. My blurted response to her was, "If you can't move your mountain, beautify it." That phrase has been going through my head for some time.

If our life is a mountain, how do we beautify our life? How do we change the things in us that seem insurmountable? Unchangeable, chained down? Burdened? Horrible? Explicit? Hopeless? How do we change those things? Mount Lemmon is an illustration of change. It's an illustration of process and metamorphosis. In a physical diagram you can drive along, it shows life-sustaining differences at various levels of elevation. Human beings are able to sustain different types of life at different points of throughout our life. I could see that clearly on the mountain. It's not realization that's easy to hold on to in the valley.

Sitting one thousand feet short of the summit, the low laying clouds seem but an arm stretch away. I listened as the wind picked up. As I talked through my thoughts, the breeze became brisk and strong. I've always think of the breeze whistling through trees as God's response to what I'm saying. If that should be the case, I was on right track when these words came to me.

This mountain has various areas different types of growth. If we view our life as being illustrated by this mountain, we would probably have more patience with ourselves. We would probably have more understanding of our processes. As well as more appreciation for the things we must go through in order to grow, in order to survive, in order to thrive, and in order to change. In order to praise God absolutely, fully, completely in valleys! In the valley – that's where we praise God.

I'm overlooking a valley as I share this message. The pine forest is in the foreground. Heavy white clouds hover overhead. Not sure if the valley directly below me is Tucson or if I'm looking at another town on the opposite side of the mountain. Doesn't matter. People are the same on either side of the mountain. As I traveled up Mount Lemmon, I thought about how many people aspire to the heights of life. They aspire to sit in the corner office at the top of the skyscraper. They aspire to live on top of the mountain. They aspire to fly over everybody in the best and the fastest jet planes. But no one really stops to share how they got through their valleys. We all have to travel low roads, some longer and deeper than others. We all have low spots where we have to figure out life, maneuver through somehow, someway. We grit our teeth, grunt, trudge on, and throw our backs into the effort of moving forward inch by inch until we break down or break through. Ideally, we will make it to where ever or whatever our top is. Lately, as a resident of one of the top floors of a skyscraper in lower Manhattan, as an employee of the top banking firms in the world, I've been looking out of one the windows overlooking the Hudson River, the City of New York and Jersey City across the river on the expanse of land below. Wondering, what if this space – New York City – this job, this point of my life, what if all this is indeed the mountaintop that the enemy has shown me in order to divert me away from the growth, the process and the everlasting glory God has for me some place else. I've come to think of New York City as my desert. It's been a true desert, but not one that has killed me fully of hope.

COMING DOWN THE MOUNTAIN

Having spent the morning driving up and down Mount Lemmon, pausing to enjoy the pullouts, taking time to sit, speak and take photos, I was incredibly glad I hadn't allow my consternation of heights to rule me. The morning and refined message were both needed and appreciated.

Initially, I had hoped to share words at the very top of the mountain, but the road basically ended at the ski lodge about 8,000 feet up. The words shared along the drive were sufficient to convey the message about climbing mountains, perspectives, and prospering in the valleys of life.

Mount Lemmon has been a wonderful illustration of process, growth and areas of life. It has various kinds of topsoil. Various levels of growth. Various types of vegetation at different levels. It brings to mind that in our own lives, as we produce the fruit of God's blessings, and both prepare ourselves and allow God to prepare us for our harvest time, there will be different levels and different areas of growth during different times throughout our lives. We have to embrace that. We have to understand that… or not understand it. Simply know that it is. We have to stop being so hard on ourselves as we traverse this life. As we produce the fruit we didn't know we had inside of us from seeds that were deposited from things we thought were destroying us.

Life truly is a wonderful cycle. When the end of one journey is the beginning of the next, new life is forever on the horizon.

Listen to: *Made a Way* by Travis Greene

I AM ENOUGH
⋆
RETURNING TO THE VALLEY

THE END OF A WONDER-FILLED YEAR

The biggest take-away from a year of wonder-focused living was finally seeing and accepting myself as being enough for my life. The concept has been an ongoing theme in my journals for several years. The more I challenged my thoughts, the more I wrote about self-acknowledgement…until a declaration emerged. *Who I am, what I am, how I am is enough for me!*

For fifteen to twenty years prior, I had been consumed with the idea of finding someone to share my life with – perhaps even find someone to validate my existence. In the absence of a romantic life partner, I was sufficiently satisfied with any relationship that could essentially justify my life – family, friends, mentors, co-workers, community, believers. You name it, I pursued folks in every arena, hoping against hope they would choose to pursue me in return. Their wanting me in their lives helped define my purpose and provide direction for a possible future.

The best result of focusing on *wonder*, is realizing that should I remain alone for the rest of my days, I'm good with that. None of my dreams, opportunities or possibilities are diminished by being a solo, unattached human being in this world.

Life is a gift from the Most High. God has blessed me with His Breath, His Spirit and His Image. He crafted me with a compassionate heart, reflective mind, earnest soul and enlightened spirit. He continually replenishes me with faith, love, mercy, understanding, comprehension, and knowledge. He guides me in wisdom with a gracious generosity. He formed me with a nature bent towards compassion, service and sharing. He's tempered me with an empathetic sensitivity that grieves and rejoices with others.

God created a wonder when He created me and it's beyond time to accept myself as such. The same is true for you.

Many people are unable to empathize with themselves which makes the concept of being compassionate towards others incomprehensible to them. Such people are incapable of understanding anything of substance.

Robyn Davidson wrote in her memoir, *Tracks*, which chronicled her solo trek of seventeen hundred miles across an Australian desert, "It is not what you carry on your journey, it's about what you leave behind." This has proven true on my journey. With each year that passes, I learn to let go of more. In the letting go, I see myself clearer.

∞ ∞ ∞

During Christmas week 2015, I was laid low with a chest cold. Yet, despite phlegm-choked congestion, I felt good, healthy and on the verge of regenerating. That week became a simultaneous process of purging and refreshing.

On Christmas day, I ventured outside to walk to Harlem Meer, a pond located at the northeast corner of Central Park a couple of blocks from my home. It began to drizzle. With a peaceful calm, I sat on a bench, opened my umbrella and watched the rain drops pelt the pond. It was a balmy sixty-five degrees which was unusually warm for December in New York. The day before the temperature was in the seventies. According to the Weather Channel, it was the warmest New York Christmas on record. Indeed, if not for the Christmas tree in the middle of Harlem Meer, anyone looking at a photo would think it was an overcast autumn day.

Eleven months earlier, I had begun the project that would become *Desert of Solitude* with a tearfully earnest video message. My goal was to explore and overcome my melancholy.

Though some residue of sadness remained by year end, it was not nearly as potent as it had been.

Choosing not to focus on what I believed my life lacked made all the difference. Seeking wonder made for a wonder-filled year. More than being a year of milestones, 2015 was the year I began to appreciate the ordinary!

That being said, the desire to share my life didn't dissipate. Yes, it would have been great to share my joy and bounty with a sibling, friend, mate or child – but that's not my story. The absence of a special someone doesn't diminish my value, negate who I am or what I have to share. And honestly, I've been tired of putting my life on hold; waiting for someone to show up to make it better. I accept that I've been set apart, refined by adversity and strengthened by faith. My journey has led to an appreciation for solitude and a respect for my solo status in the world. It's taught me to enjoy my own successes, strengths and uniqueness with vibrancy, knowledge of my wholeness and awareness of my sufficiency.

You, too, are enough for you. Wherever God has placed you is where you are meant to be. Whatever your quirks, know that they contribute to your uniqueness. Though we may continually long for something more, something else, or something different, we should not linger or despair in that longing. It's okay to want, it's not okay to tether yourself to an idea of lack. It's tempting to visualize amazing alternatives to our lives, but it's important to make sure temptations don't usurp God's place in your life. When we resist the ways of the Lord, we force ourselves into situations that are not for us in that moment. Insisting on our own way is a rejection of His will. The difficult situations created by our rebellion spill over into relationships that are impacted by our poor choices. Eventually, this leads to emotional and spiritual despair.

If you remember nothing else, remember you are enough for your life. You are enough for where you are. You are enough for who you are going to be. The person you are being developed into, is going to be so satisfied with the results of your journey. You are enough as you are. God created you as you are. You are lacking nothing.

At the end of my wonder-filled year, I was amazed by the awesomeness of God's provision. It's incredible to think of His unimaginable foresight in taking us through our lives step-by-step and revealing our purposes to us moment by moment. We mortals have no idea what tomorrow will bring, but God has mapped out the intimate details of all human and spiritual existence throughout the span of time. It's incomprehensible that we could possibly matter in the vastness of just the creation we are aware of. The wonder of it all is, not only do we matter, we are deeply loved.

Listen to: *So Will I (100 Billion X)* by Amanda Cook & Bethel Music

RESISTANCE IS FUTILE, CHANGE IS INEVITABLE

Change is one of the only guarantees we have in life, yet we all resist change for most of our lives. During some self-reflection, I acknowledged that I have become rather complacent in areas of my life. A couple of years ago, I saw that I was moving towards complacency, and I desperately tried to spark myself to steer clear of that life-hole very few ever escape from. I didn't want to become comfortable with where I was in life or satisfied with what I had. I thought such comfort and satisfaction meant that the desire to strive for more or better would be extinguished indefinitely. But resistance proved to be futile. I was indeed assimilated into the complacent culture surrounding me. Often during this period, I despondently asked God "Is this it? Is this all I have to look forward to?" He never quite said, "Yes," but slowly my vision of the future got dimmer and dimmer until the present day was all I could focus on.

Now I can say with confidence that many seeds were planted and nurtured during my season of complacency. I know God was working on me even though I felt like a lump on log.

Fast forward, I sense another change coming. I'm not resisting now. I am eager for this transition, and I welcome it. My vision is widening beyond the day again and I'm open to whatever doors and experiences are revealed to me.

Change is inevitable, so resisting the evolutionary changes life takes us through is futile. But there is something we can do as we stumble through our processes. We can better prepare ourselves to receive the best each season of life has for us by letting go of our expectations of what the coming season will look and feel like. By letting go of our expectations, we become free to simply experience the changing elements in our life moment by moment and day by day. In this way we will learn to appreciate that we are exactly where we need to be, learning what we need to learn, growing in a way God has designed us to grow.

BATTLING COMFORT

February 3, 2018
In four days movers will arrive to load my New York City life onto a truck and transport it twenty-four hundred miles across the country to Marana, Arizona, twenty-six miles northwest of Tucson. A week and a half later I will follow the transport by plane and begin the next chapter of my life.

Before this move, I thought the end of Desert of Solitude was the realization and message of being enough for life. Understanding that God has embedded Himself so deeply in me that everything I need will manifest at the appropriate time. Because God's sufficiency allows a fluid journey which produces fruit throughout the process, the destination becomes a footnote. This book was intended to explore my dryness and barrenness. Accepting and embracing my ordinariness. Pulling up roots of resentment, depression, frustration and loneliness to more fully appreciate my blooming relationship with my Creator. What I'm experiencing now, is the need to close a loop and end a cycle.

In the beginning I was. At the end I AM.

∞ ∞ ∞

Early on September 1, 2005, I left Milwaukee, Wisconsin with everything I owned, and no intention to return, in a small U-Haul truck. A friend followed behind with my car. We arrived in the Bronx at my new apartment late the next afternoon. The move that changed the trajectory of my life was a fourteen-hour road trip split across two days.

There was perhaps two months of rent in my checking account, basically two-thousand dollars which didn't account for car expenses or food. For eighteen months prior to moving, I had been unemployed so I was functioning on wide-eyed dreams and unemployment insurance, and yard sale proceeds. That year I reported sixty-five hundred dollars on my income taxes; the least amount since starting full-time work in college. I thought moving with almost nothing and hoping to make something of my life on the other side would be the hardest leap of faith I could ever take.

In July 2017, I purchased my second home in Arizona while still inhabiting my first home in New York. Initially, I thought I would remain in the City to work. It was that paycheck, after all, that not only financed my life but allowed me to think beyond state lines and time zones for what I wanted in my life.

During each of the last three years in New York, I earned more than one-hundred-thousand dollars. When my base salary broke eighty-thousand dollars a few years earlier, the realization that I was solidly in the middle class tax bracket was a shock to my inner-poor-girl system. Being underprivileged from birth had its own comforts – chiefly, knowing what each day would bring. Struggle as a way of life means doing what needs to be done with what you have. Planning, hope and expectation weren't priorities. Ease and leisure were unheard of.

During my last year-end compensation discussion with my manager in December 2017, there was an extended pause as I stared in bemusement at my new base salary on a slip of paper she had given me. The raise took me to one-hundred-twelve-thousand dollars. Though overtime was strongly discouraged, my annual OT income had ranged between eight and twelve thousand dollars throughout my ten years with the company. Raising my eyes to my manager, I said quietly, "I guess I'm no longer the poor girl from Milwaukee."

With a slight smirk and a mild shake of her head, she replied, "No. You're no longer that girl."

Knowing and feeling are two different things.

∞ ∞ ∞

Coming to terms with the timing of my move to the Tucson Metro Area was unexpectedly difficult. Knowing full well there was no employment market to pay me what I had become used to meant I had to cut my expenses drastically.

The part of me that hustled my butt off in New York was terrified of having to start all over again with no job on the horizon. That part of me was okay staying in the City at my job for another year or more to pay off bills and put away more money.

That part of me actually had more faith in my income – the mighty, worldly dollar – than in God.

The other part of me was horrified that there was such a sharp internal division. My spirit was troubled that my flesh was wrestling my it into the background. Foolishly, I believed, I had brought my flesh and spirit into perpetual agreement, but Operation Exit NYC showed me clearly that my flesh is not consistently faithful.

After more than a dozen years, building a life and career, it was impossible to immediately dig up the roots I had so deliberately planted.

The simple truth was, I needed my income. Like many New Yorkers, I lived up to the limit of my paycheck so a missed check could do some damage. My goal with the second house was to rent it out for a couple of years to free myself of the expense. But after spending my winter vacation in the new house, I realized I wanted to experience the fullness of starting over in a completely new space. I needed to reinvent myself. And I wanted to give myself the time and opportunity to do so.

Unfortunately, none of my schedules lined up. Due to a government subsidy on my co-op building, if I sold my East Harlem co-op before September 2018, I would receive no profit from the sale. After that date, I would receive fifty percent of the profit from the sale; government agencies received the other fifty percent. To receive all of the resale profits, I would have to hold the property for another ten years. There was no way I would last that long. As much as I loved the City, I was barely holding myself together emotionally, psychologically or spiritually. I was okay walking away with what I could at that point.

It would have been prudent to stay on the job until I could sell the co-op for a profit. But prudence isn't faith. My spirit was urging me to leave New York immediately. My inner debates centered around trusting God to provide especially when I couldn't see anything on the other side of a decision.

Despite submitting many employment applications, seeking out managers in my company for whom I could work remotely, putting in feelers with colleagues and colleagues of colleagues, I was unable to secure a job in the Tucson area. That didn't deter me. I figured once I was there full-time, finding a new role would be a breeze.

Leaving my job before selling my co-op apartment was an extremely risky gamble. Being on my own for so long made risky things seem like the daily struggles I was used to. So I became just another thing that had to be done with the resources available to me.

The apartment didn't sell in any kind of reasonable time. After maintaining two mortgages and related household expenses without full-time employment for over a year, foreclosure became a looming probability. The thought of losing everything I had worked a dozen years for was devastating. Attempting to anticipate every which way life could implode, immobilized me. I defaulted to survival mode. Since no jobs were calling in Tucson, I returned to New York to make whatever money I could.

In Matthew 19, a young man with many possessions walked away from Jesus after being told he would have to sell everything he owned and give the money to the poor in order to follow Jesus. The young man and his dilemma stayed with me as I throughout the time I split between Arizona and New York. I was ashamed much like Peter must have been when he realized that he had indeed deny Jesus three times before the rooster crowed, just as Jesus had predicted he would (Matthew 26:75).

Fear began to smother me. Drowning in debt, choking on life, I was ready to give up. In the end, the things that weren't working out exposed the condition of my faith. The entire year and half long transition from East Harlem to Marana was incredibly humbling.

Floundering faith hadn't been part of my walk, but it should've been expected. How can we be strengthened if we aren't tested?

From a faith perspective, my paralysis was illogical. I know nothing I have is mine; everything I have is a blessing of grace. God had blessed me and provided for me yet I didn't want to trust Him with what He had given me.

Even with that deep sure knowledge, I still thought I could pause what God had set in motion until I accomplished what I wanted to accomplish. Even being sure God held me firmly in His hand, it was a struggle to quit my job and go where I had been shown to go. Even with historical experience of God's work in my life, my six-figure salary kept trying to trump my single-digit faith.

It was stunning that it was harder for me to trust God as a person of some financial means than it had been when everything I owned fit into a short U-Haul truck.

∞ ∞ ∞

If there's a secret to my survival and faith, it's that I keep moving. Waiting for someone to save me has never worked in my favor. Lessons early in life taught me that the longer I stay down, the harder it is to get back up. That doesn't mean I know which way to go or even when exactly to move.

The weekend of February 3, 2018 my congregation hosted its annual women's conference. The theme was *Gripped by Grace*, and the keynote speaker was Pastor Esther Ibanga from Joss, Nigeria. She spoke twice that weekend – at the conference on Saturday and again during Sunday's afternoon service. The first message was on the grace theme, the second was titled *"The Cave-Dwellers Are Coming Out."*

I arrived late to the conference on Saturday and was extremely dismayed to walk into the main sanctuary as Pastor Ibanga began her closing prayer and alter call. Even that snippet triggered something in me. Immediately, I knew she spoke clarifying words.

Pastor Ibanga was talking about endings, beginnings, cycles and coming full circle. I was in the process of closing the New York chapter of my life. Loops I hadn't been aware of were also being closed. But up until that moment, there was still something about this time that hadn't been properly sealed and set aside.

"We must be ready to go when He says," Pastor Ibanga said emphatically. "Do you know you need grace to step back? You need grace to let Him take over. You need grace to let Him work it out. Because our human minds are limited in understanding," she continued with maternal forcefulness. "We don't know, and can't see, the future. Just when we think He's killing us, He's actually working something out. Because until we die, and come to the end of ourselves there's no life that will come out."

"Hear the voice of the Master. Come and receive grace in this time. Grace for your need, your assignment, your situation, your home, your city, your church, your future, your destination. I don't know what you heard this morning. I don't know what He's calling you to. I don't know what excuses you have been giving. I don't know what bargains you have been offering to the Lord. 'Lord, let me do this first, then I'll come. Let me get married first, then I'll serve you. Let me buy a house. Let me have my children.' No more excuses. Just come."

Her words summarized my life and my hopes. Indeed, she summarized this whole portion of my journey. I was already on my way, already taking action to heed the call on my life, but her words added a level of urgency and excitement I hadn't yet experienced. She confirmed purpose and provided clarity and understanding. With that, it was time to get up and leave New York City, my desert and proving ground.

∞ ∞ ∞

There was no doubt my apartment would sell for a price I was content with. However, the length of time it took to close a deal made me frantic. However, there are blessings in every season. Being extremely mobile is a one great benefit of being single and without children. Not having a quick sale meant I had a place to stay while working to stay afloat financially. I was extremely grateful for all the blessings interwoven with hard times.

A few days after the Women's Conference, all my possessions were on a truck en route to Marana, Arizona. I followed by plane a couple of weeks later. I didn't think I would be back in New York until the fall to list the apartment for sale. To my extreme disappointment, complications with the roommate I left in the apartment and building management had me returning much sooner and staying far longer than I wanted.

In early fall I received two great offers, but the agent I had thought her job was getting offers, not closing sales, so the first deal fell apart and the second offeror walked away.

I returned to Arizona furious and forlorn. My apartment sat empty through the winter.

During the months I spent in Marana that first year, I worked on getting my real estate and foster parent licenses. I had uprooted and tossed my whole life up in the air with a seemingly not-too-well-thought-out goal of changing everything about how I lived. My primary focus was creating space and making room for a home and family. Spending my thirties in the City that Never Sleeps did nothing for family-building and as much as I loved my co-op in East Harlem, I couldn't foster in it. Therefore, I determined that I needed to change my environment to something that supported my goals. I was also determined to learn a trade I could work from home anywhere in the country in addition to monetizing my creative works.

Basically, I was in the process of reinventing myself or, perhaps more accurately, embracing God's rewrite of my story. It was harder process than I could have possibly imagined and destroyed me in many ways, in areas I had no awareness of holding pride in.

"Father, please tell me what my next step is," this quiet bedtime prayer held all my uncertainty. For most of the year, I had been asking Him to tell me what to do. I could see the mid-range picture, but I couldn't see how to get there without losing financial and material ground. The morning following my earnest plea, I awoke with a straight-forward answer in my spirit, *"I have already given you a way out."* With that, I got up and went about my Father's business with some confidence.

The hardest lesson learned during my eighteen-month-long move from New York to Arizona was that though my spirit is always willing to move when, where, and how God instructs, my flesh remains in lockstep to the ground it is formed from. Spiritually, I know *everything* is God's plan, positioning and timing. I knew then as I know now, my home in Marana and the transcontinental move were not the *big* things. Neither was selling my Harlem co-op the *primary* thing. They were merely steps to dislodge me from the ideas of home, safety and comfort.

My current stretch of unemployment will soon hit the three-year mark. Double the time I had been unemployed before moving to New York from Wisconsin. Arizona has yielded me much, but income has not been part of the bounty. What I know about God and His work in my life is that everything is a cycle. All my lessons repeat on multiple levels and with increasing difficulty. If the last cycle of draught and increase is anything to go by, my coming abundance is going to be incredibly awesome.

Meditation Verse: Matthew 19:27-30

Then Peter said in reply, "Look, we have left everything and followed you. What then will we have?" Jesus said to them, "Truly I tell you, at the renewal of all things, when the Son of Man is seated on the throne of his glory, you who have followed me will also sit on twelve thrones, judging the twelve tribes of Israel. And everyone who has left houses or brothers or sisters or father or mother or children or fields, for my name's sake, will receive a hundredfold, and will inherit eternal life. But many who are first will be last, and the last will be first.

WOMAN, BE RESTORED.

Spending my day at the Woman Be Restored Conference at Times Square Church. This year it started with a two-hour morning break-out session. I chose the Relationship Restoration breakout teaching. I missed most of the first hour - I thought there would be a warm of singing before we got into the meat of the conference. My thinking was wrong. So was my attitude. I walked in on the teaching saying that our ability to forgive is based on our capacity to forgive. My listening walls immediately went up and I typed in my notes, "capacity vs. understanding." Meaning we have the capacity to do everything God instructs us to do, we are limited only by our understanding of who God Is and the Power He has to Perform in our life. We have to understand that saying "yes" and "amen" to God will take us places (internally and externally, spiritually and physically) we can't even imagine or envision.

While my attitude was busy saying no to the teaching in the room by countering the points with my own, God broke in with a whisper, "Thank you for Peewee."

Before I know it, I'm searching my phone for this post I wrote in October 2016. I shook my head slightly on the negative even as my hand was going in the air for permission to speak.

My hand played cat and mouse with the air several times before I was called on. I ended up being the last to speak before we closed the meeting in prayer. I think it was fitting to close on a cry of thanksgiving. I started by stating that forgiveness is an expression of love and I offered it to my dad, Peewee, as an offering of love for my deceased mother who loved him to her death. Forgiveness is a process and many people will try to dictate or force their interpretations on you about their idea of what forgiveness looks, feels or sounds like. Then I read the paragraph beginning with "So on to now."

October 2, 2016
Thank You for Peewee.

My dad has been coming to mind strongly and often lately.

I wrote a piece about him a few years ago as a submission for a father/daughter project. Sometime after his death, I had a series of dreams about him, disturbing dreams actually. Dreams where I was locked up and still a sexual object for him. The dreams didn't stop until I forcibly removed myself from the home he had me locked up in and blew the home up from a helicopter with a rocket launcher.

I awoke from that final dream feeling quite badass and liberated.

Despite the effort I made following his release from prison to build a father/daughter relationship with him, most of my thoughts of him are devoid of fondness. My greatest sadness about him is that there is no longer any opportunity to reconcile with him again. Our relationship blew up after my brother died in 2007 because of Peewee's decision to honor his own brother at my brother's funeral. His brother had also sexually violated me in my youth. My brother was not fond of him. And even if they had been in communication as Peewee's sister recently tried to tell me, Antione would not have approved of the way his sister's rapist was given a place of honor to speak through a relative of his love for his nephew at his funeral as his unprepared sister realized too late what was going on.

Peewee and I fell out over that sneak attack. What I snapped at him outside the funeral home as we walked out was, "Even now, with the death of your son, you chose not to put your children before your brother and sister. When will you put us first?" Although he had no rights of fatherhood, I had already named him as legal next of kin for my brother in order to help with funeral preparations until I was able to arrive in Gary. I insisted in the street the day of my brother's funeral that he put his grandchildren first and sign the paperwork to have my brother's cremated ashes sent to his daughters. He agreed and we walked back into the funeral home to complete the paper work. After that I told him he and I were done.

He died three years later. To my knowledge he made no effort to mend our breach. When he knew he was dying he called his brother and sister. Even on his deathbed he didn't ask for me. I saw that as a choice... as in he chose who he wanted to see and be with in the end. As in, he never did get around to putting his children first - before his brother and sister.

And for that ending, my thoughts of him are often filled with resentment and a deep sense of rejection. Wow. I hadn't been able to follow my thoughts through to this revelation before. His sister and perhaps others thought that my feelings towards Peewee were based on his sexual abuse of me in my youth. When she finally spoke to me about it a few years ago, I told her what I shared here and added that he had been forgiven long ago for his abusive violation of me.

Moving forward to now. I'm sitting in the sanctuary streaming silent tears. During service, after a phenomenal message on ethics, integrity, loyalty and righteousness by Elder

Jerry Hampton, I prayed during the singing of "You Are My Strength." I began crying and thanking God for everything He has done for me. For my humbling and my affliction. *"Thank you for hearing me. Thank you for responding! Thank you for the pastor. Thank You for this!"* The word was phenomenal during that service and during the morning service also - the message flowed through both. The song took me to another level. *"Thank you for keeping me. Thank you for everything You Are in me. Thank you for forming me into the woman I Am and for everything You're doing to make me the woman I Am becoming."* And before I knew what was coming up from the deep well of my soul, these words passed my lips, *"Thank you for Peewee!"* Perhaps I stunned myself for a millisecond, but almost immediately I affirmed my thanksgiving by repeating my thanks twice more. *"Thank You for Peewee, Father! Thank you for Peewee."*

Perhaps this is the reconciliation my spirit, body and life needed: Acknowledgement that even Peewee has been a blessing to my life.

I then gave thanks for Akmad, the long-forgiven uncle I want nothing to do with. I gave thanks for their sister who has a special place in my heart but holds none of my trust. I gave thanks for my mother who is always a blessing in my sight. I gave thanks for all the family God has blessed me with who have repeatedly rejected and mocked me. They have all been my training ground. The rod of my affliction. Without them what would I know or understand of the true darkness of the human spirit? And by contrast, what would I appreciate in the pure light of God's grace, mercy and redemptive powers?

Recent thoughts about Peewee

When I began packing up my East Harlem apartment in anticipation of a cross country move to Tucson, Arizona, I noticed I had a medium size box full of greeting cards and stationery.

The things I enjoy most in life were introduced to me by Peewee. My first box of stationery was powdery pink parchment he gave me for Christmas when I was about eleven years old. I got my first bike at age seven and he let me help him put it together. Afterwards, he took me outside and taught me how to ride it. My love of sci-fi comes from watching *Star Trek* with Peewee. It's amazing that memories of Peewee at his fatherly best dominate more as time goes by. It's not that I've forgotten him at his worst, I've simply chosen to see him as he was – a flawed human being whom God also loved enough to sacrifice His Only Son for.

Perhaps this is the manifestation of healing and the revelation of grace.

Sermons: *Spiritual Depression* by Carter Conlon
Ethics: Part 3 by Jerry Hampton

Listen to: *Hidden* by United Pursuit

BUILDING A STRUCTURE

I dreamed about building a structure....

God always gives us a word to perform. We may not always hear it, see it or know what we're doing when we get it, but as long as we're sure to put our trust in Him, He will get us to where He wants us to go.

One consistent element of my writing, especially my journaling, is my written words regarding my life are often either prophetic or revelatory. I don't have a sense of which words define my life when I write them, but in moments of review and reflection, I can see the results clearly. The dots connect clearly from when I first received an urge (word or vision) to do something, to my becoming aware that I am being prepared to take action, to the action being completed.

On the first Saturday spent in my new home in Marana, Arizona, I was reminded of a forgotten dream from nearly three years prior. It was the end of the first week as a full-time resident of my new town. The actual seventh day was when confirmation was received that a Word had been completed in my life. I really had no idea I was hearing correctly, performing accurately or moving in the right direction. I struggled long and hard with taking the final step – moving from New York City to Tucson. There was no struggle with the first steps or middle ones. Only eagerness, a sense of purpose and a need to follow-through. The final actions carried the most anxiety because of their finality, perhaps because of the level of commitment and trust required to let go of the life I had been building for over twelve years.

I'm quite certain I wouldn't have understood this until I was on completed side of the executed instructions. The dots weren't connecting while I was still in New York. I didn't see the fullness of anything there.

This week, I've been doing a final review and edit of this volume, *Desert of Solitude: Refreshed by Grace*. Aside from writing everything in the book, I've read and shuffled the material numerous times. At some point I may have connected the line "building a structure" to my new construction home, but certainly not like I did today. My granddad died at the end of the year I received this message. Around that time, I assumed my mom's visit in my dream was about his departure.

However, mom has never visited before a death. She has often visited to provide a sense of comfort and insight. She always represents a pivot or answers an unknown question. I can't always decipher with certainty what her presence in my dreams mean, but there's always a very strong sense of what the message intends to convey. [Let me clarify here that I don't believe my mom's ghost or spirit is visiting me. I have long believed that God speaks to me through her image because she has been the best representation of love in my life here on Earth. When I see her there is purity and trust. Never any ulterior motive. She always s comes for my good or protection.]

On the morning of March 15 during my thirty-ninth year, I wrote down what I remembered of a dream the night before:

> "I dreamed about building a structure…. I was building a structure next to my bed in my home. It reached eleven stories. Then it started falling down. Mom was in the kitchen cooking. Then she was in her room. At the end of the sequence, she took shower."

Eighteen months later I visited Tucson for the first time. Three months after that I went into contract to build a house in a place called Dove Mountain which sits in the Tortolita Mountains (my translation: *Little Dove* or *Dove of Peace*). Throughout the home construction in Tucson, I posted progress images of the build on my bedroom wall in East Harlem. At some point during this process, I moved my bed to put my headboard up against the "vision" wall.

One thing I know: I tried hard to build a full life in New York City. After nearly two years living in the City, I began working for the company I stayed with until the day before I left for Tucson, Arizona. At the time of my relocation and job exit, I was in my eleventh year with the company. The last two years were rife with resentment and bitterness due to the lack of advancement support despite my tenure, experience and education.

Building. Collapse. Shelter. Nourishment. Cleansing. The message and vision were received three years before they were understood. Understanding came at the appointed time.

Meditation Verse: Habakkuk 2:2-3
Write the vision; make it plain on tablets, so that a runner may read it. For there is still a vision for the appointed time; it speaks of the end and does not lie. If it seems to tarry, wait for it; it will surely come, it will not delay.

Listen to: Build My Life by Housefires III

STARTING OFF FRESH

For the last five years or so I've taken a two week vacation straddling the last week of the year and first week of the new year. I don't often travel during this time. If I do, it's only for a few days in the middle of my break. My first goal for the time off was to enjoy my home and local attractions because vacations and weekend trips always took me away. After years of using all my time off traveling, visiting, or generally moving around and realizing very little to none of my limited time was spent being still, resting, refreshing or reconnecting with myself, I began shutting down at the end of the year.

During this years' break I've been much busier than I wanted to be, but it is also a pivot season. That being said, a few days ago I simply stopped the busy work, picked up my Bible and allowed myself to sleep in.

This last year has been all about being enough for my life, refreshment and grace. What does it mean to be enough? What is refreshment? How does one embrace grace?

For me, being enough for my life means everything I need to function, grow and excel in my endeavors is within me. I am complete. I am equipped. I able, capable, ready and willing to do what needs to be done to move forward in life.

Refreshment comes from rest. It's not just about doing nothing. Resting is willfully stopping and choosing to be still. Breathing. Recalibrating.

Embracing grace is about accepting your vulnerabilities, shortfalls and weaknesses. In relation to my year-end shut down, grace is present when I reflect on the last year. How have I fallen short on my goals? What did I want that wasn't achieved? Did I do what I'm able to do and let go of the things out of my control?

There's also grace in planning for the next year. How can I progress on last year's goals? How can I move any ball forward? Do I still want what eluded me last year? How have my priorities changed? How do I distribute my time, energy and resources? What do I let go of or put on the back burner?

Reflection, self-evaluation and goal-setting have long been part of my year-end process. What's new is showing myself some TLC while allowing myself time and space to process my life.

The greatest thing I've learned during this pivot season is the importance of giving myself time, space and opportunity. No one else will ever do this for me at any satisfactory level.

ROAD TRIP: RIDING SHOTGUN

October 3, 2018

Travel was one of my first loves. I remember telling my mom at a young age that I wanted to visit all the states, each continent and as many countries as possible before I die. The desire to see the world likely comes from the frequent moves my family made in my youth. So much so that folks often ask if my parents were in the military. They weren't. They were simply okay trying something new for a better life. After making life moves with family, school trips with classmates seemed to be a good next step. Which led to vacations with friends throughout my twenties. My thirties were dedicated to exploring myself and solo trips became my therapy... until the therapeutic benefits disappeared. After a while, asking strangers to take horrible snapshots of me in front of historic landmarks lost its charm. I was tired of group travel with various personalities because the first couple of days were usually spent trying to get to know each other, while the last few days were spent putting distance between self and everyone else so we could all enjoy our own personalized experiences.

When solo travel fell out of favor with me, the only pleasure trip I could talk myself into for a five-year period was a self-planned hop-on/hop-off train tour along the French and Italian Riviera to celebrate my 40th birthday.

Absolutely no complaints about that trip. As the mother of all vacays, it was also the first time I consciously road shotgun with God. The whole trip was about embracing my solo status and a reminder to celebrate myself even in the absence of others.

Over the last two years, my life has been all about transition and transformation, which are happening at multiple layers currently. The biggest layer is moving from New York City to a suburb of Tucson, Arizona. Throughout the last year, I've traveled between the two cities preparing to end my life in one and begin anew in the other.

Because August is my birthday month, I view it as my primary new year and a symbol of renewal. For that reason, it was important to spend August in the new place. It proved to be a much needed gift of time and space to myself. Before returning to New York City to sell my apartment in the autumn, I decided to take a road trip. The idea started off small-ish. A quick – perhaps overnight – trip to the Grand Canyon. Five hours each way split over two days seemed almost leisurely to me. It turned into a six-day excursion I now call my Grand Tour of Arizona. Road trips and national parks are going to be a huge part of my future.

At the beginning of my trip, words began settling in me. These words were a mediation throughout my travel:

Pilgrimage.
Communion.
Silence.
Peace.

∞ ∞ ∞

I felt a need to declutter my mind, my heart, my soul. A need to be more purposeful about decluttering my life. I didn't think about fasting until I was on the road. At that point I was already tiring fast so not eating was out of the question. As I reflect back, the week before I began my road trip, I did indeed fast from life. I shut down. I refused to check email or follow up with the major stressors in my life. I decompressed. I vegged on TV. I did some gardening, some cleaning. Generally, I allowed myself to simply and quietly occupy my space.

That was a beautiful gift.

The Grand Canyon has become a symbol of perseverance and focus in my life. When I lived in Arizona as a child, we never visited the Canyon. For my relocation, I wanted to be a tourist early on, to see the wonder of my new home state before I fell into new routines.

I am so grateful for the time and opportunity to see some of the amazingly beautiful National Parks and monuments throughout Northern Arizona and the stunning landscape variations from the south to the north of the state. (Many photos will be shared on my Images + Life photo blog under the tag "Exploring Arizona.") My Grand Tour of Arizona consisted of stops at Sunset Crater Volcano, the South Rim of the Grand Canyon, Navajo National Monument, Monument Valley, Antelope Canyon, Horseshoe Bend, Lake Powell and the dam that created it, and the North Rim of the Grand Canyon. I camped in my car for the first two nights, found a bed and breakfast on the third night, then splurged on hotel rooms. Nearly three days were spent on Navajo Nation Land. My first camp fire was started at Grand Canyon Desert View camp site. I LOVED that spot! My fire burned for less than five minutes total, despite lighting it up about twenty times. Most amazing and unexpected was the boat ride I took on the lake in the middle of the desert! Who knew? There was so much natural beauty over such a vast amount of land, I grew tired trying to chase it all.

Within the first day or so, I knew this would become a regular, most likely annual, trip for me. Acknowledging that allowed me to relax a bit. There was no need to try to see everything or do more than my body was prepared to do. I made the trip all about photography. Capturing sunrises, sunsets and dark skies were my primary goals each day. The secondary photo goal was to capture some decent self-portraits. Note to self: hair and make-up should be part of the routine when attempting self-portraits on vacay.

This year has been exhilarating in many ways. I've purposefully taken action to change my life into something that represents my heart, spirit, vision and purpose. It's taken a lot of energy and focus, so much so, I keep thinking I'm failing when I allow too many distractions or eagerly change or adjust plans as things come up. However, when I look around after detours, I see that I have not been pushed off-course. I'm exactly where I need to be. I'm developing and moving at a pace that has been calibrated for me. After all, I am not behind the wheel of my life. I'm riding shotgun. It may appear that I'm in control, but I'm not. It may seem like I can screw all this hard work up, but I can't. I've already surrendered to the one who controls the universe. Any moment of uncertainty or chaos in my life is not going to disrupt the plans He already has in motion for me. Believing that, knowing it, and remembering it brings comfort and peace in a solitude full of communion with my Heavenly Father. My life, my pilgrimage, my journey is unfolding before me. With each step, I discover more and more good things that have been deposited in me for my good.

Be blessed as you go.

STRUGGLE & TRIUMPH

We all carry a flame of passion within us that we struggle to bring (lift) into the physical world (our lives). Oftentimes it feels like we're diving headfirst off a cliff... or we don't move forward because we fear falling on our face... or we fear losing face. However, if we can only summon the courage to keep going, or to get up after a fall, or numerous falls, we will eventually finish. We will complete what we started. We will triumph. We will win more than gold. We faced our biggest fears, wrestled with our most deadly demons, dove deep within ourselves and rose again victorious! Our prize will be the sure knowledge that we are more than conquerors for we have overcome ourselves.

I GIVE GOOD LOVE

While having a late brunch at Melba's restaurant in Harlem, Whitney Houston's *You Give Good Love* came on overhead. Three other women were in the restaurant with their men, and we all seemed to burst out in unison on the first note: "I found out what I've been missing / Always on the run..."

This was a hair brush in the mirror song for me when it came out in the mid-80's. However, on that particular day, it made me very introspective. As I sang along in a moderate tone, I noticed the other women were looking at their men and smiling the words into their eyes as they added their voices the chorus.

Before brunch, I had a conversation with a friend about the spirits of manipulation and control. The topic was troubling me because people in every area of my life were exhibiting the influence of these destructive spirits. During that morning conversation, I had shared with my friend the story of a young man I met in my early twenties shortly after my mother died. His personality and desire for a relationship with me were more than I was equipped to handle during that period in my life, so he ended up overwhelming me emotionally. He was ready for marriage and children and spoke of taking me to Nigeria to meet his mother. I was focused on surviving moment to moment, trying to cope with the grief of losing my losing my mother and the responsibility of guardianship for my teenage sister. I asked for time. He insisted the time was now. I shut down and disconnected.

Where would I be... who would I be... had I allowed him to control my story?

I know I wouldn't resemble the woman I am today.

My friend gifted me with the observation, "Had he worked with you as a partner instead of trying to dominate you, he could have won you and I'm sure you would have followed him anywhere in the world - simply because he was your man and he had worked to make you comfortable with his manhood."

Very true.

The type of man he was then would be wonderful for me now - attentive, present, direct, decisive, focused, determined, demanding. I'm not concerned with losing myself in another's personality anymore. Mostly because I demand to be seen and accepted for who I am. And in being who I am, I too have become a forceful personality - attentive, alert, direct, no nonsense, independent with a true desire for a mutually dependent and respectful relationship. In embracing and nurturing all of me, I have become the best lover of me. I've learned to give good love to myself and that has become the greatest possible love a person can have in this world.

Listen to: *I Didn't Know My Own Strength* by Whitney Houston
You Give Good Love by Whitney Houston

WOMAN, YOU ARE ENOUGH.

My mom died shortly after my twenty-first birthday. I have now lived as long without her physical presence as I had with her. Having to navigate the world my whole adult life without a mother's love, guidance, and support has been extremely difficult and lonely. It has also been the impetus propelling me into a relationship with my Heavenly Father through His Son and Holy Spirit. The mother's love I lost in the world, I found in the Spirit.

This message is for all the mothers, and women in general, out there who are struggling with any aspect of their identity and responsibilities: **You are enough.**

Dear Woman:

You are equipped to provide all the true necessities for yourself and your family.

Despite what you may think, your love will never fail your children. You will always be a light to them, even in the deepest darkest pits they may fall into, everything you represent will be a beacon to them.

Your strength is phenomenal. Even in your weakest moments, your children will look back and view you as the epitome of EVERYTHING.

You can do wrong, but no wrong will outlast your love. Remember that. Give yourself a break when you're overwhelmed.

You don't need to go beyond yourself to be the best mommy ever. You already are the best mommy ever – simply because you are the mom your child was blessed with. Know that. Embrace it.

You are a blessing. You are a lover. A nurturer. A builder. A teacher. A guide. A comforter. A savior. A survivor. You are the first true sacrifice and offering your child will ever encounter. You are the first environment of creation your child will ever experience. Your body, the most sacred of temples, hosted and presented life to the world. How awesome is that!?

Your life will be what influences your children's life the most. In the midst of your everyday, this may be a lot to think about. So, don't think about it. Just live.

Be who you are. Work on being the best person you can be - the best version of you. Do the best you can do in any given moment with the full knowledge and acceptance that your best varies depending on the time of day, time of month, time of year and a million other factors. Whatever your best is in any given moment is enough.

Your children understand more than you know. They appreciate you more than they may ever be able to express. You represent everything to them – their beginning, their end, their in-between. You are the fabric they will weave their lives from. You are the start line and the line they will return to continuously throughout the relay of life. To your little champs, you are the MVP.

Not far from the tree
During my short time with my mother, she planted the following seeds and lessons in me, and they are still flourishing today:
- She challenged me to be myself
- She supported me when I spoke up for myself
- She rebuked my pride and instilled a sense of humbleness and service in me

- She insisted I respect everyone no matter their actions against me or those I love
- She showed me the pain and value of forgiveness and how it is inseparable from love
- She encouraged me to dream of futures I couldn't see or comprehend
- She exhibited discipline and patience to me
- She demonstrated hard-work and perseverance
- She practiced generosity, grace and kindness
- She modeled for me the satisfaction of building a life from your own efforts and appreciating all you have even when what you have is counted as nothing by others.

I can go on as I am still learning so much from Mom. There's so much I didn't comprehend in my youth that is becoming clear now and bearing fruit in my spirit. I am so very grateful for the timelessness of her grace and generosity in sharing herself.

EPILOGUE

SUNSET SILHOUETTES

JOURNALING THROUGH THE JOURNEY

August 9, 2019
New York, NY

My mind is all aflutter with clamoring thoughts... but first I give thanks.

Father God, thank you for all You are! Thank you for keeping me, for providing for me. Thank You for looking out for me when I'm ready to give up all semblance of hope.

My closing is scheduled for next week and now I can think. I can breathe. I wish I had planned this time because it's a good point for a fast. The last two sermons brought up a lot in me. A lot of thoughts about rejection and how different my life would be with people in it.

I'm recognizing trauma for what it is and what it has done to me.

My sister avoiding me for over a decade has been the most deep-seated, hard-to-face rejection of my life.

One of my best friends from high school treating me as a second rate, after-thought option to fill in for her white best friends from middle school and college has changed my commitment to female friendships.

Three older women I've long thought of as "second mothers" each telling me in their own way I had no real place in their lives crippled me emotionally.

Remembering how I traveled across the country to visit my paternal grandmother in the hospital shortly before she died, how I sat patiently at her bedside for four hours, hoping to have one last conversation as she kept her eyes closed and faked sleep, is still painful nearly a decade later. Watching her stir herself and engage with her children when they arrived felt like a betrayal to the special relationship I thought we had. She had no words for me even when she knew she was dying. Her son, Peewee, had also refused to acknowledge me when he lay dying two years prior. He reached out to his siblings and died surrounded by the family he had chosen throughout his life.

Then there was the time my youngest aunt had security escort me out of the hospital my maternal grandfather was dying in simply because she could.

And there was the time I was the only relative at an uncle's wedding and he acted like he wished I wasn't there.

Basically, I was flooded with thoughts of all the disrespect, emotional, psychological and spiritual harm inflicted on me in all my important relationships.

The footnotes of harm can go on and on. Though the rejection has stung each time, the disregard and dismissal have always been unexpected from each of these people.

These instances and more have each happened in their own space and time. Separate and unknown to each of the actors. After each incident I dealt with what I could and buried the rest or thought about what I couldn't ignore, then filed it away as another great emotional injustice in my life.

This week I realized the anger – deep seated and ferocious – stemmed mostly from the trauma accumulated over the years from these relationship abuses. I've endured habitual emotional violence in all my major relationships throughout my whole life.

What a revelation!

Suffering from accumulated pain while thinking my anger stemmed only from the state of the world. Dealing with the little I could handle left a whole bunch of stuff to fester under the surface through years of layering. That's how I keep getting pulled in fast and deep. My darkness is a quagmire.

Sadly, I asked to be able to love people. From prior experience I should've been ready for the worst. Reflecting from a long view, I can understand how many fall to the wayside. How giving up can be perceived as a road to comfort. Yet and still, there's no doubt there is literally nothing and no one waiting for me on the other side of You, Father God. You're all I have. So, despite my trauma and uncertainty, I keep plodding ahead as I'm able. After all, if I'm in You and You're in me, then I'm already all in, right?

My sense of worthiness was wrapped up in all the hurt, anger and rejection. Reasoning that if the people who know me best don't love me or care about my well-being, then how can some newbie care about me?

What man would love a woman whose own dad didn't love or protect her? What kind of wife can a woman be when she's never had an enjoyable voluntary sexual encounter? What kind of friend can a woman be when her own sister disowns her? I am the common denominator in all my relationships therefore there must be something inherently wrong with me, right?

My reasoning concluded it's my fault no one loves me. What is it about me that's so utterly unlovable? What a sad irony that an unloved person prayed to be a lover of people. No one can give what they don't have. All these debilitating, shame-filled thoughts loop ceaselessly in the background of my life.

Perhaps kernels of pride rise from rejection. An understanding of being created in greatness and being rejected for Who I AM. Knowing my higher self is rejected more often than my personhood, doesn't lessen the sting. What is it about the person I am that makes me so disposable?

Despite airing these rhetorical questions, I will continue on the path I'm on – searching and seeking You in my fullness and emptiness. Should my life remain one of solitude, then so be it.

By Your Grace, I am able to remind myself I am blessed and highly favored. My life is good. I offered only the best of myself to all these people. The best of my understanding and intentions. I am not lost without them. My existence is not lacking. I know all this.

Having identified the deeply rooted anger and trauma has lightened me immeasurably and made space for a more vigorous pursuit of healing.

Thank You for giving me this week to gather myself - my thoughts, my frustrations, my pain and trauma. Thank You for the time and space to explore, examine and itemize the roots. Thank You for making me sit and rest. Thank You for giving me the time to be creative and work on my art forms. It's so hard for me to stop moving, but when You cause me to pause, it's a full stop that's never regretted or resented.

Thank You for caring for me, Abba. Thank You for keeping me and guiding me on Your path of life to a greater life in You. Thank You for the gifts and talents You have blessed me with. I am nothing without You, but without others I remain one of Your masterpieces. Thank You for Your Grace, Mercy, Love, Character, Nature, Joy, Understanding, Provision, Faithfulness and Guidance. I appreciate You, Father God. I honor You. I bless You. I surrender fully to You. I am Yours. I receive and embrace You as mine. Thank You, Creator, for making me the way You have. Designed to be who I am – salt, light, flesh, spirit – a blessing in this world.

I breathe in and out knowing Your Breath and Spirit flow through me. Thank You, Abba for sharing Your breath with me.

For counting me worthy to bear and represent Your likeness in the Earth. Thank You Abba for the mind, heart and spirit that pants after you daily; that aches when I get off track. Thank You for continually reeling me back in, turning me in the direction I should go. Lighting my fire to motivate and encourage action. Thank You, Abba, for all You do and all You are. In the name of Jesus – Your Son, my Savior – and by Your Most Gracious and overwhelming Holy Spirit, my Guide, Amen. Amen. Amen.

August 11, 2019
New York, NY

Today, I attended the 10:00am and 3:00 p.m. services. The second service is now ending. The early service was a word I need to go home and listen to again. The afternoon service promised to be a word, but it didn't flesh out the way I needed or expected it to.

Pastor Claude Haud preached "Faith to Heal from Offenses" this morning. I absolutely needed that message! He spoke of offenses as being traps that can potentially derail you. Block purpose. Delay destiny. He spoke of love growing cold from offenses left unforgiven.

It hit me right in the heart. My attention was fractured this morning, but had I been fully present, the message probably would have keeled me over since it came so soon after I catalogued painfully defining interactions I completely took offense to. Such offense in fact that I distanced myself from all of the people who caused me deep emotional harm.

That's going to have to be a study....

In the afternoon, Nik Godshall shared a message titled, "Is Love Tolerant?" He had some interesting points, but I think he was speaking firmly from a conservative American religious viewpoint.

During his prayer he referred to Christianity as a "religion" several times. I think that's where the majority fall off. One cannot practice love really. One must accept love into one's heart, mind and spirit. We must surrender to the Spirit of God (Love) so that the Spirit of God (Love) can flow through us. It is through and by the Spirit that we are witnesses of God, His Glory and the Work He is conducting in the Earth and within us as individuals. That is not religion. There's no formula of activities that produce a certain "love" outcome.

The state of our hearts, minds and souls matters. Everyone's path to cleanliness, holiness, sanctification and righteousness is going to be different. Ergo, no one-size-fits-most formula.

The biggest trouble I have with his message, is the idea that love is something we can give or do or be separate from God, which is implied by asking, "Is Love Tolerant?" We all know God is long-suffering for His Creation, so the answer is, "Yes, Love is tolerant." However, that was not the delivery. Love was presented as an expression of general acceptance by good Christians. If you're a good Christian, your love will correct, not alienate. This isn't untrue, but the road to the conclusion is suspect.

God doesn't call us to be "tolerant." He calls us to BE Love and informs us that by the love we show one another – our neighbors, strangers, family and friends – people will recognize Him in us – as His Children and co-workers.

One of the hardest things about Christianity is trying to define who we are within worldly or cultural norms. Tolerance is a world concept intended for people with no greater understanding to get along. Those of us who believe Jesus is the personification of God's Word are already greater than tolerant. We are representatives of Light and Love tasked with embracing our neighbors and bringing them to our Lord.

August 13, 2019
Flight: New York, NY to Tucson, AZ

In the air, on the way home to Marana with no immediate ties to New York City anymore. No need to be there. No job. No property. No obligation to return. Unfettered, finally and happily, so.

The closing on my co-op apartment sale finally happened after eighteen months of straddling two properties on different sides of the country. The actual close was surprisingly smooth. The buyer was happy and I'm ecstatic!

This has been such a stressful time for me but on this side of it I am completely appreciative of the struggle and everything I've learned in the process about myself, real estate, co-op sales and the New York City housing market.

Last weekend I was unsettled, anxious and fearful that nothing would work out in time for me to salvage my life. I knew the closing would happen, but how many more setbacks and delays would I have to endure before the sale was finalized? This weekend, I knew in my spirit all is well. For the last few days, my Spirit has been singing praise songs – even now, as I write, I hear in a loop: "The Lord's Right Hand has done many things for us! The Lord's Right Hand is lifted high!" The praise songs change but the ecstasy of worship flows through me continuously.

Thank You, Father God for the journey and the process. It's hard sometimes – excruciating – getting through, but persevering is so very worth it!

August 14, 2019
Marana, AZ

Good morning, Father! What a Glorious Morning You've made! A new day that feels like an absolutely BRAND NEW DAY! Thank You for new days, new dawns, new beginnings! Thank You for making all things new, for shining light in the darkness, for giving hope and making a way in every situation. Thank you for being the Way. Amen! Glory to You always, Father.

August 27, 2019
Road Trip: Santa Monica, CA

I took a road trip to release all the things I needed to let go of. My spirit was longing for water, so I took a road trip to the ocean. I drove I-10 from Marana to San Diego. The highway ended at the Pacific Ocean. So wonderful! I arrived in time to enjoy the sunset from a seaside cliff. My soul was pleased.

For the last week, I've explored California. Now I'm at Santa Monica pier, finally sitting on a beach. I couldn't leave without stepping into the ocean to say a prayer and give thanks. I needed to touch water and baptize my feet – rededicate my journey, my heart and my purpose – reaffirm myself as Your vessel, Father God. Thank You for the journey. Thank You for the growth. Thank You for Your Grace. Thank You for the experiences, lessons, understanding, sight and vision. I'm truly looking forward to everything you have in store for me.

All praises to You, Father. In the name of Your Son, my Savior, the Amen, and by Your Most Gracious Holy Spirit, Thank You. Amen. Amen. Amen.

Your daughter,
LaShawnda

ABOUT LASHAWNDA JONES

IMAGE BY DEIDRE WILSON, LAS VEGAS, 2014

LaShawnda Jones is an observer who documents her observations in words and images. As an independent author/publisher for *Harvest Books* and independent photographer for *Harvest Photo*, LaShawnda's work focuses on women, spiritual growth, social justice, and the beauty of everyday life. Through themes of love, relationships, self-discovery, spirituality, and social commentary, she shares her thoughts, experiences, and reflections. Her choice mediums are blogging, books, calendars, art prints, greeting cards and apparel.

    LaShawnda has been journalling since she was six years old. By twelve, she was writing short stories on a seven-line Brother Word Processor.

    For her eleventh birthday, she received a Vivitar 110 point and shoot camera which marks the beginning of her love for candid photography. In late 2014, she became passionate about photographing demonstrations, marches and protests around the country. In 2021, she released her first photo essay book, *I AM WOMAN: Expressions of Black Womanhood in America.*

In 2024, she released her third collection of poetry, *Alone | All In One: A Solitary Journey* which is an excellent companion read for *Desert of Solitude: Refreshed by Grace (2018).* There are some shared themes that are explored in diverse ways within the two formats. In some areas, *Desert of Solitude* presents the seedling of thoughts that are fleshed out in *Alone | All In One.*

This revision of *Desert of Solitude* has added context and content due to the gift of hindsight. However, the author was careful to maintain the integrity of her experiences and understandings at the time of initial writing.

LaShawnda grew up in the Midwest, in several cities around Lake Michigan and in Mesa, Arizona. She matured during fourteen years in New York City followed by three mellowing years in Marana, Arizona. In 2021, she returned to Milwaukee, WI where she attended high school and college.

For more information about LaShawnda Jones, her blog, books, and photography, please visit **Harvest-Life.org** and **Harvest-Photo.org**.

Lists of Meditation Verses, referenced sermons and songs are available for download on Harvest-Life.org
[=>Books=>Desert of Solitude]

CONNECT
Email: HarvestLife2020@gmail.com
Instagram: @HarvestBooks1 | @HarvestPhoto1
Threads: @HarvestBooks1

BLOGS
Harvest-Life.org
Harvest-Photo.org
LaShawndaJones.wordpress.com
AmericaRisingBlog.wordpress.com

BOOKS
Alone | All in One: A Solitary Journey
I AM WOMAN: Expressions of Black Womanhood in America
Desert of Solitude: Refreshed by Grace
My God and Me: Listening, Learning and Growing on My Journey
The Process of Asking for, Receiving & Giving Love & Forgiveness
Clichés: A Life in Verse
Fantasies: Wide Awake

Buy Books
Amazon
BN.com
Harvest-Life.org/shop

PHOTO ART PRINTS
Harvest Life Store: Harvest-Life.org/shop

END NOTES

i Adapted from unknown prose by unknown author.
   I asked for strength and God gave me difficulties to make me strong.
   I asked for wisdom and God gave me problems to solve.
   I asked for prosperity and God gave me brawn and brains to work.
   I asked for courage and God gave me dangers to overcome.
   I asked for patience and God placed me in situations where I was forced to wait.
   I asked for love and God gave me troubled people to help.
   I asked for favors and God gave me opportunities.
   I asked for everything so I could enjoy life.
   Instead, He gave me life so I could enjoy everything.
   I received nothing I wanted, I received everything I needed.

2 Elizabeth Cady Stanton and Susan B. Anthony, Declaration of Sentiments and Resolutions, Woman's Rights Convention, Seneca Falls, New York, July 19-20, 1848; http://ecssba.rutgers.edu/docs/seneca.html

3 https://en.wikipedia.org/wiki/African-American_women%27s_suffrage_movement#:~:text=African%2DAmerican%20women%20began%20to,York%20Female%20Anti%2DSlavery%20Society.

4 Elizabeth Cady Stanton and Susan B. Anthony, Declaration of Sentiments and Resolutions, Woman's Rights Convention, Seneca Falls, New York, July 19-20, 1848; http://en.wikipedia.org/wiki/Declaration_of_Sentiments

5 http://en.wikipedia.org/wiki/Feminist_movement ; http://en.wikipedia.org/wiki/Women's_suffrage

6 http://www.pacificu.edu/magazine_archives/2008/fall/echoes/feminism.cfm
7 http://www.pacificu.edu/magazine_archives/2008/fall/echoes/feminism.cfm
8 http://www.pacificu.edu/magazine_archives/2008/fall/echoes/feminism.cfm
9 http://en.wikipedia.org/wiki/Third-wave_feminism

10 Dr. Martin Luther King, Jr, Letter from a Birmingham Jail, Alabama, 1963. http://www.mlkonline.net/jail.html. Accessed 11/1/2012.

11 http://www.vday.org/annualreport11/live/index.html

12 http://www.rainn.org/public-policy/legislative-agenda

13 U.S. Bureau of Justice Statistics, Sex Offenses and Offenders. 1997

14 National Institute of Justice & Centers for Disease Control & Prevention. Prevalence, Incidence and Consequences of Violence Against Women Survey. 1998.

15 http://www.rescue.org/our-work/gender-based-violence-programs

16 http://www.rescue.org/our-work/gender-based-violence-programs

[17] Rumain Brisbon, 34-year-old father of four, was dropping off dinner for his family when he was shot and killed by police officers in Phoenix, Arizona. No charges against the officer. Source: USAToday.com

[18] Tamir Rice was twelve and playing on a playground with a BB gun in Cleveland, Ohio when a police officer pulled up and shot and killed him without a word. The officer was not charged for murdering Tamir Rice. Two and half years later, he was fired for lying on his application. Source: NBC26.com

[19] Eric Garner, 43-year-old married father of four, was suspected of selling single cigarettes. He was swarmed and attacked by six police officers, one of which choked him to death while he repeatedly stated, "I can't breathe." The officer was not indicted. Source: NYTimes.com

[20] Freddy Gray was 25 years old when he was arrested for possession of a switchblade. He died in police custody after receiving spinal injuries and falling into a coma in police custody. Six officers were charged, none convicted.

[21] Sandra Bland, 28 years old, was on a road trip from Naperville, IL to Prairie View A&M University in Texas for a job interview. She was pulled over for an alleged minor traffic infraction then beaten by the arresting officer on the side of the road. Three days later she was dead in the jail. Source: LATimes.com

[22] Sources: CBS Sunday Morning: Livestrong After Lance; Showtime Documentary: Lance Armstrong: Stop at Nothing

www.ingramcontent.com/pod-product-compliance
Lightning Source LLC
Chambersburg PA
CBHW022123290426
44112CB00008B/793